IMPERIAL GAMES IN
TIBET

Dilip Sinha is a former diplomat, author and public speaker. He served as the head of India's United Nations affairs during its Security Council membership and was Ambassador to the UN in Geneva, where he was elected Vice President of the Human Rights Council and Vice Chairman of the South Centre. Sinha steered India's responses to the crises in Libya and Syria within the Security Council and Sri Lanka in the HRC. In the course of his diplomatic career, he led India's relations with Pakistan, Afghanistan and Iran and held assignments in Germany, Egypt, Pakistan, Brazil, Bangladesh and Greece. He is the author of *Legitimacy of Power: The Permanence of Five in the Security Council*.

Advance Praise for *Imperial Games in Tibet*

'An authoritative and objective account of the Great Game among the powers over Tibet since the seventeenth century. It is a salutary and, sometimes, depressing tale. This meticulous work of history, grounded in archival work, reminds us of the complex course of previous rounds of great power rivalry. There are lessons here from the devastating consequences of competition among the larger empires and states on those, like Tibet, who chose not to participate or who played the game badly. Tibet was one of the few nations in Asia not to be recognized as transitioning to a modern Westphalian state. Dilip Sinha is particularly acute on China's key role as a player of some skill in the Great Game, not a victim of imperialism but imperial herself. This is a book to be read carefully as we enter another age of contention among the powers in Asia and the world'

**Shivshankar Menon, former National Security Advisor
and Foreign Secretary of India**

'*Imperial Games in Tibet* persuasively investigates the "root causes" of the global apathy towards Tibet and the manner in which the imperial powers – Britain, China and Russia – have played devious games that advanced their own interests at the cost of trampling over Tibetan aspirations for equitable statehood and sovereignty.

Written in a lucid manner leavened with the rigour of a diligent researcher, the book empathetically illuminates an often-forgotten geopolitical and ethical issue. It will be of considerable value to the specialist and lay person alike'

**Commodore C. Uday Bhaskar (retd.), Director,
Society for Policy Studies, and former Director of
Institute for Defence Studies and Analyses**

'In focusing on the complex geopolitics of Tibet's history, Dilip Sinha shines a light on the forgotten role of the great power politics in shaping the region's tragedy. Sinha's rich narrative, backed by solid research, unpacks the fickle alliances and fierce rivalries between the British, Russian and Chinese empires that have shaped the evolution of Tibet in the modern era. Sinha offers deep insights into independent India's inability to sustain the complex strategic legacy of the British Raj in Tibet and the continuing costs of that failure. As great power rivalry returns to India's land frontiers, Sinha's history helps us reflect on the strategic future of inner Asia'

Prof C. Raja Mohan, Institute of South Asian Studies, Singapore

'Dilip Sinha leaves no doubt about where his sympathies lie. To him, Tibet is clearly a victim of major powers, including India, giving priority to their own interests rather than to Tibet's legitimate rights. Sinha, who has earlier written a much-praised book about the workings of the Security Council, also regards this as one of the unacknowledged failures of the UN. But he also draws our attention to the contribution of the Tibetan ruling elite itself to what he rightly terms a "tragic chapter". He backs his conclusions with impressive, wide-ranging research.

Debates will continue about the manner in which Nehru handled the problem but the question remains: Would any other decision by him have prevented the takeover of Tibet by the very determined and powerful China?'

**Vinod C. Khanna, former Ambassador, former Director-General,
India Taipei Association, and Emeritus Fellow,
Institute of Chinese Studies, Delhi**

IMPERIAL GAMES IN

TIBET

The Struggle for Statehood and Sovereignty

DILIP SINHA

MACMILLAN

First published 2024 by Macmillan
an imprint of Pan Macmillan Publishing India Private Limited
707 Kailash Building
26 K. G. Marg, Delhi 110001
www.panmacmillan.co.in

Pan Macmillan, The Smithson, 6 Briset Street, London EC1M 5NR
Associated companies throughout the world
www.panmacmillan.com

ISBN 978-81-19300-53-2

Maps of Tibet (eastern and western regions) by Mohammad Hassan
All photographs featured in the book are in the public domain.

Maps on pages xiv–v, 58, 74 and 174–75 courtesy the UK National Archives

1 3 5 7 9 8 6 4 2

Typeset in Adobe Caslon Pro by SÜRYA, New Delhi

Printed in India by Gopsons Papers Pvt. Ltd., Noida

Contents

List of Maps

Timeline (1700–2000)

	British Empire/India	Russian Empire	Chinese Empire	Tibet
1700s			Russian Orthodox Mission in Beijing	
1720s		Treaty of Kiakhta in Manchuria		First and second Chinese invasions of Tibet. Stationing of Amban.
1750s	British conquest of India starts. Battle of Plassey.		Invasion of East Turkestan	Third Chinese invasion of Tibet
1790s				Fourth Chinese invasion of Tibet
1820s			Jahangir's revolt in Kashgaria	
1840s	First Afghan War	Conquest of Kazakhstan is completed	First Opium War	Jammu–Kashmir invades Tibet
1850s	Indian Revolt	Crimean War	Taiping Rebellion	Nepal invades Tibet

1860s			East Turkestan breaks away. Britain invades Beijing.	
1870s		Conquest of Tashkent. Formation of Turkestan province.	Tongzhi Restoration	
1880s	Second Afghan War	Russia–Turkey War	Reconquest of East Turkestan	
1890s	Anglo-Chinese Convention of Sikkim Border	Britain–Russia agreement on Wakhan Corridor	Japan invades China	
1900s	Britain invades Tibet	Japan's victory over Russia		
1910s	Simla Convention	Collapse of Romanov dynasty. Formation of USSR.	Abdication of Qing dynasty	Declaration of Independence
1920s			Civil War – Nationalists vs Communists	
1930s			Japan invades China	
1940s	India's independence		Victory of Communist Party in Civil War	
1950s	Panchsheel agreement with China			China invades Tibet. Khampa Rebellion. Flight of Dalai Lama.
1960s			War with India	
1980s				Riots in Lhasa. Dalai Lama awarded the Nobel Peace Prize.

1990s		Disintegration of USSR. Independence of Central Asian republics.		
2000s				Protests in Tibet and elsewhere

A Note on Spellings

China uses the Sinicized names of its rulers and dynasties, masking their foreign origin. The Yuan dynasty, for example, was Mongol, as China was part of the Mongol empire during its reign. The Qing dynasty originated in Manchuria, which became a part of China at the end of the nineteenth century. Likewise, the Tang dynasty was half Turkic. To emphasize their foreign origin, the book refers to them using their original names.

Chinese emperors are commonly known by the title of their reigns rather than personal names. Hongli was the most powerful ruler of the Manchu Qing dynasty, but here, he is referred to as the Qianlong (Ch'ien-lung) emperor.

It has always been difficult to transcribe Chinese names and words into the Latin (Roman) script. There are two prevalent systems at present. First, the Wade–Giles, named after the two Englishmen who devised it. Thomas F. Wade, a British diplomat and linguist, created the system before it was slightly revised by Herbert A. Giles, another diplomat, in 1912.* It continues to be used in Hong Kong and Taiwan, where its pronunciation conforms to the local language, Cantonese. In the 1930s, a new system – reflecting Mandarin pronunciation under the Hanyu pinyin (Han language phonetics) system – was developed in Moscow and eventually adopted by the People's Republic of China (PRC). In books written in English prior to the adoption of the pinyin

---

* Wade became the first professor of Chinese at Cambridge University, with Giles succeeding him.

system, Wade–Giles remains the prevalent style. I have followed the current pinyin system, with the Wade–Giles transcription included in parentheses.

The Tibetan script is alphabetical and can be romanized according to the pronunciation of respective words. But Tibetan names also frequently contain silent consonants that are typically ignored in transcription. Thus, the celebrated Tibetan king Songtsen Gampo's name is spelt Srong Btsan Sgam Po in Tibetan. It is also romanized as Srongtsen Gampo. The Chinese romanize Tibetan names with the Mandarin accent, writing Gampo as Songzan Ganbu. This book follows the spellings used by the Central Tibetan Administration based in Dharamsala, Himachal Pradesh, for all Tibetan names.

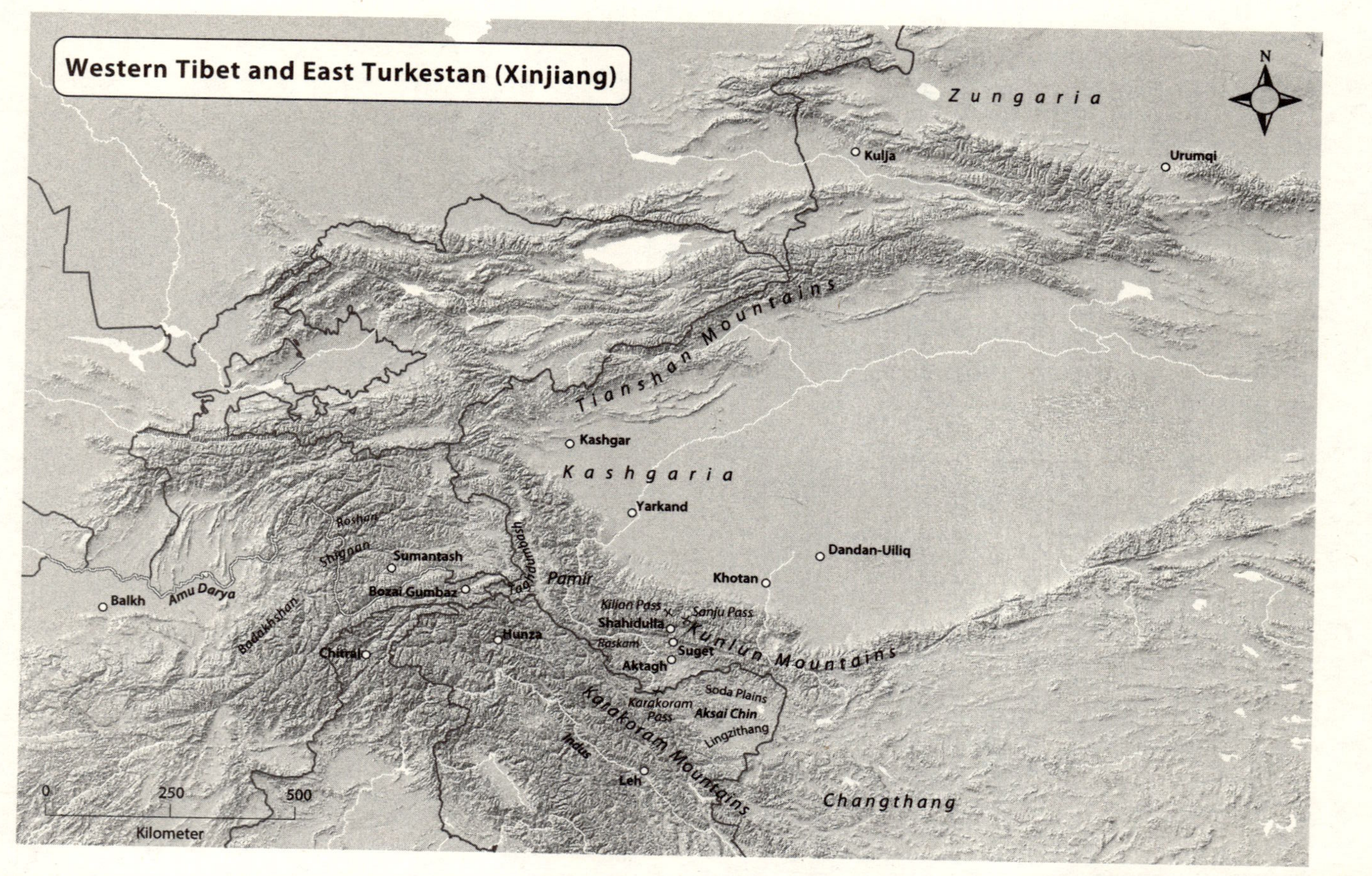

Western Tibet and East Turkestan (Xinjiang)
N
Zungaria
Kulja
Urumqi
Tianshan Mountains
Kashgar
Kashgaria
Yarkand
Dandan-Uiliq
Khotan
Roshan
Shignan
Sumantash
Pamir
Balkh
Amu Darya
Bozai Gumbaz
Tashkurghan
Badakhshan
Chitral
Hunza
Kilian Pass
Sanju Pass
Shahidulla
Baskam
Suget
Kunlun Mountains
Aktagh
Soda Plains
Karakoram Pass
Aksai Chin
Lingzithang
Karakoram Mountains
Indus
Leh
Changthang
0   250   500
Kilometer

Eastern Tibet
N
Changthang
Amdo
Huang He
Kham
Chamdo
Mekong
Salween
Yangtze
Tachienlu
U-Tsang
Lhasa
Tsangpo
Shigatse
Gyantse
Khamba Dzong
Yatung
Tawang
Chumbi Valley
Gnathang
Himalaya
0
250
500
Kilometer

A cartoon of the Afghan leader Amir Sher Ali with his
'friends' Russia and Britain, 1878

INTRODUCTION
The Game

In October 1950, China invaded Tibet. Its military marched into the eastern town of Chamdo, which capitulated after a brief resistance. Although the provincial governor was taken to Beijing, the Chinese army decided not to advance to Lhasa, instead initiating negotiations for Tibet's surrender. Meanwhile, the Tibetan government, led by the fifteen-year-old Dalai Lama – who had fled to Yatung near the Indian border – made appeals to Britain, India, the United States and the United Nations for help. None came to its rescue. The matter was brought up in the UN General Assembly, only to be postponed after a perfunctory discussion. Tibet was presented with an agreement of surrender, ultimately signed in May 1951, and by September, the Chinese army entered Lhasa.

The lack of international support for Tibet, and the unquestioning acceptance of China's claim over it, represents a tragic chapter in modern history – one of the unacknowledged failures of the UN. For India, it has created an endless security nightmare.

The current constellation of countries in Central Asia, the vast interior of the world's largest continent, was shaped in the last century by two dramatic upheavals: in 1950 and 1991. The first was engineered by Russia, the primary power within the Soviet Union, which helped the Chinese Communist Party (CCP) win the civil war in China and reconquer Tibet, East Turkestan and Manchuria – all of which had gained independence after the collapse of the Qing (Ch'ing) or Manchu dynasty in 1912. Russia maintained control over Mongolia, even though it had been claimed by China, but allowed it to retain Inner Mongolia, the southern region. The second round of change took place when the Soviet Union collapsed, with five republics rising on its ruins in Central Asia: Kazakhstan, Uzbekistan, Kyrgyzstan, Tajikistan and Turkmenistan. It was during this convulsion that Mongolia emerged from Russia's shadow.

India shares its northern frontier with two Central Asian countries – Tibet and East Turkestan, referred to as Xinjiang (Sinkiang) by China. After its conquest of India in the mid-nineteenth century, Britain began demarcating its land borders with the other imperial powers – Russia and China. Through diplomatic negotiations and military encounters, these three imperial powers drew the contours of the Central Asian countries and the northern borders of India.

In the early nineteenth century, Central Asia stood as one of the few regions in the world uncolonized by Europeans. China had conquered its eastern part in the previous century. The western portion, comprising independent Mongol and Turkic khanates, was steadily taken over by Russia. Britain's interest in the region developed when it reached the northern frontier of India and started to view Russia's expansion not only as a threat to its Indian empire but also to its global supremacy. As a result, Tibet and East Turkestan became its primary concerns.

Military invasions by these powers for empire-building ambitions and diplomatic manipulations to create spheres of influence sealed Tibet's fate, the country with which India shared its longest frontier. Their imperial games replaced peaceful Tibet with an expansionist China as India's largest neighbour. A similar fate befell East Turkestan, and its border with India was also settled during this period. The effects of these events are still keenly felt by the people of these countries, and the border between India and China remains one of the longest and most disputed in the world.

The rivalry between Britain and Russia, the defining feature of nineteenth-century geopolitics, is remembered as the 'Great Game' in Central Asia. The term was coined by British intelligence officer Arthur Conolly and popularized by the grand poet of the British colonial era, Rudyard Kipling. The two countries played cat-and-mouse throughout Central Asia in the second half of the nineteenth century. China, an unwieldy, tottering empire, was brought into the game when it suited the two primary players. This triangular contest was similar to, and influenced by, the Anglo-Russian rivalry in West Asia, where the third party was Ottoman Turkey – once the terror of Europe, but by the nineteenth century, on the brink of collapse. Britain propped it up for nearly a century simply to prevent it from falling into Russia's hands.

Less well known is Britain and Russia's grudging cooperation with China. Today, China portrays itself as a victim of imperialism, referring to this period as the 'century of humiliation'.[1] This narrative minimizes its key role as an imperial player – and, in retrospect, the shrewdest of the three. Unlike many other Asian countries, it was never colonized by Europe. It has also maintained its independence as the only one of the three empires to have survived relatively intact to this day.

Fickle Alliances, Fierce Rivalries

The first significant interaction between Britain and Russia occurred in 1815 when they joined forces to trounce Napoleon Bonaparte. Despite their continued cooperation in the Concert of Europe – Europe's post-Napoleon security arrangement – Russia's rise turned them into bitter rivals. Always on the lookout for a warm-water port, Russia attempted to gain access to the Mediterranean Sea through Istanbul, the Ottoman capital. In the Crimean War (1853–1856), Britain, in alliance with France, thwarted Russia to maintain its naval supremacy. Frustrated, Russia turned its attention to the east – Central Asia – only to find Britain an even more determined adversary.

Who were the Qings, the dynasty ruling China at the time? In the seventeenth century, China was conquered by the Manchus, the Mongols' neighbours and fierce enemies living up north in

Manchuria. After overthrowing the Mings, the last Han dynasty to rule China, the Manchus established a vast empire. They invaded East Turkestan, inhabited by Turkic and Mongol tribes, in the mid-eighteenth century, designating it the 'Western region', around the same time the British began their conquest of India. Expanding to include Tibet and Mongolia, they created one of the largest empires in Chinese history. And they chose a Chinese name: Qing.

By the middle of the nineteenth century, however, the Manchu empire was crumbling. Following the First Opium War of 1839–1842, Britain occupied Hong Kong. Other European countries seized trading privileges on the east coast, and Russia encroached on its territory to the north and west. East Turkestan and several outlying provinces had let go of their yoke, and they could no longer protect Tibet from raids by the rulers of Nepal and Jammu and Kashmir. Britain feared that Russia would annex China's Central Asian colonies. For China, the most serious threat was internal – a devastating civil war, the Taiping Rebellion, which pitted the Han-dominated south against the Manchu-dominated north.

The year 1860 marked a watershed moment in changing Britain's policy towards China. A British army occupied its capital, the first foreign army to do so in more than two centuries. It was led by James Bruce, a Scot whose father, the seventh Earl of Elgin, had ripped down the marble friezes from Athens' Parthenon temple and sold them to the British government. The eighth earl was sent to punish the Manchu ruler for failing to implement a treaty he had signed. En route from London, though, he was diverted to India, where a revolt had broken out in 1857. After helping suppress the Indian uprising, he proceeded to China. Seizing Beijing, he followed in his father's footsteps by destroying the magnificent Summer Palace. He was rewarded with a viceroyalty in India.

Britain's occupation of Beijing should have ended the Qing dynasty, but remarkably, it thrived and lasted another fifty years. It successfully suppressed the Taiping and other rebellions, reclaiming its lost provinces and colonies. What spurred this miraculous turnaround? How did China bounce back and evade colonization, unlike many other Asian countries? What was its secret to playing the imperial power game so adroitly?

The answers lie in the broader geopolitical gameboard. The Anglo-Russian rivalry in Central Asia exerted a profound impact across the continent as a whole. Britain's fear for the security of its empire in India, fuelled by a seemingly distant Russian threat, drove most of its late nineteenth- and early twentieth-century foreign policy. Worries about Russia's designs on India arose as early as 1800, when it first considered a military expedition to India. Though the invasion never materialized, Britain began to view any Russian move in Central Asia with suspicion. India became the pivot around which relations between these two empires revolved, drawing China into the fray and spelling doom for many small, unfortunate Central Asian nations – Tibet among them.

Britain recognized that the Manchu empire had become the 'sick man of Asia', just like Ottoman Turkey in Europe. China lacked the military strength to contain Russia's expansion in Central Asia. But so did Britain, which had to weigh Russia's physical proximity to China when wargaming any possible military encounter. And despite being the master of oceans, Britain was vulnerable on land. Its defeat in the First Anglo-Afghan War (1839–1842) had chastened its ambitions, instilling little confidence about taking on the Russian army deep within the Asian continent. Britain feared that China's collapse would lead to a land grab by European powers, with Russia gaining the upper hand.

Throughout the 1800s, Britain was the world's foremost power. Yet, by the middle of the century, it had been weathered by upheavals in three of the largest countries in the world – India, China and the United States. India was its most prized colony, while China and the US its chief trading partners.

In India, the uprising against the rule of the East India Company had caused panic in Britain, while civil wars threatened to disintegrate China and the US. To save the East India Company, the British government sent troops to crush the Indian revolt and take over the country's governance. In the US, it declared neutrality, seeking to minimize the impact of the war on its trade. However, China posed the most complex challenge. Britain sought to expand trade to compensate for its losses in the American market, but in the process of forcing open China, it launched an invasion of Beijing. The Manchu emperor and his courtiers had fled to their homeland of Manchuria. The mighty Chinese empire lay at its feet.

For Britain, this was a critical moment in its dealings with China. Having only recently regained control over India, it was hesitant to annex another large country. The invasion of Beijing had been carried out jointly with France, which provided crucial support. Russia was hovering across the frontier, waiting for the empire to fall apart. Britain had to decide how to deal with its prey while also ensuring the safety of its own forces inside the country, where it operated with little knowledge of the terrain. Beyond the Great Wall lay vast steppes roamed by fierce Mongol and Turkic warriors. Russia had established itself in Siberia, and its envoys had been visiting Beijing for a long time. Although Britain was reluctant to occupy Beijing, how could it avoid leaving behind a vacuum that Russia could fill?

Britain needed allies in the Far East to counter Russia, but this was never an easy task in fractious Europe. Its only geopolitical constant in the nineteenth century was the rivalry with Russia. Despite their long and intense competition, they never came to blows in Central Asia, unlike in Europe, where they fought at least one major war.[2] So, how did the British–Russian rivalry shape the national destinies of Central Asia? What was the impact on Tibet?

Playground for the Great Game

Tibet has fascinated the world for centuries due to its forbidding terrain and mystical remoteness. This towering highland to the north has traditionally served as India's longest land frontier. Although Tibet was once an imperial power, the arrival of Buddhism ushered in a reclusive pacificism. The proliferation of monasteries made it vulnerable to foreign intervention, as the lamas were willing to seek outside assistance to settle internal disputes. The

Mongols invaded Tibet in the thirteenth century, and the Manchus arrived in the eighteenth century. Both groups conquered China and ruled Tibet from Beijing. By the mid-nineteenth century, when our story begins, Manchu China had nominal control over Tibet.

The once-hermit country was swept into the Great Game, becoming a hotbed of imperial intrigue. Charles Bell, a leading Tibetologist in Britain, expressed worry that if Tibet fell under Russian control, Britain would need 'to maintain considerable bodies of troops at great expense in damp, unhealthy regions' to defend India.[3] Lhasa's proximity to India, particularly Kolkata – the capital of British India until 1911 – concerned the British officials in India. But Britain worked hard to avoid a military confrontation with Russia, preferring to address its challenges through diplomacy and strategic alliances.

Whether Britain ever contemplated making Tibet an independent country is a hotly debated subject, especially in India, where many believe that Britain intended to use Tibet as a buffer against China, a prudent policy abandoned by independent India. An American historian supported this view shortly after China's invasion of India in 1962: 'Imperial British policy had envisaged the maintenance of a Tibetan autonomy that would keep Tibet as a buffer between China and India.'[4] But why would a powerful country like British require a buffer against China? Didn't Britain have more to fear from an independent Tibet? According to the imperial mindset of the time, any country that was not under an empire was free game – a no-man's land. Minor kingdoms were seen as invitations for neighbouring empires to conquer, serving as magnets for major power rivalries. Small countries and communities that had earlier lived independently, were soon subjected to the arm-twisting envoys of imperial powers – or worse, trampled by their armies. Cartographers arbitrarily drew lines on maps, assigning territories to empires based on geographical contours or geometric lines, regardless of who lived there or how they were related historically.

As part of this policy, Britain sought to bring all the lesser kingdoms on India's borders within its domain. But its defeat in Afghanistan had hightened awareness of the dangers lurking in the mountains. The topography of Tibet was much more formidable and unknown. Fighting Russia in the cold mountains was a daunting prospect. Britain needed to devise a solution that was both acceptable to itself and the other imperial powers. Stubborn lamas, unwilling to open their country to trade, were not its cup of tea. Despite its weakened state, imperial China was more in Britain's league and easier to deal with.

Statehood and Sovereignty

Tibet's status in international relations remains disputed. The critical question is whether it's a separate country or a part of China. Most countries, including India, consider it an autonomous region of China. But autonomy does not imply independence. An autonomous region cannot claim to be a state under international law, nor does it count as a colony under foreign occupation.

What exactly is statehood? Or, what determines a country's independence in international relations? A state is regarded as a legal person under international law. It is, by definition, a sovereign entity with equal status and ability to engage in relations with other states. 'The sovereignty and equality of states represent the basic constitutional doctrine of the law of nations, which governs a community consisting primarily of states having a uniform legal personality.'[5] State sovereignty also implies that other countries and international organizations cannot interfere in its internal affairs. Even the UN, under its charter, is prohibited from intervening in matters primarily within a state's domestic jurisdiction, except for enforcement measures relating to the maintenance of international peace and security, as per Article 2.7.

This state-based international order began to take shape in Europe following the Peace of Westphalia treaties in 1648.[6] As to what entitles a territory or a people to be recognized as a state under international law, there is no consensus. The UN Charter does not attempt to define a state – despite being an association of states. In 1933, the Montevideo Convention on the Rights and Duties of States attempted to define statehood thus:

> The State as a person of international law should possess the following qualifications: (a) a permanent population; (b) a defined territory; (c) government; and (d) capacity to enter into relations with other States' (Article 1).

This remains one of the most comprehensive definitions of statehood, applying the capacity to enter into relations with other states as an essential qualification, over sovereignty.[7] While population, territory and government are relatively easy to identify, sovereignty is a much more amorphous and contested concept. The UN, like its predecessor, the League of Nations, does not list sovereignty as a qualification for membership. The League offered membership to any 'fully self-governing State, Dominion or Colony' (Article 1). UN membership is open to all 'peace-loving states' that accept the Charter's obligations and are 'able and willing' to carry them out. Thus, India became a founding member of both the League and the UN while still being part of the British empire. Ukraine and Byelorussia joined the UN even though they were constituent countries of the Soviet Union at the time.

A state that grants extensive extra-territorial rights to another cannot claim to be sovereign; one that cedes its foreign affairs to another would fall into the same category. But in certain instances, a state has continued to be recognized as such, despite considerable dilution of its sovereignty. After the Second World War, Germany was bifurcated and occupied by foreign powers, yet both regions were accorded recognition as states and admitted to the UN. Members of the European Union regard themselves as sovereign states, rather than federating units, even though they have ceded significant authority to the EU.

In spite of these flexibilities, exceptions and divergent interpretations, the standards applied to Tibet's claim to statehood have remained extremely stringent. Tibet is considered to have been under Chinese 'suzerainty' for an indeterminate period and thus lacking the necessary attributes of statehood. But the term suzerainty itself is not recognized in modern international law. It was popular in the nineteenth century, describing the emperors' authority over their tributary states. The Ottomans, for example, were said to have suzerainty over the Balkan countries of Europe. India made anti-colonialism the central pillar of its foreign policy, standing up for the rights of countries against colonial powers. Yet, it did not deem China's occupation of Tibet to be an act of colonization, instead toeing the British line.

The lamas, being monks, described their relationship with the Mongols and the Manchus in ecclesiastical terms – as a priest–patron connection. But such abstruse relationships receive no recognition in international politics. To assert its right to statehood, a state has to claim sovereignty and enter into diplomatic relations with other countries. As a result, theocratic Tibet was inconsistent in demanding recognition of its sovereignty and often unsure of its legitimacy.

Britain firmed up its Tibet policy early in the twentieth century, during the dying years of Manchu rule. Despite its best efforts, Britain could not persuade China to maintain control over this distant country. It juggled strategies to achieve a complex set of goals, including preventing the disintegration of the Manchu empire, blocking the southward march of Russia and opening up trade within the reclusive Tibet. Finally, it settled on the imperial construct of 'suzerainty' to define Tibet's relationship with China, while conducting dealings directly with it.

After India gained independence, it faced an irredentist China that was no longer content with stationing a ceremonial representative in Lhasa. The Tibetan government was supplanted by Han Chinese functionaries of the Communist Party serving as administrators. China also laid claim to extensive Indian territory bordering Tibet, which was inhabited by Buddhist people who revered the Dalai Lama. This contrasted its own policy of annexing large parts of Tibet and denying the Dalai Lama traditional monastic privileges in China.

Although independent India retained the British policy, while Britain had extracted several trading rights in Tibet and enforced them using its army, India's military weakness and lack of political will soon resulted in the loss of those rights. The newly independent nation also inherited borders that were vaguely demarcated or agreed upon by the three imperial powers. With Britain no longer interested in the region and Russia offering unstinting support to its fellow communist nation, India faced a formidable challenge. Communist China condemned Western imperialism but claimed the Manchu mantle and aggressively pursued shadowy claims over neighbouring countries under the guise of liberating their oppressed people.

In his seminal history of humankind, Yuval Noah Harari offers a perceptive insight into China: 'The ultimate achievement of the Chinese empire is that it is still alive and kicking, yet it is hard to see it as an empire except in outlying areas such as Tibet and Xinjiang.'[8] Harari only includes Tibet and Xinjiang as colonies of the Chinese empire, leaving out autonomous regions like Inner Mongolia and Yunnan. This omission is likely because the immigration of the Han Chinese has changed the demographics of Inner Mongolia, Yunnan and the three provinces of the erstwhile Manchuria. The same fate awaits Tibet and Xinjiang.

This book investigates the root causes of the international community's apathy towards Tibet and its refusal to respond to the latter's pleas against China's occupation. Importantly, it delves into the games played in Central Asia by the three imperial powers – Britain, China and Russia – that have fundamentally shaped the postulates of Tibet's international status.

1

Tibet: Monastic Heights

Nestled between the Himalaya and the Kunlun Mountains, and several towering ranges, Tibet is the world's highest plateau. Unsurprisingly, it is known as the 'roof of the world'. To the east run the mighty Mekong and Yangtse rivers, and the mountain ranges from north to south form the frontier with China. With an average elevation of 4,000 metres, it covers 1.2 million square kilometres – roughly the size of South Africa. Tibetans claim their territory to be 2.5 million square kilometres, including the provinces of Amdo and Kham annexed by China. It is the source of some of Asia's mightiest rivers, all of them better known by their names in downstream countries: Senge Khabab (Indus), Yarlung Tsangpo (Brahmaputra), Drichu (Yangtse), Machu (Huang He), Gyalmo Ngulchu (Salween) and Zachu (Mekong). Its 46,000 glaciers account for nearly 15 per cent of the world's total and are a vital source of fresh water. Lakes, or *tso* in Tibetan, dot the entire country. A number of these lakes, which have no outlet in the mountainous terrain and thus turn salty, are called *tsa-ka* or salt pits.

In Tibet, the country is referred to as 'Böd'. The term 'Tibet' originates from 'Tubbat', as it was called in the past by its neighbours – the Turks, Iranians and Arabs, possibly derived from 'Tö Bö', which translates to Upper Tibet. Other cultures have adopted their own versions of Böd. It was known as 'Thumbed' among the Mongols and 'Tufan' among the Chinese. Indians called it 'Tibbat', which the British later adapted to Tibet. In the nineteenth century, it was spelt 'Thibet'.

The Chinese name, 'Tufan', is formed by two Chinese characters – *tu* and *fan*. The second can also be pronounced as *pö*, making it a close phonetic transliteration of Böd. This was how S. W. Bushell, a British physician at the British Legation in Beijing in the nineteenth century, interpreted it.[1] Early Tibetans were called 'Tubo' in China. According to Bushell, Tibet was home to various tribes in ancient times, as noted by Chinese researcher Ma Tuanlin. In 634 CE, Tibet sent its initial mission to China to the court of the Tang emperor Taizong. The Tang chronicles contain detailed mentions of the interactions between the two regions. In 641 CE, the Tang emperor solidified political relations by offering a princess to the Tibetan king.

Tibet's current size is smaller than before its annexation by the PRC in 1950. In 1895, in an assessment of trade prospects with Tibet, the Bradford Chamber of Commerce estimated the country's area to be about 700,000 square miles (1.8 million square kilometres) and its population between 6 and 7 million.[2] After conquering Tibet, China merged parts of the Amdo and Kham provinces into the neighbouring Chinese provinces of Qinghai and Sichuan.

China now refers to Tibet as Xizang, from the name of its central province, Tsang. Xizang can be translated as West Zang (Zang being the Chinese transliteration of Tsang and *xi* meaning west). China also employs *Zang* to derive other terms relating to Tibet, such as *zangwen* (for the Tibetan language) and *zangzu* (for the Tibetan people). It has notably started referring to the state of Arunachal Pradesh as Zang-nan, or South Tibet.

Despite claiming that Tibet has been a part of China since ancient times, the Chinese always referred to the Tibetans as 'barbarians' – as they did all other foreigners. The early Chinese termed their neighbours – two Tibetan groups, two Turkish and a Mongolian as the 'Five Barbarians'. This practice continued until recent times. Tibetans reciprocated in kind, but privately, referring to the Chinese as 'beggars'.[3]

Tibetan Language

China maintains that the Tibetan language is part of the Sino-Tibetan family – one of the twenty-eight languages of China's ethnic minorities, including Yi, Zhuang, Bouyei, Dai, Miao and Yao. It classifies Uygur, Kazak, Mongolian, Manchu and Korean under a different category, under the Altaic family.[4]

The *Cambridge Encyclopedia of Language* groups Tibetan and Chinese in the same Sino-Tibetan family, stating that the Sinitic part includes various Chinese languages (which China calls 'dialects'). Tibetan is also included as one of them, while noting that 'The membership and classification of the Sino-Tibetan family of languages is highly controversial.'[5] Rinchen Dolma Taring, a Tibetan who travelled extensively in China in the 1950s, commented: 'Our written and spoken language is nothing like Chinese, though many people think that there is some resemblance. Tibetan grammar is very complex and the written language is often beautiful.'[6]

Tibetan is closer to Burmese, Tai and Miao-Yao. These languages are part of the Tibeto-Burman family, comprising nearly 300 dialects. Some studies place Tibetan in the Altaic family, given its similarities with Mongolian. The languages closest to Tibetan are Sikkimese and Bhutanese, which are mutually intelligible to their native speakers. Burmese and some languages in India's north-eastern states are also close enough to Tibetan to merit classification in the same family.[7]

While the debate on the origin of the Tibetan language rages on – China will never accept that it is not an offshoot of its own language – there can be no dispute about the origin of the Tibetan script, which is fundamentally different from the ideograms or characters used to write Chinese. The Tibetan script is alphabetical and is believed to be derived from the Shāradā script of the Brahmi family, once popular in north-west India.

Blossoming of Buddhism

When the British first tried to enter Tibet in the nineteenth century, it was a closed country tightly controlled by the lamas, who were hostile to all foreigners, especially non-Buddhists. Sarat Chandra Das, an Indian employed by the British to explore Tibet at the time, estimated that there were 19,000 monks in the country, of whom 16,500 lived in the three main monasteries.

Buddhism came to Tibet in the fifth century CE during the reign of Thori Nyatsen, the twenty-eighth king of the Yarlung dynasty. According to a legend, a casket containing the mantra of *Avalokiteśvara*, the patron and protector of Tibet, fell on the royal palace from heaven. The king could not read the script but he kept the relic. The earliest evidence of Buddhism, however, is the arrival of two texts, *Chintāmani Dharani* and *Pang Koneyama*, which were brought over by an Indian pandit (religious scholar) and translated into Tibetan.[8] Buddhism came closer to the people and became a state affair in the seventh century, under the reign of Songtsen Gampo, the thirty-third king of the Yarlung dynasty. His marriages to both a Nepalese and a Chinese princess may have influenced his conversion to Buddhism.

Soon Buddhism became a defining feature of Tibet, developing unique characteristics. Tibet has been chiefly responsible for Buddhism's spread throughout Central Asia and China. There are four main sects of Tibetan Buddhism:

1. *Nyingma* (meaning 'the old'): Founded by Padmasambhava, a tantric Buddhist from the Swat Valley in northwest India (now in Pakistan) in the eighth century CE. Its followers wore red hats.

2. *Sakya*: Founded by Kon Chogyal Pho (1034–1102 CE), with the Sakya monastery (or Grey Earth monastery) established in Tsang province in 1073 CE.

3. *Kagyu* (meaning 'orally transmitted'): Founded by Marpa (the great translator, 1110–1193 CE). Its followers are known as Black Hats.

4. *Gelug* (the sect to which the Dalai Lama and most Tibetans belong): Its founder, Tsongkhapa Lobsang Dragpa (1357–1419), followed the teachings of a Buddhist

from Vikramshila University in Bihar, Atiśa, known in Tibet as Jowoge, the Noble Lord. He stressed celibacy, abstinence and austere living. The first Dalai Lama was Gedun Drupa, a disciple of Tsongkhapa. He built the Tashilhunpo Monastery in Shigatse, which later became the seat of the Panchen Lama. The Dalai Lama is revered as the reincarnation of Chenrezig, Lord of Compassion. Members of this sect wear yellow hats.

Tibetan Buddhism is closest to that practised in Mongolia. The Indian historian B. N. Puri noted the similarities between Tibetan and Mongolian Buddhism, writing that there 'seems to be no difference between the two in deities, doctrines or observances'. Mongolian lamas often recite their scriptures in Tibetan – even though they exist in their native language as well.[9]

Early History

The Tibetan calendar starts from 127 BCE, the date of accession of the first king – Nyatri Tsenpo.[10] This is shortly after the decline of the Mauryans in India. Nyatri was proclaimed king by the people of the Yarlung Valley, in southern Tibet. Legend has it that Nyatri, a god-like being belonging to a royal family related to the Buddha, descended from heaven using a sky-rope. He started the Yarlung dynasty, which spanned forty-one rulers and endured until 842 CE, when its last king, Lang Dharma, was killed by a discontented Buddhist monk. In Tibetan legends, India is considered the 'land of the gods'.

Old Tibetan texts discovered in Central Asia reveal that in the eighth and ninth centuries the Tibetan presence extended to the Kashgaria region in modern Xinjiang, including towns like Khotan and Lobnor, and Dunhuang in the Gansu province. This was during the reign of Songtsen Gampo – 'Songtsen the Wise' – who Tibetans look upon as their first great king. His father had expanded the kingdom from the Yarlung Valley to occupy most of central Tibet. Songtsen continued this expansion into Amdo, in north-east Tibet, stretching his kingdom to the border of the Tang empire in China.

Songtsen Gampo, recognized for his role in the spread of Buddhism in Tibet, was a pioneering king. He commissioned an Indian scholar to develop a script for the Tibetan language. With the help of Narendradeva, a Nepalese king who had taken shelter in his court, he had Lhasa's Jokhang temple built on the model of a temple in Nepal. Songtsen then sent Narendradeva back with a Tibetan army to reinstate him to his Nepalese throne.

Tibetan sources reveal that in the last year of his rule, Songtsen Gampo attacked northern India and defeated the King of Kannauj, Arjuna (who had succeeded Harshavardhana, a patron of Buddhism). The provocation for this invasion was the slaughter of a Buddhist scholar from China, Wang Hiuen-Tse, and his thirty-member team, in Kannauj. Wang had come to India after the extremely successful visit of the Chinese Buddhist scholar Xuanzang (known in India as Hiuen Tsang). By then Harshavardhana had died and his minister, Arjuna – who was not well disposed towards Buddhists – had succeeded him. These killings prompted a swift retaliation by Songtsen Gampo, who defeated Arjuna at Hirahati in Bihar and deposed him.

Contact with China

Although China was united for the first time under the Qin dynasty in the third century BCE, it took almost a millennium for its first contact with Tibet to be recorded. This occurred in the seventh century CE, under the Tangs, in the form of a matrimonial alliance. Earlier contacts before this had been confined to occasional Tibetan raids into China.

The Tang dynasty was founded by a general by the name of Li Yuan in an outlying province of the Sui kingdom of China (581–618 CE). Li Yuan rebelled and declared himself emperor in 618 CE, with the title 'Gaozu'. He set up his capital at Chang'an (modern Xian). A son from his Turkic wife, Li Shimin, later overthrew him and ruled as Emperor Taizong, beginning his reign by subjugating the Turkic people, then conquering northern and central China. Under him, it became one of the most powerful empires in Chinese history, its extent unequalled for centuries until the arrival of the Mongols. The ethnic links of the Tang with outside groups enabled it to open China to direct contact – not only with the 'barbarians' on China's borders but also with the distant civilizations of India and West Asia. The Tang era was one of enlightenment and prosperity for China, bringing conquests and other interactions with neighbouring countries. It was during this period that Xuanzang came to study at Nalanda University. According to Edwin Reischauer, a Harvard historian and US diplomat, 'Never again until the twentieth century was China to prove so responsive to foreign influences.'[11] The dynasty lasted nearly three centuries.

While Tibetans acknowledge that Buddhism came from India, China has its own version, attributing it to Songtsen's Tang wife. In 641 CE, Taizong – who was Buddhist – gave a princess of his family, Wen Cheng, in marriage to Songtsen. She brought to Lhasa as her dowry a life-size statue of the Buddha – made of gold, silver, zinc, iron and copper – and had it installed in a custom-built temple. Later, it was transferred to the Jokhang temple, where it remains today. Tibetan legend, however, traces the source of the statue to the Indian kingdom of Magadh, from where it was sent to China as a gift.[12]

China's imperial records state that Wen Cheng also brought '360 classic texts … 60 varieties of books on construction and industrial arts, 100 medical prescriptions for 404 diseases, six types of medical tools, four medical books, and large amounts of silk and clothing'.[13] The princess started 'civilizing' the Tibetans by introducing them to the refinements of Chinese culture. Chinese historians regard this as the start of Tibet becoming Buddhist and proof of its Chinese origin, seeking to portray it as a two-way cultural exchange. The Han people picked up ball games from the Tibetans, and Han women learned how to do their hair and makeup.

Around 700 CE, another Tibetan ruler, Tridu Tsugtsen, married Jin Cheng (also a Tang princess) during the rule of the Tang emperor, Zhong Zong. She brought with her not merely silk fabrics and artisans but also Confucian classics such as the *Book of*

Odes, Book of Rites and Zuo Qiuming's *Commentary on the Spring and Autumn Annals*.[14] Confucianism, however, did not take root in Tibet.

Despite such supposedly warm marital and religious ties, relations between China and Tibet were hardly friendly during this period. In the middle of the eighth century, the Tang empire was shaken by the revolt of one of its generals, An Lushan, who declared himself emperor in 756 CE. The Tang emperor, with the help of the Uyghurs, regained the throne the following year – but his authority had been gravely undermined. Trisong Deutsen, the Tibetan ruler, took advantage of this and attacked China, occupying Dunhuang and, in 763 CE, raiding the Tang capital, Chang'an. Although he did not occupy the city, he plundered it several times.

Trisong Deutsen strengthened Buddhism in Tibet with the help of another Indian Buddhist, Padmasambhava, who had a stormy stay in the region, trying to prove the supremacy of his skills by taming demons. His work and rituals gained popularity, and he became recognized as the 'Precious Teacher' – Guru Rimpoche.[15] Deutsen also established a large monastery at Samye in the Tsangpo valley, which displayed architectural features from India, Nepal and China.

During Trisong Deutsen's reign, Buddhist scholars from China and India fought for supremacy. It is said that he brought the two sides together in a debate organized at the Samye monastery. Kamalashila represented the Indian school and Moheyan, a scholar from Dunhuang, his Zen school. The Tibetan version of the story goes that Kamalashila was declared the victor. But Chinese records claim that the Tibetan king gave his blessings to the Chinese teacher. Deutsen also organized the translation of Buddhist scriptures from Sanskrit and Pali to Tibetan. This remains one of the biggest enterprises of its kind in the medieval world. Deutsen's patronage of Buddhism enabled its spread throughout Central Asia among the Mongols and later the Manchus, who revered Tibet as the fountain of Buddhist learning. Sadly, though, most texts in Tibet were destroyed during China's Cultural Revolution in the 1960s.

In 822 CE, Tritsuk Deutsen – popularly known as Ralpachen, the 'long-haired' – entered into a treaty with the Tang ruler of China. The agreement, written in Chinese and Tibetan on a stone pillar in the Jokhang temple, stated: 'The two countries, Tibet and China, guard the land and the frontier now in their possession. All to the east of that frontier is the land of Greater China, and all to the west is indeed the land of Greater Tibet. Thereafter both sides shall not struggle like enemies, shall not lead armies into war and shall not invade and seize each other's territory.'[16]

Tibet continued to enjoy a flourishing relationship with various Buddhist monasteries in India, particularly Nalanda and Vikramshila, until the twelfth century. Tibetan Buddhist holy texts comprise the *Kangyur*, which includes 108 volumes containing the words of the Buddha, and the 225-volume *Tengyur,* which collects his teachings.[17]

The decline of Buddhism in India – combined with the long Muslim rule – weakened ties with Tibet. In 1206, Muhammad bin Bakhtiyar Khalji, a Turkish chieftain who had overrun northern India, invaded Tibet. His army was decimated in the cold. The rise of Islamic rulers in north India, and the establishment of Buddhism as the state religion in China by Kublai Khan, drew Tibet closer to China. Tibetan lamas turned to patrons in China and Mongolia.

So, how independent was Tibet in this period? Chinese historians Wang Jiawei and Nyima Gyaincain, who have explored China's historical claim to Tibet, acknowledge that the two countries were independent during the Tang era and the Tang did not have official rule over the Tubo.[18]

The Chinese Civilization Centre of Hong Kong also confirms the separate status of Tibet during the Tang period:

> Later, many wars broke out between the Tubo regime and the Tang Dynasty, and the Tubo army marched as far as Chang'an. The intermittent outbreaks of war and peace between the Tubo regime and the Tang Dynasty deepened their understanding and promoted economic exchange. In the early ninth century, the Tubo regime and the Tang Dynasty formed an alliance.[19]

Another Chinese historian, Bai Shouyi, writes:

In 822 [CE], the Tufan ruler met with the emissary of the Tang Emperor Mu Zong at Lhasa to discuss the alliance between the Tufan and the Tang, and a Monument of Unity was erected in front of the Jokhang Monastery the following year. Later, the Tufan was torn by a prolonged split, which ended only in the second half of the thirteenth century when it accepted the rule of the Yuan Empire.[20]

No significant contact between China and Tibet is known to have taken place after the Tang dynasty until the thirteenth century, when Mongolia conquered both countries. Wang and Gyaincain state that Buddhism declined in Tibet after the Tang dynasty before reviving in the tenth century via two routes: the Lower Route from China and the Upper Route from India. The Upper Route provided the Buddhist texts, which were translated into Tibetan, while the Lower Route 'played a role in the construction of monasteries in Tsang, the recruiting of monks, and the conducting of Buddhist activities'.[21] This description of the Indian route as the Upper Route, gives the impression that even this route was from the north, rather than across the Himalayas in the south.

In the first decade of the twentieth century, traces of this ancient history – and its realities – would become easy to see when the French army major Vicomte D'Ollone travelled through Yunnan, Sichuan (Szechuan), Tibet and Mongolia. He left behind a graphic account of the country and meeting the Thirteenth Dalai Lama in exile in Mongolia. It is evident from his travelogue that, culturally, Tibet was quite distinct from China and was, for all practical purposes, independent. D'Ollone wrote:

All the western provinces of the Middle Empire are merely territories won by conquest from non-Chinese populations. Yet the word 'won' is deceptive. The Chinese are content to occupy the fertile valleys where the superiority of their arms, their organisation, and their numbers assures them of the advantage; and there they have built strong fortresses, connected by roads across the more accessible passes.[22]

D'Ollone also described the separate identities of Chinese and Tibetan people, stating that, 'On the frontier of the Si-Fan China comes clearly and definitely to a stop, and even where the Imperial authority is recognised, it is known only as a foreign suzerainty.'

He asserted that the people of Tibet were connected by 'one common trait which at once distinguishes them from all their neighbours: they practise the religion of Lamaism'.[23] In the border region of China, the authority of the Chinese emperor was respected but resented. D'Ollone called the town of 'Ta-Tsien-Lu',[24] which had both a Tibetan king and a Chinese prefect, the 'gateway to Tibet'. A bridge at 'Lu-Ting-Kiao' on the 'Ta-Tu-ho' River was the only link between Tibet and China. D'Ollone observed that Tibetan architecture, too, was quite distinct from Chinese.

In the village of Kiang-Kyu, he found numerous Buddhist structures and statues that were heavily influenced by Indian culture. He wrote: 'No doubt the Buddhist apostles were accompanied from India by the first sculptors, who carved out of the rock, in the Hindoo manner, these extraordinary monuments: unprecedented in China, and containing characteristic details of the Graeco-Buddhist type.'[25] This village was in what is now the Sichuan province of China.

At Len-Chu (Lanzhou), the capital of Kansu (Gansu) province, D'Ollone saw a picturesque bridge made of boats – about two hundred yards long – on the Yellow River (Huang He) that marked the border between China and Mongolia. He met the Dalai Lama [the thirteenth] at Wu-Tai-Shan, the 'mountain with five terraces', a renowned monastery where he stayed while waiting for an invitation from the Chinese emperor to go to Beijing. Their conversation was somewhat circuitous, first translated from French to Chinese (by a Chinese interpreter), then to Mongolian (by a lama), after which another lama transmitted the words in Tibetan to the Dalai Lama.

D'Ollone's description of the Dalai Lama's ceremonial journey from Len-Chu to Beijing reflects his status in China as a religious leader rather than a vassal:

> Everywhere I saw triumphal arches of verdure, decorated with lanterns, oriflammes, and inscriptions, and the whole desert seemed to be transformed into a pleasure-garden ... Generals, governors, and viceroys attended his passage, and a veritable army was assembled to do him honour.[26]

Tibet and Ladakh

The links between Tibet and Ladakh can be traced to the seventh and eighth centuries. Ladakh was the route connecting Tibet to Kashgaria in East Turkestan. There is evidence of Tibet conquering Ladakh and extending as far as Gilgit and Baltistan. The origin of Buddhist monastic institutions in Ladakh dates back to the tenth century, and their growth is clearly influenced by Tibetan culture.[27]

During the Mughal era, Ladakh was ruled by a Buddhist king. In 1679, under Shah Jahan's reign, Tibet attacked Ladakh due to its alleged interference in western Tibet, prompting the latter to appeal for the assistance of the Mughal governor of Kashmir. The arrival of the Moghul forces helped ward off the Tibetan threat. With a treaty in 1684, Ladakh and Tibet were able to broadly define their borders, assigning Guge, Purang and Rudok to Tibet. Ladakh got a monopoly over the wool trade in western Tibet.

Gulab Singh, the governor of Jammu–Kashmir (then a part of Ranjit Singh's kingdom of Punjab), annexed Ladakh in 1834. In 1841, his general, Zorawar Singh, attacked Tibet and reached as far as Taklakot (Purang), near Lake Mansarovar (Mapam Yutso). Tibet, ostensibly part of the Manchu empire, looked to it for help. But China, in the midst of the First Opium War with Britain, was in no position to do so. So, the Tibetans bided their time, then annihilated the invading army in the bitter cold of winter. Zorawar Singh was among the 3,000 soldiers who perished. The victorious Tibetan forces chased the fleeing survivors into Ladakh. Although

Gulab Singh's forces returned the following year and recovered Ladakh.

An agreement was reached between the two sides in 1842 to respect the 'old, established frontiers' of Ladakh and Tibet. The right of Ladakhis to exchange tributes with Lhasa was reconfirmed, as was keeping the border open to trade. The Letters of Agreement, one in Tibetan and the other in Ladakhi, noted: 'No restriction shall be laid on the mutual export and import of commodities e.g., tea, piece-goods, etc., and trading shall be allowed according to the old, established customs.' Transport and accommodation were to be provided to each side's envoys.[28]

The ruler of Jammu–Kashmir sent an envoy to Lhasa every three years with presents for the Dalai Lama. However, the Chinese court records described these as a tribute to their emperor.[29]

2

Mongol Empire: Connecting Eurasia

The story of imperial conquest in Central Asia starts with the Mongols, who have a long history with Tibet. Mongol chronicles trace back their royal house to mythical Tibetan rulers and an Indian king.[1] Mongolia was the first foreign country to conquer Tibet.

In the thirteenth century, Mongolia was unified by Chinggis Khan (also spelt Genghis Khan), who built one of the largest empires known to the world.[2] The Mongols dominated Asia and Eastern Europe for several centuries, changing the course of history. At its height, the Mongol empire stretched from China to eastern Europe.

Chinggis Khan began his conquests by uniting Mongolia and attacking the Jin kingdom in northern China – a Manchurian Jurchen tribe that ruled over northern China, with Beijing as its capital (southern China was under the Song, a Han dynasty).[3] After Chinggis' death, his four sons divided the empire. In 1240, Godan Khan, Chinggis Khan's grandson and governor of northern China, sent an army to conquer Tibet, but Tibetan Buddhism soon became a bond between the two countries. The Mongols valued Tibetan monks for their learning and the rich treasure of Buddhist scriptures. When Godan was looking for a Buddhist scholar, the Radreng monastery sent Kunga Gyaltsen – a sixty-two-year-old monk, venerated as Sakya Pandita for his knowledge of Buddhism. Godan appointed several of his associates to his administration.

After Godan's death in 1251, his cousin, Kublai, seized power in China and launched his own dynasty in 1271 with a Sinicized name, Yuan – derived from Da Qianyuan, meaning 'the Great Original Force'. He retained the capital of the Jin dynasty and renamed it Dadu, 'the Great Capital'. His empire became one of the two largest ever to be ruled from Beijing, the other being the empire of the Manchus.

Kublai Khan strengthened the connection between the Mongols and Tibetan Buddhism by appointing a nephew of Sakya Pandita, Chogyal Phagpa, as his personal tutor. He vested him with the title of 'Imperial Preceptor', thus making Tibetan Buddhism the state religion of China. Kublai Khan instructed Phagpa to create a script for the Mongolian language to make it more suitable for governing China. The script, however, did not survive his dynasty's rule.

As many as fourteen Lamas of the Sakya School received the title Imperial Preceptor and Kublai Khan had several Tibetan temples built in Dadu. The Mongol rulers of China administered Tibet through the department of Buddhist and Tibetan affairs, with most staff being either Tibetan or Mongol. His patronage enabled the Sakya clergy to establish control over Tibet in temporal matters as well.

The priest-patron (*cho-yon* in Tibetan) relationship, which started with the Mongol conquest of China, had its downsides for Tibet. In political terms, it reduced it to a vassal of Mongol rulers. Their patronage of Tibetan monks led to the rise of monasteries vying for favour, giving rise to bitter rivalries that remained in check only as long as the Mongols themselves were united. Once they were pushed out of China by the Ming dynasty in 1368, internecine warfare arose among the Mongols, affecting the monasteries as well.

Dalai Lama and the Mongols

Mongol association with Tibetan Buddhism took a critical political turn in the sixteenth century with the founding of the Gelug sect. In 1566, Secen Hongtaiji, a Mongol chieftain, came to Tibet and converted to Buddhism. On his return, he advised the ruler of the Tumed Mongols, Altan Khan (1502–1582), to use Buddhism to strengthen his position among his peers. In 1578, Altan Khan invited Sonam Gyatso, the head of the Gelug sect, to visit his capital, Hohhot (now in Inner Mongolia). The two struck a deal of mutual support. Altan Khan recognized him as the pre-eminent lama of Tibet, conferring the title *Dalai*, meaning ocean.[4] The full title was *Dalai Lama Vajradhara*, or 'the All-embracing Lama, the Holder of the Thunderbolt'.[5] In turn, Gyatso declared Altan Khan to be the reincarnation of Kublai Khan.[6] Altan Khan also conferred, retrospectively, the title on Sonam Gyatso's two predecessors – Gedun Drupa and Gedun Gyatso.

The Chinese have their own version of these events. They maintain that, at the request of Altan Khan, it was the Ming emperor who conferred the title of Dalai Lama on Sonam Gyatso. But this is highly unlikely since Altan Khan and the Mings were enemies. Besides, what reason would the Chinese have to bestow a Mongol title on a Tibetan lama?

Sonam Gyatso remained at Altan Khan's court to spread Buddhism among the Mongols. This elevated his status among them – but also increased Mongol interference in Tibetan affairs. He died in Mongolia in 1588, after which Altan Khan's grandson was declared his incarnation as the fourth Dalai Lama. But the Mongol Lama had a difficult time finding acceptance among Tibetans. He also did not keep good health in Tibet's climate and died at age twenty-seven. It is suspected that he was poisoned.

Having a Mongol chieftain as its head brought disrepute to the Gelug sect and increased its dependent status. Eventually, Tibet's Tsang province rose in revolt. Its ruler, Karma Puntsog Namgyal – a patron of the rival Karma Kagyu sect – raised a strong army to resist the Mongols.

Fortunately, the Mongol Dalai Lama's reincarnation was found in an aristocratic Tibetan family. The Fifth Dalai Lama, Ngawang Lobsang Gyatso (1617–1682), enjoyed wider acceptance. But in 1641 a new threat emerged on Tibet's borders – Gushri Khan, another Mongol ruler. The Gelug sect sided with him in expectation of garnering support against the Karma Kagyu sect and the Tsang ruler.

The Fifth Dalai Lama had to restore both the ecclesiastical prestige of his sect and its temporal authority. He used his Mongol connections to subdue the powerful Tsang region after a protracted struggle. Although he enjoyed great respect – and is considered one of the greatest Dalai Lamas – he did not have temporal powers in his early years. The Great Fifth, as he is popularly called in Tibet, was still regarded as merely the spiritual preceptor of the Mongol king Gushri Khan, who had proclaimed himself the ruler of Tibet after defeating the Tsang king. He created the office of a governor, *desi*, to handle all political matters.

This was the cho-yon relationship in operation, and no contradiction was seen by the people between his authority and that of the Mongol king. But the Great Fifth was uncomfortable with Mongol control and soon found a new ally to counter it. The Manchus, who had overthrown the Mings in China in 1644 CE, found the Tibetan connection useful in organizing their religious order in China and in countering their traditional rivals, the Mongols.

The Great Fifth took the title of *Chenrezig*, the Embodiment of Compassion (the Tibetan equivalent of Avalokiteśvara). He moved his seat to Lhasa and selected Marpori Hill as the site for his palace, which he named Potala, after the legendary hilltop abode of the Avalokiteśvara in Kanyakumari in India. The monasteries, called *gompas*, became the centres of administration, replacing the earlier feudal *dzong* (fort or citadel). The Great Fifth left his earlier monastery in Shigatse, Tashilhunpo, to his tutor, Choki Gyaltsen, and conferred on him the title of Panchen Lama (a learned scholar). The title was also conferred posthumously on his three previous incarnations, making him fourth in the line.[7]

Chinese historians do not deny the cho-yon relationship but insist it was between a sovereign and his subject. Whatever the nature of the relationship, it is undeniable that Tibetan monks like Phagpa of the Sakya sect were treated with great reverence by

Mongol and Manchu rulers. Even the Ming rulers held them in high esteem. They were bestowed high honours and given lavish gifts. Kublai Khan, twice in two years, gave gifts of gold, silver and pearls to him and other Tibetan monks. Since the monks were not temporal rulers of Tibet, their relationship with the Mongol emperors could not be the determinant of the country's political status. This had been settled earlier by the Mongol military conquest of Tibet. Under the Mongols, the status of Tibet was no different from that of China: both were ruled by a third power.

3

Chinese Empire: Conquering Barbarians

The Chinese call their country Zhongguo, the Middle Kingdom. 'China' is a name used by foreigners since ancient times, with Chīna appearing in early Sanskrit texts. Its mainland consists of the vast plains of three rivers: Huang He, Yangtze and Zhujiang. North of the plains are the steppes that stretch from Xinjiang (East Turkestan) to Manchuria. To the west is the plateau of Tibet, where the Huang He and the Yangtse rivers originate. These mighty rivers and mountain ranges running north-south separate the Tibetan plateau from China's plains. The earliest civilizational remains found in China are around the Huang He, a region considered the birthplace of Chinese civilization. To the east, there is the 'Eastern Sea', which protected China until modern times. But the steppes, inhabited by hardy horse-riding nomads – the 'barbarians' (Huns, Mongols, Turks and Tibetans) – were a perpetual source of invasion. From ancient times, marauders from the steppes ravaged the rich plains of China and ruled over its people for long periods, forcing migrations to the south.

The river plains are inhabited by people who call themselves Han. They were historically agricultural people whose staple food was rice. The steppes and highlands are inhabited by Tibetans, Turks, Mongols, Manchus and several other smaller communities who, except the Tibetans, were nomadic herdsmen. These cultures have distinct histories and ethnicities. Even the southern province of Yunnan, which is geographically the northern extension of Southeast Asia, consists largely of high plateau. After Xinjiang, it has the largest Muslim population in China.

China's external boundaries have never been constant and have varied with the power and ambition of its ruling dynasties. The Han Chinese were generally content to protect their river plains by building a northern wall on the edge of the steppes. It was rebuilt by the Ming dynasty (Han Chinese), and came to be called the Great Wall. The nomads on the other side retained control of the steppes, though the largest Chinese empires were under the Tang, Mongol and Manchu dynasties – all of which originated in the steppes and commanded both sides of the wall.

An American missionary, Samuel Wells Williams, wrote at length on China and the Chinese language in the mid-nineteenth century:

> The Chinese themselves divide their empire into three principal parts, rather by the different form of government which they adopt in each, than by any geographical arrangement.
>
> 1. The *Eighteen Provinces*, or that which is more strictly called China, or China Proper; it is, with trivial additions, the country which was conquered by the Manchus in 1664 [sic].
> 2. *Manchuria,* or the native country of the Manchus, lying north of the gulf of Liautung and east of the Inner Daourian Mountains to the Pacific.
> 3. *Colonial Possessions,* including Mongolia, Īlí (comprising Sungaria and Eastern Turkestan), Koko-nor and Tibet.[1]

In his monumental two-volume work, *A History of China*, published in 1844, Thomas Thornton, a member of London's Royal Asiatic Society, described China as 'an almost circular area of from five hundred to six hundred leagues[2] in diameter, watered from west to east by two great navigable rivers, taking their sources from the lofty mountains of Tibet'.[3] Regarding the Yunling mountain range, he added: 'The Yun-ling chain ... runs from north to south, and constitutes a real natural barrier between China and Tibet.'[4] The Yunling chain in Yunnan province runs between the Mekong River to the west (which flows into South-East Asia) and the Yangtse River to the east (which turns into China). In the north, Thornton identified the great chain of the Yin Mountains as the 'boundary between China, the country of the Mongols, and the Desert'.

When describing the courses of China's two mighty rivers, the Yangtse and the Huang He, Thornton wrote: 'They both take their rise *beyond the limits of the empire*, in the mountains of Tibet, which form part of the great hill-country of the Himalaya [*emphasis added*]'.[5]

Chinese Language

The Chinese language, with numerous mutually unintelligible dialects, is predominantly spoken in the plains. Mandarin, the dialect currently deemed official and enforced throughout the country, is spoken in the north. What binds these dialects is the Chinese script, universally recognizable throughout the country. It consists of ideograms (also called characters) that were first pictographic but have now become symbolic and non-alphabetical. The ideograms are read differently in different dialects (as a result, today's Chinese films carry subtitles in Chinese – even within the country – to enable the speakers of other dialects to read the dialogue).

Writing foreign names is difficult in any language but impossible in Chinese. During the Opium War, Canton's Governor General Qi Gong (Ch'i Kung), wrote about the problem:

> Foreign languages have sounds for which no [Chinese] character exists to represent them, and in each instance of this we take the nearest corresponding character and add a *kou* [mouth] radical to its left side, and in punctuating it one must reverse the order. Foreign sounds do not match the sound of Chinese characters, and the Cantonese dialect differs from those in other provinces, and still more it is distinct from Tibetan.[6]

As described by General Qi, the Chinese use an unorthodox method to write foreign names. They reduce the name to two or three syllables and use the Chinese ideogram closest in sound for each syllable. The family name is written first in Chinese.

For example, Chinggis Khan's name became Tai Zu in Chinese and Kublai Khan's, Shi Za or Shi Zu. The Manchus resisted using this system for long. The Qianlong emperor, the most powerful ruler of the Manchu dynasty, transcribed foreign words using the Manchu script. But as the Manchus became Sinicized, they adopted the Chinese practice.

Rule by 'Barbarians'

The first known kingdom in China is Xia, founded around 2000 BCE. Little is known about these people, but some archaeological finds in the Huang He plains have affirmed that they are not entirely mythical. The earliest surviving Chinese written characters are from the period of the Shang dynasty, which followed the Xia. The third dynasty – the Zhou (eleventh to third century BCE) – introduced their deity, *Tian* (meaning heaven) and the Zhao ruler called himself the Son of Heaven (*Tian-zi*). But this was not a period of unity in China; the country was frequently overrun by invaders and split into warring states.

The Zhou period is considered to be the birth of Chinese civilization as we know it. The greatest Chinese philosopher, Kung Fu-zi – better known as Confucius (551–479 BCE) – expounded his ideas of social and political order during this age as the core of Han culture and civilization took shape.

China was unified for the first time in the third century BCE under the Qin dynasty. After he consolidated his hold over the Huang He River basin, Shi Huang Di declared himself the emperor in 221 BCE. He then conquered the Yangtse River plains and the Zhujiang River further south. He also built part of the Great Wall to protect against nomadic Hun tribes. But his dynasty was short-lived. In 206 BCE, the Han dynasty overthrew his son. The Qin and the Han dynasties extended their power into the southern coastal regions inhabited by the Yue peoples, bringing with them their culture and system of writing: 'Though extensive borrowing occurred, northern Chinese (Mandarin) never succeeded in replacing the Yue languages, which continue to this day in the form of Chinese dialects (including Wu, Min, and Cantonese).'[7] Over time, the Yue languages became monosyllabic and tonal, like Mandarin.

Several Chinese ruling dynasties originated from the 'barbarians' of the steppes. They conquered China and, combining with their homelands, built large empires. These dynasties preferred to keep the capital in the north. The Manchurian Jin dynasty made its base where modern Beijing is now located and the Mongols, who replaced them, retained it as their capital. The Ming, a Han dynasty from the south, preserved it as the capital but maintained a large military presence in Beijing to counter persistent Mongol raids. They thus had two bases: Nan-jing (meaning southern capital) and Bei-jing (northern capital).

The migrating 'barbarians' steadily got absorbed into the vast human ocean of China's Han civilization. The migration pattern in China's history has moved from north to south due to the relentless pressure of invasions from the steppes. The southward migration of the Han Chinese increased the Chinese character of the coastal population. It also led to China's expansion. The northern conquerors retained an interest in their homelands and extended their rule in those regions. The Turko-Chinese Tang dynasty overthrew the Sui in the seventh century CE and expanded its empire deep into Central Asia, ruling there for three centuries. In the thirteenth and fourteenth centuries the Mongol Yuan dynasty, and the Manchu Qing dynasty from 1644 CE to 1912 CE, did the same. China now treats the conquests by these dynasties as being part of the divine 'motherland'.

The conquering 'barbarians' also extended China's empire to the south. Yunnan, with its capital at Dali, was an independent kingdom between China and Burma till the Mongol conquest in the thirteenth century. The kings of Dali adopted the name

Gāndhāra for their kingdom, after the historical region of northwest India (now in Afghanistan), and considered themselves descendants of the legendary Indian emperor, Ashoka. The Mongol prince, Uriyangkadai, conquered Yunnan and added it to Kublai Khan's empire. Many of his soldiers were Muslims from Central Asia who settled in Yunnan. Although Han Chinese migration has changed the population mix of the province, Muslims continue to be a significant minority there.[8] Kublai Khan appointed Syed Shams-el-Din Omar as its first governor. He claimed to be a descendant of the Prophet, and his tomb included an inscription in Arabic. Nearby, there were remains of a seven-storey stupa in granite, dating back to the Song dynasty, with an inscription in Sanskrit. There were also several inscriptions in Tibetan, testifying to Tibet's historical influence in the region.

Such large empires had to be ruled through divine myths, which each dynasty strengthened. The Middle Kingdom, comprising the Chinese cultural area, claimed to be the centre of the world – surrounded by tributary states. Its emperor was the Son of Heaven, who presided over a hierarchical international order. Gifts sent by foreign rulers were called tributes, and it was mandatory for the envoy bringing them to perform the ceremonial *kowtow* to the emperor (more on this below). This was deemed in China to be an expression of submission by the foreign ruler. Court chronicles recorded all diplomatic contact as an acceptance of Chinese sovereignty. The fact that for most of its history, China was either divided into smaller kingdoms or ruled by foreign 'barbarians' did not change the narrative. Whoever conquered the country was Sinicized and accepted as the Son of Heaven.

In the late nineteenth century, a British diplomat in China, Hugh Fraser, divided the states dependent on China into three categories, according to the degree of their dependence:

Thibet, where the Government is directed by a Chinese Envoy, stands alone in the first rank; Annam and Corea, whose sovereigns [accept] investiture at the hands of the Emperor, but over whose subjects, even in China, the Imperial authorities do not seem to claim a right to exercise jurisdiction, come next; and lastly Burma and Nepaul, who merely send complimentary tribute at intervals in token of amity and deference to a powerful neighbour.[9]

Chinese emperors saw the tributary system as a fair arrangement – they provided trading privileges, political legitimacy and protection to the vassal in exchange for recognition of their overlordship. The periodic tribute paid to China was more than compensated by generous return gifts. Modern China continues to regard this as a just and pragmatic basis for an international order founded on equitable moral precepts.

The Qianlong emperor declared 'Hindustan' to be a vassal state and in 1790, as part of celebrations to mark his eightieth birthday, he wrote that Hindustan had 'sent an agent to the court to present a tributary memorial and tribute'.[10] It is not known which Indian kingdom sent this envoy, since India was known in China by different names through the ages.

In the last millennium, the largest empires of China were formed during the rule of the Mongols and the Manchus, and it is on the basis of their imperial conquests that modern China lays claim to territories outside its mainland. The Mongols who set up the Yuan dynasty, and the Manchus who took the name Qing, were foreigners who conquered and ruled over China. In contrast, the Han dynasties in this period – the Song and the Ming – were content to rule over China proper (the twenty-three provinces of Han China).

Earlier, under the Han and Tang dynasties, there had been successful expeditions into the Turkish areas of Central Asia, but these were brief and had no lasting impact. East Turkestan – made a province in 1884 and named Xinjiang – came under stable rule from Beijing only during the Manchu period. The Tang dynasty, which had also ruled over large parts of Turkestan, was half Turkic.

Towards the end of Manchu rule, Manchuria was split into three provinces – Liaoning, Jilin and Heilongjiang – and was fully absorbed into China. China still looks at Mongolia, which it calls Outer Mongolia, as a Chinese province forcibly snatched by Russia. This stretches even into modern times. During Soviet leader Mikhail Gorbachev's visit to China in May 1989, Deng Xiaoping mentioned Outer Mongolia as one of the territories that Russia had taken from it.

The Kowtow

The practice of the kowtow before the Chinese emperor deserves special mention here. Foreign envoys in the Manchu Qing court were required to kneel on the ground thrice, tapping their head on the floor three times with each kneel. The ritual was imposed on all foreign envoys and considered a demonstration of submission by their ruler to the Chinese emperor. When Qing emperors agreed to receive European envoys in the seventeenth century, courtiers insisted that the envoys perform the kowtow, which they agreed to in their eagerness to gain trading rights.

At the time, China had no comprehension of Europe, whose people were referred to as 'hairy barbarians' that came from across the 'western ocean'. The Chinese believed there were two oceans, the eastern and the western. Of the seventeen missions from the West between 1655 and 1795, 'all but one yielded to the Chinese demand and performed the *kowtow* to the emperor'.[11] In 1858, Britain put an end to the kowtow in the Treaty of Tientsin (Tianjin), which stated that the ambassador or any other diplomatic agent would not be required to 'perform any ceremony derogatory to him as representing the Sovereign of an independent nation, on a footing of equality with that of China'.[12]

Ming Dynasty

China remained restive under Mongol rule, which lasted about a hundred years. In 1368, the successors of Kublai Khan were overthrown by Zhu Yuanzhang, a resident of Anhui province, who founded his own dynasty and called it Ming (meaning 'radiant'). It lasted nearly three centuries, until 1644, and was the last Han dynasty to rule China.

After driving the Mongols out of Dadu, the Mings renamed the city Beiping, meaning North Pacified. The Mongols retreated to the steppes and made Hohhot, in Inner Mongolia, their base. The Ming ruler, Zhu Yuanzhang (Chu Yüan-chang), ruled from Nanjing with the imperial title of Hongwu, one of the few rulers to unify China from the south. His son, who ruled as the Yongle emperor, moved the capital to Beiping and renamed it Beijing (spelt Peking in the Wade-Giles system) – meaning North Capital – to be in a better position to deal with the Mongols, who continually raided China and found ingenious ways to overcome the Great Wall. In 1550, Altan Khan skirted the wall and attacked Beijing. The city's walls held, but he ravaged the countryside. In 1449, the Ming Zhengtong emperor (1436–1449) was defeated and taken prisoner by another Mongol ruler, Esen, at Tumu in Hebei province. He was later released.

Continuing to be raided by the Mongols, the Mings had to expend enormous energy and resources to build defences against them. They reconstructed walls on the border with Mongolia, strengthening them with brick and stone, and erected watch towers. The location of the Great Wall is an authoritative indication of the northern frontier of China as perceived over the centuries by the Chinese themselves. It was built broadly along the southern edge of the Gobi Desert to protect the fertile plains from invasion. Before 1429, there are no references in Ming records to the Great Wall, though it is believed that the Qin dynasty had built some portions of it in the third century BCE. Keay writes: 'The "Great Wall" was unquestionably a Ming creation, both in terms of its construction and of its later repute.'[13] In the fifteenth century, the Ming extended the wall along the border with Manchuria for protection against the Manchu tribes. This section came to be called the Liaodong Wall.

In 1610, the visiting Jesuit missionary Matteo Ricci noted the presence of a 405 miles (650 kilometres) long wall. While China now regards the Great Wall as a tourist site, 'Mongolian historians insist that the Chinese and Mongols always were completely distinct political, geographical, and cultural units of equal status, demarcated by the Great Wall.'[14]

The Mings organized China into eleven provinces that remained approximately the same throughout their extended rule. Tibet was not one of them (along with the Mongol territories, it had broken away after the collapse of the Yuan dynasty). The Mings were not interested in maintaining the level of commercial and cultural contact that the Yuans had with Central Asia. Their main preoccupation was defending themselves against the Mongols. Tibet had very little official contact with the Mings. But as with the Mongols, the Mings were fascinated by the religious beliefs and practices of Tibet and even invited the Fifth Karmapa Lama to visit.[15] More journeys eastward by lamas followed. But 'neither in the economic nor in the political realms did the Tibetans perceive themselves to be subjects of the Ming court'.[16]

The authority of the Sakya clergy in Tibet declined with the overthrow of Mongol rule in China. Wang and Gyaincain write that 'the Ming Dynasty refrained from acting like the Yuan dynasty, which gave special support only to the Sagya Sect'.[17] They instead widened contact with Tibetan monasteries by sending gifts. Chinese historians maintain that the monks paid tribute to the Ming rulers and that Tibet remained a tributary state as under the Yuan dynasty.

The Ming period is considered a golden age of Chinese history. Although they faced serious threats from the north, they were able to expand their empire southwards. They conquered northern Vietnam, which they named *Annam* (meaning the 'pacified south', a misnomer since the region kept rebelling).

Manchu Conquest of China

In the seventeenth century, the Jurchens from Manchuria became a serious threat to the declining Mings. They frequently breached the Liaodong Wall and raided China. In 1644, they crossed it in force and captured Beijing.

The Jin dynasty that had ruled northern China before the Mongol Yuan dynasty was also Jurchen. The Jurchen language is considered part of the Tungusic group and is linked with neighbouring languages like Turkic, Mongolian, Japanese and Korean.[18] A Korean emissary, Sin Chung-il – who visited the tribes in 1595 – found them heavily influenced by Mongol and Han cultures. They used the Mongol script in preference to the one developed by the Jin dynasty. Some of the educated people among them could speak Chinese. Through their Mongol neighbours, they had become familiar with Tibetan Buddhism and Confucian values from China, though traditional shamanism remained their dominant faith.[19]

The Jurchens had watched their more successful cousins, the Mongols, build vast empires and acquire immense power since the days of Chinggis Khan. But by the sixteenth century, Mongol power had declined. Nurgaci (also written as Nurhaci, 1559–1626) united the Jurchen tribes and declared himself a *Khan*, a title used by the Mongols. He patronized the Sakya sect, as did the Mongols, and its monks were present at the coronation ceremony of his successor, Hung Taiji, who consolidated the earlier unification and declared himself emperor – *Khagan,* or Khan-of-khans.

After one of his victories over the Mongols, Hung Taiji also made himself a patron of the *Mahākāla* cult. He forbade his people to call themselves Jurchen, due to its association with the vassals of the Chinese and adopted a new name – Manchu. While the origin of this name is obscure, it is said to be derived from the Sanskrit word *mañjuśri* denoting good luck from the Buddhist faith. The following year, Hung Taiji took on the name Qing (meaning 'pure' or 'clear') for his dynasty. He also had its genealogy compiled and claimed a shared ancestry with the Mongols and the Koreans. Having established his credentials, he turned his attention to China, where the Ming dynasty was in terminal decline. Inept rulers, moral degradation, high taxes, famines, intrigues in the court and rebellions in the provinces had sapped the country.

Hung Taiji carried out a series of successful raids into China. But he died in 1643, leaving the conquest of China to his younger brother, Dorgon, who crossed the Great Wall the following year and occupied Beijing. The last Ming emperor hanged himself. Hung Taiji's five-year-old son, Fulin, reigned as the Shunzhi emperor with the help of his mother and Dorgon.

Mongol–Manchu Rivalry

After the Manchus conquered China, they got direct access to Tibet and the opportunity to use its religious power to bear upon the Mongols. The Manchus knew the importance of Tibetan Buddhism among the Mongols: 'Since the time of Nurgaci it had been clear that legitimate rule over the Mongols depended upon patronizing Tibetan lamas, whom Altan Khan had established as the spiritual guides of the Mongols'.[20]

Within a few years of conquering China – during the reign of the Shunzhi emperor – the Manchus formalized the ruler-monk relationship with the Dalai Lama. This served the interests of both sides: the Dalai Lama could fend off rival sects in Tibet and the Manchus derived political legitimacy among his followers.

To help in organizing his religious and administrative affairs, the Shunzhi emperor invited the Fifth Dalai Lama (the Great Fifth) to visit Beijing. This was also intended to wean Tibet away from the Mongols. Himself looking for an opportunity to throw off the Mongol yoke, the Great Fifth went to Beijing in 1651. The emperor bestowed high honours on him during his long stay.

Chinese historians depict this as a visit by a vassal paying obeisance to a sovereign, but Tibetan sources maintain that this was in the cho-yon tradition, and the two leaders met as equals. In any case, the firmness with which the Great Fifth went about establishing his authority in Tibet, and setting up a theocratic government, betrayed few signs of subordination.

Tragically, a series of disputed Dalai Lama scenarios followed the Great Fifth's death in 1682. Sangye Gyatso, rumoured to be his illegitimate son, became a power broker. An internal power struggle ensued in which both the Mongols and the Manchus were actively involved. Sangye Gyatso selected Tsangyang Gyatso as the sixth

A painting at the Potala Palace of the Fifth Dalai Lama meeting the Shunzhi Emperor in Beijing, 1653

Dalai Lama and appointed himself regent. He invited Latsang Khan, grandson of Gushri Khan, to help him. He also hid the news of the Great Fifth's death from the Kangxi (K'ang-hsi) emperor – Shunzhi's successor in Beijing – who was enraged when he found out about it sixteen years later.

Sangye Gyatso soon developed differences with Latsang Khan, but he was defeated and killed in 1705. The young Dalai Lama, Tsangyang Gyatso, was also no match for the Mongols. He turned to the Manchus for help but died on his way to Beijing. Latsang Khan tried to instal a new Dalai Lama, believed to be his son, but found himself overthrown by a rival Mongol tribe, the Zungars.

Under Tsewang Rabdan (1697–1727), the Zungars invaded Tibet in 1717. This enraged the Kangxi emperor, and he sent a force to expel them. The Zungars thwarted the first two Manchu invasions of Tibet. But in the spring of 1720, the emperor made a two-pronged attack – one from Qinghai in the north and the other from Sichuan in the east. The army from Sichuan reached Lhasa by autumn and routed the Zungars. This was the first time that a Chinese or, more accurately, a Manchu army had entered Lhasa.

The Kangxi emperor endeared himself to the Gelugpa lamas by installing a boy selected by them as the Seventh Dalai Lama. An imperial resident called the *amban* (meaning high official in Manchu language) was stationed in Lhasa. The emperor also reorganized the government under the nominal authority of the Dalai Lama, with a four-member council, the kashag, holding administrative powers. He elevated the Fifth Panchen Lama to a position of near equivalence to the Dalai Lama, an act designed to help manage the administration during the Dalai Lama's minority, but it also created a rival centre of power. The bulk of the Manchu forces withdrew after three years.

The Tibetans soon revolted against the Manchus, prompting the Yongzheng (Yung-cheng) emperor who had succeeded Kangxi in Beijing, to send an army of 15,000 to suppress them. The emperor now stationed two ambans, backed by a military escort of 2,000 men, to keep an eye on the government. He also detached the Amdo and Kham provinces from Tibet and merged them into Qinghai and Sichuan, with some areas incorporated into Yunnan. The Dalai Lama was exiled to Kham province, and Pholhanas, a member of the council, was made the effective ruler. By 1727, Panchen Lama had control over three large districts in Tsang province, marking the beginning of China's rule in Tibet.

Monasteries Enmeshed in Power Struggles

There was relative peace in Tibet for twenty years under Pholhanas. On his death, however, another uprising erupted in Lhasa, resulting in one of the ambans getting killed and the suicide of the other. Once again, a Manchu army was sent to Lhasa. The Qianlong emperor, who had succeeded Yongzheng, thought it wise to restore temporal powers to the Dalai Lama, though he also reasserted the role of the kashag and the amban.

The Tibetan monasteries prized Manchu patronage, as it expanded their reach throughout the empire. In turn, the Manchus revered the Tibetan lamas as much as the Mongol khans did. Tibetan monasteries were already present in the neighbouring regions of Tibet – Gansu, Sichuan, East Turkestan and Mongolia. Under Manchu patronage, they spread to Manchuria and Han China, where the Tibetan holy texts were translated into the Chinese, Mongol and Manchu languages.

The Qianlong emperor was also the religious head of his empire. He claimed the right to approve the heads of all major religious organizations – the Dalai Lama, the chief Taoist and the Kong (the descendant of Confucius). He considered Ashoka, the Buddhist Indian emperor of the third century BCE, his role model and dedicated his conquests to the Buddha.

A devout patron of Buddhism, he sponsored the translations of the sacred Buddhist texts, the *Tripitakas*, from Tibetan into the Manchu and Mongolian languages, along with the original commentaries written about them. Buddhist temples were constructed, and several hundred Buddhist monks from Tibet and elsewhere were invited to study in China. Qianlong used Buddhism's appeal to establish his moral authority universally, not only among the Chinese but also among the Mongols and other neighbouring people. He severed Tibet's links with the Mongols, declaring that incarnations of the living Buddha would only be found among Tibetans, thus precluding Mongols from being recognized as the Dalai Lama any longer.

After the Fifth, a succession of Dalai Lamas died young and, between the Fifth and the Twelfth, only two lived beyond the age of twenty-four. While perhaps a coincidence, the introduction of the regency system created a centre of power that would be diminished if a Dalai Lama became strong. The Manchu rulers used the Panchen Lama as the regent of the Dalai Lamas during their minorities. The Panchen Lamas, holding a lower religious stature and less authority among the people of Tibet, were more amenable to serving the goals of the Manchus, who honoured them and worked through them during the minority of a Dalai Lama. China refers to the Panchen Lama as the Bainqen Erdeni and maintains that it was the Kangxi emperor who first conferred the title in 1713, although this was the fifth Panchen Lama.

The Manchus also interfered in the process of selecting the Dalai Lama. In 1793, the Qianlong emperor sent a golden urn to be used in the casting of lots by which the Dalai Lama was chosen. The urn was used in the selection of three Dalai Lamas, from the Tenth to the Twelfth.

The ambans had a small Chinese, mostly Manchu, staff to assist them and a small military contingent. The emperor often appointed two ambans, to keep an eye on each other. The Tibetans hated the ambans because of their arrogance and extortion of the people. According to Sarat Chandra Das, who often travelled to Tibet, the ambans were 'the terror of the Tibetans, who abhor[red] them from the depth of their hearts'.[21] In one incident, the people of Shigatse attacked the amban and his entourage when he tried to extort money from them. He was rescued by the local Tibetan force.

Tibet needed the Manchus for protection against the predations of the rulers of Nepal and Kashmir. When the English disappointed them by refusing to restrain Nepal from invading in 1791, they fell back on the Manchu emperor for support. To protect themselves from diseases like smallpox – which distant foreigners like Europeans brought with them – and to protect their monastic religion and polity, Tibetans were in agreement with the Manchus on maintaining their reclusiveness.

Conquest of East Turkestan (Xinjiang)

Today, the Xinjiang Uyghur Autonomous Region – about half the size of India – is a Chinese autonomous region, split in the middle by the Tianshan Mountains. The northern part was once referred to as Zungaria (also spelt Zungharia, Dzungaria or Jungaria) and, until the nineteenth century, remained mainly populated by Mongol people. The southern part was referred to as Kashgaria, after its main city of Kashgar, and inhabited by Turkic people, the largest among them being the Uyghurs (the region is also called Uyghuristan).

Currently, the name East Turkestan is more popular, as it encompasses other Turkic inhabitants like the Kazakh and Kyrgyz. Tucked within the Tianshan Mountains is the Ili Valley, originally predominantly Kazakh but now also inhabited by the Han Chinese. Yining, formerly known as Kulja (or Kuldja), is its main city.

The Kunlun Mountains were regarded as the southern border of East Turkestan both by the British and the Chinese. In a paper presented at the Central Asian Society in 1907, a British army officer, Major Clarence D. Bruce, referring to the region as 'Chinese Turkestan', described it as surrounded by the Kunlun Mountains on the south, the Altai Mountains and the Pamirs on the west, and the Tianshan Mountains on the north. On the east, the region merged into the desert and there was no natural boundary. Bruce outlined the southern border as 'an almost impassable wall formed by the Kuen Lun mountains'. From India, he identified a route via Leh and the Karakoram Pass as the main access to the region, with another via Gilgit and Hunza, which was used less often.[22]

East Turkestan has also historically served as the main land route to China. Small oases along the north and south of the Taklamakan and Gobi deserts enabled caravans and armies to traverse the distance of 4,000 kilometres.

The Uyghurs, who regard themselves as a separate nation, have repeatedly revolted against Chinese rule. In earlier times, they referred to themselves simply as *Musalmáns* (Muslims); the term Uyghurs only came to be applied to them in the twentieth century. They are distinct from the Muslim Chinese of Gansu and Shanxi provinces, who are called Hui in China.[23] Due to its military strength and the ethnic divisions among the local people – especially between the Mongols and the Muslim Chinese – China was able to maintain control over these provinces. Chinese settlers lived close to the river, while the Mongols and Dungans were driven into the foothills. They dreaded the Chinese soldiers, who continually looted them and protected Chinese settlers.[24]

Kashgaria was a major centre of Indian civilization in the past. Places like Uttarakuru, Parasika, Rishika and Parama Kamboja – referred to in Indian epics like the Ramayana and the Mahabharata – have been identified in this region. It was the eastern fringe of the Indo-Greek kingdoms left behind by Alexander (the Great) in the fourth century BCE. During this period, it became an important centre of Buddhist learning.

The three main towns of Kashgaria – Kashgar, Yarkand and Khotan – are located along the southwestern edge of the Taklamakan Desert. They were closely linked to the civilizations in the Amu Darya (Oxus River) basin further to the west and acted as the centre of the Turan civilization, which in the third and second millenniums BCE was a contemporary of Sumer (Mesopotamia) and the Indus Valley (India). Archaeological finds also affirm close cultural ties with India. Buddhism was the dominant religion in the region before Islam arrived in the tenth century, though Buddhism continued to be practised until the sixteenth century.

After the Indo-Europeans, the region was occupied by Huns (called Hiung-nu by the Chinese). The Huns also occupied Mongolia and large parts of China. Emperor Wu Ti of China's Han dynasty invaded it in 115 BCE. China called the region Xi-yu – the western territory – and claims that its rulers accepted Chinese sovereignty until 36 BCE, basing its claim on the 'tribute' paid by its rulers to the Chinese emperor. Despite these assertions, though, China's military presence was challenged by others in the region.

In the first century CE, Kashgaria became part of the Kushan empire of India, ruled by Kanishka, who made it an important centre of Buddhist learning. In Turfan and Kucha in northern Kashgaria, Sarvastivada became popular, while in Khotan, Mahayana became the dominant Buddhist doctrine. Buddhism spread to China via this route and several Chinese scholars, including Xuanzang, travelled to India to study Buddhism. The almost complete text of a Sanskrit treatise from this period, *Mahāratnakuta-Dharmaparyāya* (or *Kashyapapari-varta*), was discovered in this region.[25]

The Russian army officer Colonel Aleksey N. Kuropatkin made an extensive survey of Kashgaria in the 1870s, describing the region as covering 19,000 square miles (49,000 square kilometres) bounded by the Pamir to the west, Tianshan Mountains to the north, the Kunlun Mountains to the south and the Altai Tag to the east. He estimated the population to be 1.2 million, writing that the region was originally inhabited by Indo-European people.

From the second century CE, people of Mongol descent entered the region. In the eighth century, Arabs invaded it. Kuropatkin found a wide variety of traditional inhabitants belonging mainly to the Turkic race. The more modern inhabitants were Chinese, Dungans and immigrants from the Khokand region of western

Turkestan. The Chinese were primarily engaged in extracting natural resources like gold and naphtha. Russian goods were dominant in the markets, though Indian muslin was imported. The Turkish language was spoken all over Kashgaria in a dialect different from other Central Asian dialects, the difference arising from the admixture of some Chinese words.

Towards the end of the nineteenth century, the Hungarian-born British archaeologist Marc Aurel Stein carried out extensive surveys in East Turkestan. In Tashkurghan, which is in the Sarikol region of Kashgaria adjoining Afghanistan, he found the remains of an ancient *stupa* ascribed by local tradition to the Indian emperor Ashoka. He unearthed copper coins of early Khotan kings showing both Indian and Chinese legends in Kharoshthi script. The coins were of metal and stone, with representations of the Buddha and Buddhist divinities. Stein concluded that this was the region where Xuanzang had seen hundreds of Buddhist stupas on his journey to India.

In Dandan-Uiliq, he found frescoes resembling the later Ajanta frescoes. He collected manuscripts in various languages and scripts – Indian Brahmi, Central Asian Brahmi, Kharoshthi, Tibetan and Chinese. Notably, some Kharoshthi inscriptions were in a style similar to that prevailing in Takshashila (called Taxila by the Greeks) in Pakistan.[26] The wealth of Sanskrit literature in Brahmi and Kharoshthi scripts established 'the large place which Indian language and culture must have occupied in the administration and daily life of this region during the early centuries of our era' and continued down to the end of the eighth century.[27]

Campaigns Against Zungaria and Kashgaria

In the seventh century, the rise of a Turkic kingdom in East Turkestan coincided with the flourishing Tang dynasty in China. Enter Taizong, the second ruler of the Tang dynasty, who invaded the region he called 'Anxi' (the pacified west) in 630 CE. The Tangs had to not only deal with a restive local population but also an aggressive Tibet. In 657 CE Taizong mounted another campaign, but by 670 CE the tide turned: the Tibetans inflicted a severe defeat on his forces and occupied Kashgar. In the eighth century, the rise of the Arabs brought yet another claimant, one impassioned to spread its new religion Islam. The army of the Abbasid Caliph of Baghdad, led by Ziyad ibn Salih, inflicted a crushing defeat on the Tang army of Gao Xianzhi in a battle near Talas River in 751 CE (now in Uzbekistan). Muslims of the Naqshbandi sect began spreading throughout the region.

The capital of Xinjiang, Urumqi, is located on the eastern edge of the Tianshan Mountains. Mentioned in the Tang annals of the seventh century CE as the base of a military garrison, it underwent a name change during the Mongol era, when it was called Bishbalik.

After unifying Mongolia, East Turkestan would become one of Chinggis Khan's first conquests. Centuries later, the northern portion of Zungaria was ruled by Galdan (1676–1697), an Ölöd Mongol. By this time, Peter I (the Great) of Russia had started his expansion into Siberia and a triangular contest began with the Mongols and the Manchus. In 1678, Galdan conquered Kashgaria and then marched north into Mongolia – then ruled by the Khalkha Mongols, who were important allies of the Manchus. The Kangxi emperor wanted to come to their help, but his first goal was to secure his northern frontier where the Russians were advancing. The Treaty of Nerchinsk in 1689 defused the rising confrontation between the two empires in Siberia and left Kangxi free to go after Galdan.

In 1696, the Kangxi emperor defeated Galdan, who died the following year. But the Manchus could not consolidate their victory, as they had to redirect their attention to the conquest of southern China. Galdan was succeeded by his nephew, Tsewang Rabdan (also known as Tsewang Araptan, 1697–1727), under whom Zungaria reached its largest expanse. Rabdan entered into a marital alliance with another powerful Mongol tribe, the Türgüd, and became a renewed threat to the Manchus. His rule saw incessant wars with Russia and China, beginning with delivering some decisive blows to Russia. But the Manchus were the ascendant force of the time and, as soon as they had consolidated their hold in China, they turned to the west again.

The conquest of Zungaria was finally carried out by the Kangxi emperor's grandson, the Qianlong emperor. He was an aggressive and ambitious ruler and, fortuitously, had a favourable political environment in the neighbourhood. Peter I died in 1725 and his successors became preoccupied with events in Europe. Rabdan's death in 1727 left Zungaria vulnerable. Between 1755 and 1757, the Qianlong emperor sent two campaigns into Zungaria and was finally able to declare victory in 1759. He carried out a scorched earth policy, which Keay describes as a brutal conquest: 'Of the 600,000 Zunghars ... 40 per cent had died of smallpox, 30 per cent had been killed by the Qing armies and 20 per cent had fled across the Russian, Kazakh and Kyrghyz frontiers.'[28] Zungaria was left desolate, to be repopulated by Manchus, Han Chinese and others under the patronage of the Qing dynasty.

The Qianlong emperor then turned his attention to Kashgaria, ruled by the Khojas of the Naqshbandi sect of Sufis. Highly revered even in Afghanistan, Kashmir and nearby areas, the Khojas had been loosely supervised by the Zungar Mongols. In 1758, the Manchus demanded tribute and, upon refusal, sent an army. By the following year, the cities of Yarkand and Kashgar had come under Manchu control. The Khoja chieftain was sent to Beijing and paraded in an iron cage. The people of the region revolted again but were forcefully put down. This led to 'peace' for about sixty years.

So, what did this mean for the Manchus? By the middle of the eighteenth century, they had exterminated their old rivals, the Zungar Mongols, and in the process, had also conquered Tibet and Kashgaria. In 1768, Zungaria and Kashgaria – which till then were referred to as Anxi, the Western region – were given a new Chinese name: Xinjiang (Sinkiang in Wade-Giles), meaning New Territory.[29]

Towards the end of his long reign, the Qianlong emperor celebrated his 'Ten Great Campaigns', three in Zungaria and Kashgaria, two in Sichuan and Yunnan, two in Tibet and Nepal and one each in Taiwan, Myanmar and Vietnam. All were led by Manchu generals.

The defeat of the Zungar Mongols was an event of epochal significance for the Manchus and Central Asia. The Manchus looked upon their victory as the fulfilment of their imperial quest and the end of all threats to their empire. The American historian Perdue points out that the defeat also removed the main resistance to the expansion of the Russian empire in Siberia and Central Asia: 'The Russians could never exact unquestioned and exclusive collection rights in Siberia until their Mongol neighbour had been eliminated by the Qing.'[30] The Manchus were conscious of the Russian threat but believed it was confined to the distant north. They were oblivious to the British conquest of India, and even on learning about it, did not link it with the British they were dealing with in Canton. This realization came much later.

Manchu Administration

The Manchus built and controlled their vast empire of diverse peoples by embellishing their considerable military skills with remarkable religious tolerance, cultural eclecticism and administrative acumen. The presence of the European Jesuit missionaries enabled them to gain insights into mathematics, medicine and gunpowder technology, which they put to significant effect in military campaigns. They used the bureaucratic skills of the Han Chinese to create an efficient administrative structure and took the universalistic teachings of Buddhism from the Tibetans, along with their religious cults and beliefs, to lay claim to the allegiance of the Mongol tribes.

A study of the Manchu administration is essential to understanding how it dealt with the diverse peoples of its empire, particularly the Han Chinese. Manchu rule was more absolute than that of the Ming. They abolished the Ming office of the prime minister, replacing it with a Grand Secretariat made up of about a half-dozen advisers. Starting in 1730, they appointed grand councillors to prominent status, relegated the grand secretaries to ceremonial status and rewarded the bureaucratic skills of the

Chinese by generously elevating them to these high positions while maintaining the numerical superiority of the Manchus.

Some Chinese institutions of governance were retained, such as the competitive literary examination for entering the bureaucracy. Of the 145 grand councillors appointed during Manchu rule, seventy-two were Manchus, sixty-four Han Chinese, three Chinese bannermen[31] and six Mongols.[32] The councillors had thirty-two secretaries under them, sixteen Manchu and sixteen Chinese. Then there were six boards – civil office, revenue, rites, war, punishments and public works. Manchus and Chinese were equally represented in their senior staff. This constituted the core of the empire's central government, which was responsible for running the administration of China proper.

The Manchus had established the *Mongol Yamen* office in 1636, long before they conquered China, to manage relations with Mongolia. After the conquest of China, they retained it for administering the Mongol territories they had conquered. They renamed it *Lifan Yuan* (the Board for the Administration of Outlying Regions) to handle relations with all outer regions. It also took over relations with Russia, which was an essential component of their Mongol policy. When East Turkestan and Tibet were conquered, the Lifan Yuan took over their affairs as well. This office was under the exclusive control of Manchus. Occasionally, a Mongol prince was given a supernumerary position, but no Chinese were ever appointed to it.[33]

There was perpetual suspicion and distrust between the Manchus and the Chinese. Although there was ostensible parity in appointments to senior positions, Manchus occupied distinctly superior positions. A post reserved for a Chinese appointee could be filled by a Manchu but not the other way around. Manchus always feared subversion by the Chinese and never permitted them to rise to positions of power.

The Manchus fiercely protected their identity from being overwhelmed by the Chinese. They established the Imperial Clan Court to supervise the births, education and marriages of the

Manchu nobles, the prohibition of Manchu–Chinese intermarriages and the ban on Chinese immigration to Manchuria.[34] The Chinese resented Manchu rule, and the revolts of the nineteenth century – as the dynasty became weak – were inspired by Han ethnicity. Sinologist Immanuel C. Y. Hsü writes that even when the dynasty was strong, there was resistance: 'While many Chinese joined the Manchu government and tacitly accepted the Ch'ing rule, a great many more remained in silent opposition.'[35]

Administration was carried out in three languages – Manchu, Mongolian and Chinese. Manchu was the main language, and some documents were exclusively maintained in it. It was not until the nineteenth century that Chinese began to be more commonly used.

The Manchus treated non-Chinese ethnic groups as distinct entities and administered them differently from the Chinese. The Han Chinese were barred from entering Manchuria, with the Liaodong Wall being used to enforce the ban. They also maintained two separate armies. The first was an elite force of Manchus and Mongols that consisted of hereditary banner armies stationed in the north, close to the emperor and the Manchu elite, and in other critical areas of the empire. Ethnic Chinese were recruited in the Green Standard armies and sent mainly to the south, where they were deployed for clerical tasks like monitoring the movement of grains. Professor Wang Ke ascribes a strategic motive to this special treatment, i.e., 'to make the ethnic groups of the outlying regions the allies of the Manchus and use them to contain the massive population of Han Chinese in the interior province'.[36]

Fenby confirms the harsh treatment of the Han, stating that they 'were made to shave their foreheads and their pigtails as a sign of submission. Intermarriage was prohibited. Nor were Hans allowed to migrate to Manchuria.'[37]

The Manchus maintained the distinction between China and the empire's colonial provinces even in the local administration's organisation. China was divided into eighteen provinces, each under a governor or governor-general. Mongolia, Manchuria, Xinjiang, Taiwan, Tibet and Qinghai (the Chinese name for Amdo) were not part of this arrangement. Xinjiang was incorporated as a province of China in 1884, followed by Manchuria in 1907 (divided into three provinces). Taiwan was made a province in 1887 but lost to Japan in 1895. Thus, towards the end of Manchu rule, there were twenty-two provinces in China. Even though Manchuria and Xinjiang were eventually incorporated into the central administration of the empire, Tibet always remained out of it.

Tibet and Tibetans were also not part of the prestigious examination system in China, which was used to select the gentry that assisted governmental administration and the performance of other official responsibilities. These examinations were confined to the provinces. No Tibetan was appointed to a high office in the administration in Beijing.

The Manchu Empire reached its zenith under the Qianlong emperor. It included the whole of China under the Ming dynasty and large parts of Manchuria, Mongolia, Turkestan and Tibet. It extended over 11 million square kilometres and had a population of about 300 million. This made it approximately the size of Europe in both area and population and one of the greatest empires ever. It also regarded several neighbouring kingdoms in Asia, such as Korea, Thailand, Vietnam and Myanmar, as tributary states because they sent envoys who performed the kowtow to the emperor at court and bestowed gifts. Other countries that sent envoys were also considered to be tributary states, even infrequent ones like Russia, Portugal and Holland. After sixty years on the throne, the Qianlong emperor abdicated in 1795, so as not to exceed the rule of his illustrious grandfather, the Kangxi emperor.

China and the Manchus

China looks at the Manchu Empire, not the Manchus, with pride. It regards all its achievements as part of its national inheritance, regardless of the ethnicity of the inhabitants. Modern China claims the achievements of the empire as its historical legacy. Hsü writes:

> It proves to have been the most durable period of foreign rule
> in China, spanning 268 years as opposed to the Yüan (Mongol)

dynasty's 89. It saw the rise of the second-largest empire in Chinese history, next only to the Yüan, and provided the country with a prolonged period of peace and prosperity. This *Pax Sinica* precipitated, among other things, unprecedented population growth from 150 million in 1650 to 430 million in 1850. These territorial and demographic legacies underlie the bases of Chinese strength today.[38] [*emphasis added*]

Modern China's claim to be the inheritor of the Manchu legacy ignores the imperial nature and foreign origin of the Manchu Empire. The Manchu dynasty was Sinicized over time but never fully assimilated into the local population. Perdue writes: 'The Manchus did not assimilate to a "superior" majority Han culture but maintained their distinctiveness, through the banners and imperial rituals, while they collaborated with Han officials to maintain legitimacy and ensure adequate tax collection.'[39]

The Chinese take a selective view of the Manchu dynasty, cherry-picking features that serve their nationalist claims. The approach swings between admiration and contempt, reviling the Manchus as barbaric foreigners and a dynasty that was reactionary and feudal, yet claiming their military conquests as the fulfilment of China's nationalist entitlement. Thus, the Mongols, Uyghurs and Tibetans were minorities who were 'unified' with China by the Qing dynasty. The fact that the Han Mings had showed no interest in conquering these people, and were primarily concerned with protecting China from them, is glossed over.

Manchu rule is now viewed in China entirely from the Chinese perspective and only the records in the Chinese language are studied. Scholars of the Qing period rely on Chinese texts alone for their research and there are few experts in the Manchu language. Crossley writes in her study of the Manchus that 'as a consequence, the Qing is perhaps the last of the great empires for which vast stretches of central documents remain unreviewed, and for which major discoveries may yet be made'.[40]

While China treats the conquests of the Manchus as a form of national reunification, any treaty not to its liking is denounced as 'unequal' and declared to have been negotiated by the 'corrupt' Qing rulers. The Treaty of Nerchinsk (1689), which the Manchus negotiated after their victory over Russian forces in Manchuria, is declared to be China's success – even though Manchuria was not a part of China then. Later treaties signed by the Manchus (Aigun and St. Petersburg) are declared 'unequal' because they surrendered 'Chinese' land.

Chinese historians also have a conflicted attitude towards the Mongol rulers of Zungaria, such as Galdan and Rabdan. They claim them to be Chinese but are unable to explain why they resisted becoming a part of China so fiercely.

Dai Yi's *Concise History of the Qing Dynasty* is considered a standard history book in the People's Republic of China. The titles of two of the chapters are indicative of the official approach to the conquests of the Manchu dynasty – 'Unification of the Minority Peoples of the Border Region and the Strengthening and Development of a Multinational Empire' and 'Qing Suppression of the Zunghar Galdan's Divisive Influence and the Unification of the Northwest Region'.[41] These regions were independent when the Manchus conquered China, but Dai Yi's book treats the Russian invasions of Central Asia as attacks on Chinese territory and the resistance of the Mongol people as expressions of the people's struggle. When the Mongols resisted the Russians, they were nationalists, but when they turned against the Qing dynasty they became 'splittists' instigated by Russia.

Chinese scholar Ma Ruheng presents the official attitude of the Communist government towards the Qing dynasty as a period of the reunification of China, during which minorities were able to come within the fold of China after overcoming the seditious designs of advocates of separation like Amursana (who resisted the Manchu conquest of the Zungar Mongols):

The Qing dynasty was a period when our unified nation of many nationalities became increasingly consolidated and developed. Qianlong's suppression of Amursana's revolt continued the tasks of Kangxi and Yongzheng of protecting the unity of the nation and waging a righteous war to resist Russian aggression. This battle not only strengthened and developed the unity of the multinational state but also coincided with the demands for unity of each of the nationalities and their common wish to oppose splittism. Therefore, the victory in the war against rebellion was inevitable.[42]

Bai Shouyi adopts the same selectivity with Tibet and Xinjiang:

In 1888, Britain launched an aggressive war against Tibet, but met with stubborn resistance from the Tibetan army and civilians. More than a hundred of the aggressor troops were killed or wounded. The corrupt Qing government, however, forbade the Tibetan people to resist the invaders who continued with their aggression. In 1890, the Qing government negotiated with Britain on the border issue and signed the Sikkim-Tibet Convention. In 1893, the Qing government agreed to Britain's request to open a trading city in Tibet, and British influence infiltrated Tibet as a result.[43]

When Yakub Beg successfully occupied Kashgar, he is described as taking advantage of 'internal strife' in Xinjiang, and when Russia occupied Ili, it is accused of imposing 'colonial rule'.

Chinese historians berate Europeans for their predatory behaviour during the 'century of humiliation', ignoring the willingness of the Han Chinese to accept Western education and even convert to Christianity. Manchu oppression made them more accepting of Europeans and adapt better to the changes taking place in the world. The Manchus, given to a life of power and leisure, fell behind in education and military skills.

But before we go into the breakup of the Manchu empire we must turn to the arrival in Central Asia of the second imperial power – Russia.

A section of Eastern Turkestan, mapped in 1879 based on British and Russian surveys.
It depicts the northern border of Kashmir at Aktagh, north of Karakoram Pass.

4

Russian Empire: Quest for Warm Waters

Chinggis Khan's vast empire splintered among his four sons after his death. The eldest son, Jochi, got the western part, which came to be called the Golden Horde and ruled over Russia and Eastern Europe for two centuries. The 'Tartars', as the Mongols were called there, steeled the tiny principality known as the Duchy of Muscovy into a war machine determined to subjugate the vast steppes of Central Asia (from where the Tartars had originally come). As the duchy expanded, it came to be known as Russia, named after the Rus people inhabiting it.

Russia's aristocracy was predominantly European in orientation. Many, like Catherine II (the Great), were German in origin. But in crowded Europe, Russia had few openings for territorial expansion. Peter I (1682–1725) tried to make his country a naval power by founding the port of St Petersburg on the Baltic Sea in 1703, but it provided only limited access to the Atlantic Ocean through the often-frigid Gulf of Finland. Russia yearned for a warm-water port that could be the foundation of a maritime power to rival other European countries. It looked to the east and conquered the frozen and empty expanse of Siberia to reach the Pacific Ocean. And in the nineteenth century, as the Ottoman empire weakened, it also made repeated attempts to establish a route to the Mediterranean Sea.

Early Relations with China

Russia's conquest of Asia started under Ivan IV (the Terrible), who declared himself Tsar in 1547. Russian forces moved along the northern edge of the continent towards the Pacific Ocean. In 1554, Ivan took the title 'Lord of all Sibir' after defeating its Khan – though it took another quarter of a century to conquer the regional capital of Sibir. The area beyond it came to be called Siberia. Russia continued to expand eastwards and laid claim to the Amur Valley, with Siberian furs and minerals becoming the main economic prizes leveraged from the region.

In Siberia, Russia came into contact with China, then ruled by the Ming dynasty. In 1618, a Russian commercial mission was sent bearing gifts to the Ming court in Beijing, becoming the first European mission to reach the Chinese capital. Russia was excited about the prospect of selling furs in exchange for Chinese silk, silver and food grains. The Wanli emperor of the Ming dynasty welcomed the 'tribute' sent by the Russian 'barbarian' and invited further such missions.[1] The Mings did not feel intimidated by the Russian presence in the frosty north, which was inhabited by the Jurchens and other tribes.

Russia reached the Pacific Ocean in 1648. It steadily consolidated its presence in the sparsely populated region by building forts – Okhotsk on the Pacific coast in 1647 and Irkutsk on Lake Baykal, on the northern edge of Mongolia, in 1651. Later, Russia crossed over the Bering Strait to America and occupied what is now Alaska, which it sold to the United States in 1867.

Russia's advance into the region took seventy years. Its culmination coincided with the conquest of China by the Manchus, who were more concerned than the Ming about the incursion of the distant Russians into their homeland, Manchuria, though during the initial years of Russian expansion they were preoccupied with their own conquest of China.

After suppressing the 'Revolt of the Three Feudatories' in 1681, the Manchus turned north to deal with the Russian threat.[2] In 1685, a large force destroyed the Russian settlement of Albazin. However, keen to secure Russia's friendship and ensure its neutrality in the war he was planning against the Mongols, the Kangxi emperor reached an early settlement with Russia on a northern boundary. The Treaty of Nerchinsk, signed in 1689, set the border between Manchuria and Siberia along the Amur River (Heilong Jiang in Chinese).

It was a remarkable treaty for the period. Written in four languages – Russian, Manchu, Chinese and Latin – it defined the border between the two empires in Manchuria, identified trading points and even specified trade tariffs. The negotiation of the treaty between power brokers whose cities were as far apart as Moscow and Beijing – not to mention peoples so unfamiliar with each other – was made possible by the sagacious use of the Jesuits by the Kangxi emperor. The Manchu delegation was assisted by two Jesuits well-versed in Latin, while Russia employed the help of a Pole fluent in it.

The drafting of the treaty also required some imaginative translation. The Manchus referred to Russians as 'barbarians', implicitly unworthy of equal treatment. This hurdle was overcome by avoiding the term in the translated texts, with the Latin text being given priority. In addition, the treaty left the border to the west, between Mongolia and Siberia, undefined. This was subsequently addressed in 1727 with the Treaty of Kiakhta, which also opened prospects for Russia to trade directly with China, though the subsequent volume of trade was disappointing.[3] Ultimately, all these treaties gave the Kangxi emperor the freedom to deal with the Mongols of Zungaria in the west.

Russia had become the first European country to have regular diplomatic contact with China. Ivan Petlin led the first Russian diplomatic mission in 1618, and such missions became a regular feature of Russian relations with China. A century later, in 1715, Russian monks and students set up a Russian Orthodox mission in Beijing. Diplomatic relations, however, were not without hiccups. The Manchus insisted on Russian envoys performing the ceremonial kowtow to the emperor, justifying this as following the local tradition.

Plans to Invade India

Britain's earliest contact with Russia was in the course of its exploration of a new route to India. In 1553, about half a century after the voyages of Christopher Columbus and Vasco da Gama, British merchants sent a three-ship expedition into the Baltic Sea in the hope of discovering a northern route to India. Two of the ships perished. The third reached the mouth of the Dvina River, close to Archangel (Arkhangelsk) in Russia. Ivan IV was keen to establish ties with Western Europe, so he gave the surviving merchants liberal trade concessions. On their return to London, the Russia Company was formed to pursue trade with 'Muscovy, Persia, and Northern Lands'.

During these early years, relations between Britain and Russia were wholly commercial and genial. Both countries, through different routes, expanded their presence in Asia. Britain continued its naval expansion, while Russia marched across the continent.

Russia's advance into Asia opened the prospect of trading with India and it started getting interested as early as the late fifteenth century. Russian merchant Athanasi Nikitin had explored trade possibilities but concluded that the high cost of the long and difficult journey rendered it uneconomical. A more serious attempt was made nearly a century later by Tsar Alexis in 1675 when he sent a delegation bearing gifts and a letter to the Mughal emperor, Aurangzeb. But the delegation did not travel beyond Kabul. After another century had passed, Russia's ambition increased and Peter I planned an invasion based on his calculation that the journey by camel from the Caspian Sea to Balkh and Badakhshan would take only twelve days. But the project remained on paper. Catherine II (1762–1796) also contemplated invading India in retaliation for Britain pressuring her to give up the Ochakov fortress in Turkey in 1791.

Catherine's son, Paul I, continued her desire to confront Britain by proposing to Napoleon a joint expedition to India. Napoleon's earlier expedition to Egypt, in 1798, had exposed the Ottoman empire's vulnerability and thrown open the prospect of a land march to India. Though agreeable to the suggestion, Napoleon could not disengage from domestic problems within France. But Paul I was not deterred and, in 1801, devised his own plan to invade India. However, he was assassinated before he could execute it. His successor, Alexander I, revived the project – with France onboard. Napoleon agreed to invade India through Iran. But Britain moved swiftly to thwart the move, sending John Malcolm to Iran and Mountstuart Elphinstone to Afghanistan to persuade their rulers not to join the alliance. In 1809, Britain signed a treaty with Iran obliging it to not permit any European force to pass through its territory.

The Franco-Russian threat collapsed when Napoleon invaded Russia in 1812. By repulsing the invasion and forcing Napoleon to withdraw with heavy losses, Russia achieved a dramatic victory that drew it into the heart of European affairs. Quickly, Russia and Britain formed an alliance against France, and the Russian army was a major contributor to Napoleon's defeat. Russia emerged as a power broker in Europe, becoming an important member of the Concert of Europe, the post-war international arrangement meant to maintain peace on the continent. Reassured of its naval supremacy, Britain adopted a policy of 'splendid isolation' after Napoleon. On the European continent, it pursued a 'balance of power' policy meant to prevent any country from becoming powerful enough to challenge it. But the rise of Russia soon became a concern. Britain began perceiving Russia's expansion into Asia – and its clear quest for warm-water ports – as a threat to both its naval supremacy and empire in India.

Napoleon had exposed a chink in Britain's armour. The island country was not as powerful on land as on the seas. Britain would have to handle Russia's army with care.

Start of Britain–Russia Rivalry in Asia

Across a broad front, from the Turkish Straits to China, Britain began obstructing Russia. Their first confrontation took place in the Balkans when the Greeks revolted against Turkish rule in 1821 after four centuries of Ottoman Turkish dominance. Revolutionary movements made the conservative monarchies of Europe paranoid; they considered it more important to uphold the Ottoman empire than support the freedom struggle of a co-religionist European country.

But the Greek struggle was extremely popular among the European people. The English poet Lord Byron not only wrote poems in support of the Greeks but also fought in the war against Turkey. Russia also sympathized with the Greeks because of its religious affinity to the Greek Orthodox Church and its historical animosity towards Turkey.

Britain feared that Russia's support for the Greeks had a more sinister objective: the seizure of Turkey's ports on the Mediterranean Sea. It persuaded other members of the Concert of Europe to compel Turkey to grant independence to Greece and prevent Russia from exploiting the crisis. Greece was allowed to become independent on the condition that it accepted a German prince as its king.

A few decades later, in 1853, Russia invaded Turkey and occupied parts of its territory in the Balkans. The following year, Britain aligned with its old enemy, France, to push Russia out but they suffered serious reversals. This led to the fall of the British prime minister, Lord Aberdeen. Lord Palmerston, who believed staunchly in preserving the unity of Turkey's Ottoman empire, took over as prime minister in 1855 and pursued the war vigorously until Russia withdrew from all of its occupied territory. The Crimean War (1854–1856) later became Britain's only armed conflict in the nineteenth century with a European country other than the Napoleonic Wars.

Victory ultimately did nothing to strengthen the Ottoman empire, though it earned Britain the wrath of Russia for the rest of the century. Russia's defeat dealt a severe blow to its nascent fleet in the Black Sea and its ambition of controlling access to the Mediterranean Sea. After losing the Crimean War, Russia turned its territorial ambitions to Central Asia.

Afghanistan: Fractious and Formidable

Russia's emergence as a major power and important player in European politics whetted its appetite for empire building. Its leaders discovered that military victories in Central Asia were also useful in extracting concessions from Britain in Europe. A British explorer Archibald R. Colquhoun quoted a Russian general A. Sobolev as saying, 'The more powerful Russia becomes in Central Asia, the weaker does England become in India and, consequently, the more amenable in Europe.'[4]

Britain was also easier to handle in the interior of Asia. In 1879, the Russian Ambassador to London Count Pyotr Šuvalov expressed the view that the farther inland Britain moved into Central Asia, the more vulnerable it became: 'The English can annex Afghanistan, as far as I am concerned; the closer they get to us, the better; as soon as we can get at them on dry land, they will become a great deal more pleasant to deal with.'[5]

Russia's thrust into Central Asia had begun in 1730 when a Kazakh chieftain, Abilay (Abulkhayr), accepted the Tsar's suzerainty. For the Kazakh, this was a tactic to gain ascendancy over his local rivals – not an uncommon strategy among chieftains. This gave Russia an opening, though progress was slow until the nineteenth century. Between 1822 and 1848, Russia subdued all of what is now Kazakhstan. Further expansion gathered pace after the Crimean War as Russia sent three separate expeditions to explore Central Asia in 1857–1858, going as far as the Tianshan Mountains and Kashgaria.

At this time, Britain was preoccupied with the Indian Revolt of 1857. Russia took full advantage of this to extend its territory in Western Turkestan. After conquering Tashkent and Khokand, it moved south into Bukhara (contemporary Uzbekistan) and, in 1867, formed the province of Turkestan – comprising the Bukhara, Khokand and Khiva regions – under a governor general with Tashkent as its capital.[6]

The Russian empire had now reached the Amu Darya (Oxus River), the northern extremity of the Afghan kingdom. Britain was thoroughly alarmed. A contemporary British writer assessed Russia's threat as follows: 'Thanks to England being an island there is no fear of the Cossack setting his foot on our shores; but if the Cossack sets his foot in India, his *shadow* will darken this land, and distress and starvation will make as much havoc among the masses as if he were himself present with his ruthless sabre and spear.'[7] He assessed that Russia had 900,000 troops under arms and another 3 million that could be raised in wartime. Against this, Britain had 75,000 British and 125,000 Indian soldiers. He also noted that Britain's trade with the region had slumped ever since Russia had penetrated it.

Britain had initially hoped to use Iran and the Khanates of Bukhara and Kokand as barriers to Russia's advance and despatched emissaries to ensure their support. But these kingdoms had no love for Britain, having to deal with a more imminent threat from Russia. In the post-Napoleon peace negotiations, Russia had extracted the right to acquire some provinces in northern Iran – a feat it accomplished in 1827 after a short war. Russia, however, had offered to cease hostilities and station a military adviser in Tehran. Seeking to limit Russia's influence, Britain assured assistance to Iran in case of invasion by a European power along with military aid. But reassured of its northern frontier, Iran started making military moves towards Afghanistan. This coincided with a Russian advance towards Khiva (in modern-day Uzbekistan) – an important trade crossroads – and Britain suspected Russia of conspiring with Iran to occupy Afghanistan.

Britain decided to pre-empt Russia and, taking advantage of an internal power struggle in Afghanistan, invaded it in 1839. The *amir* or chief, Dost Mohammad, surrendered and was brought to India. Britain replaced him with his rival, Shah Shuja, who had found refuge in India. A force of 4,500 British and Indian troops and 12,000 camp followers was stationed in Kabul under General William Elphinstone.

In November 1841, there was a violent revolt in Kabul. The British were badly outnumbered and relief could not reach them in time. The entire army and camp followers, save a few, were killed within two months, Shah Shuja among them. Lord Auckland, the governor general, was recalled and replaced by Lord Ellenborough, who sent a retribution force to teach the Afghans a lesson. After much killing and destruction, the British decided it was unsafe to stay in Afghanistan and restored Dost Mohammad as the amir.

According to James, Britain chose to invade Afghanistan because of fear that Russia was about to conquer it: 'The decision to invade Afghanistan was taken in May 1838 by Auckland against a background of "universal panic", prompted by reports of the intrigue of Russian agents in Persia and Kabul and fears that Herat would be captured.'[8] Another historian Spencer Walpole wrote that the increasing influence of Russia in Tehran induced Auckland to attack Kabul and seek to instal a friendly ruler.[9]

Britain also found it difficult to deal with the rulers of Central Asian principalities. In 1840, the Amir Nasrullah of Bukhara had two British agents – Charles Stoddart and Arthur Conolly (of Great Game fame) – arrested and eventually beheaded. Britain suspected Russian collusion. As Russia's advance continued, Britain sought to consolidate its position in Afghanistan. But controlling the fractious country with powerful chieftains in Kandahar, Herat, Balkh and other areas – loosely held together by the amir of Kabul – proved difficult.

Britain's disastrous foray into Afghanistan had a profound impact on it and overwhelmingly influenced its policy in the mountainous regions of the interior of Asia. The decimation of the British army and the pathetic flight of survivors from Kabul that defined the First Anglo-Afghan War (1839–1842) deeply disturbed the British. Forty thousand troops perished, and Britain suffered the ignominy of having to accept the help of Indian businessmen in Delhi in order to arrange 'the ransoming of a group of British women and children isolated in hostile territory'.[10] It faced another serious challenge when its empire in India nearly collapsed in the revolt of 1857 – coinciding with Russia's advance towards the Hindukush Mountains. This set alarm bells ringing in London. But while the fear of Russia remained strong, there was no consensus on how to deal with it.

Russian Threat to the Raj

In 1868, General Henry Rawlinson submitted a report to his government – the *Memorandum on the Central Asian Question* – suggesting that all Russia had to do to invade India was offer Afghans and Iranians the opportunity to plunder it as Nadir Shah and Ahmad Shah Abdali had done a century earlier. He declared that Britain had been building its strategy on quicksand and doubted if Indian rulers would side with the British in the case of a Russian invasion, even cautioning against the possibility of their making common cause with Russia:

> Already the Maharájá of Cashmere, taking offence at our efforts to promote trade by insisting on a reduction of the transit duties in his dominions, is said to have suggested to them to appoint commercial agents in Yarkend, on the immediate frontier of Thibet; and if the Russians were more accessible, his example would be followed by scores of others.[11]

Rawlinson advised his government to improve its outreach to Iran and Afghanistan in order to help them become strong and friendly powers. Unfortunately, Afghanistan – whose geographical position gave it greater strategic importance – was riven with internal strife. Rawlinson recommended opening a mission in Kabul and securing the friendship of its amir. He was convinced that Russia's overtures to Iran and Afghanistan were part of a design against British interests in India, adding that East Turkestan was a possible staging post against India:

> It would undoubtedly be inconvenient to us if Russia, either by force of arms or at the invitation of the native ruler, succeeded in establishing a protectorate over East Turkestán – similar to her protectorate of the Usbeg Khanates – and were thus brought into contact, through Thibet with Cashmere, and through Wakhán with Cabul.[12]

A year after Rawlinson's report, Britain's War Office prepared a thirty-eight-page paper entitled 'Russian Advances in Asia' that contemplated building an alliance of the Central Asian khanates against Russia, while admitting Britain had little capacity to help them.

In 1868, the Liberal Party replaced the Conservatives and William Gladstone became the prime minister (1868–1874, the first of four stints). Gladstone believed in coming to an understanding with Russia in Central Asia and Foreign Secretary Lord Clarendon proposed to the Russian ambassador in London, Baron Brunnow, the creation of a buffer zone between their empires. Prince Gorchakov of Russia welcomed the proposal, but Britain wanted Afghanistan within its sphere of influence and refused to accept it as a neutral territory since that would prohibit Britain from maintaining a military presence. Negotiations began in St Petersburg in 1870, centred on the delimitation of Afghanistan's northern border. Britain proposed the Oxus River as the dividing line between the two empires, thus ensuring the Balkh and Badakhshan provinces north of the Hindukush remained part of Afghanistan. These provinces were predominantly Turkic but had been part of Ahmad Shah Abdali's empire in the previous century (though Kabul's hold on them had weakened after his death).

The talks remained inconclusive. Russia agreed to the inclusion of Badakhshan and Wakhan in Afghanistan – a significant concession – but was not willing to concede Balkh. Russians believed that the Hindukush was the natural frontier of India and not the Oxus River.[13] Eventually, Britain and Russia reached an understanding in 1873, the Granville–Gorchakov Agreement, under Clarendon's successor, Lord Granville. It restricted Russia north of the Oxus River and recognized the territory between the river and the Hindukush Mountains as belonging to Afghanistan.

But Afghanistan was a turbulent country. Kabul's control over the trans-Hindukush areas was possible only when it was adequately strong. A contemporary historian Demetrius Charles Boulger wrote that while this would check Russia's progress towards India by defining its southern limit, the effectiveness of Afghanistan's control over the Turkish population residing there could not be predicted: 'The future of Afghan Turkestan is one of the most perplexing questions in the final settlement of the Afghan crisis.' Any weakening of the regime in Kabul would enfeeble its hold over the northern region. Boulger also cautioned that Britain's withdrawal from Afghanistan would be a 'signal for disturbances in Herat and Afghan Turkestan'.[14]

At the same time, whenever strong, Afghanistan became more aggressive. In 1884, it occupied areas north of the Oxus in the Shignan, Roshan and Wakhan provinces. Russia was infuriated and occupied areas south of the river in Darwaz. Britain had a difficult time persuading both to withdraw.

Despite its agreement with Britain, Russia continued to consolidate its hold over Turkestan. It approached the French architect Ferdinand de Lesseps, who had built the Suez Canal, to explore the possibility of constructing a railway from Calais in France to Kolkata. The stretch up to Samarkand was to be constructed by Russia, and then from there to Kolkata by Britain. Some French entrepreneurs showed interest, but the British threw cold water on the idea. When the prospect of building a canal in Panama was offered, de Lesseps abandoned Central Asia and went to America.

In 1877, Russia invaded Turkey again and compelled it to make several concessions in the Treaty of San Stefano. However, when the Russian troops threatened Istanbul, Britain sent a naval force to the Bosporus Strait and stationed troops on its shores. Caught off guard, Russia prepared a contingency plan to invade India and despatched a mission to Kabul, aiming to persuade Afghanistan to join it. In response, Benjamin Disraeli, a Conservative who had replaced Gladstone by then, ended Britain's 'masterly inactivity' and indifference to Russia's expansion in Central Asia.

Britain launched its second pre-emptive attack on Afghanistan, leading to the Second Anglo-Afghan War (1878–1880). The British army occupied Kabul and succeeded in its immediate objective of replacing the amir. It stationed an administrative head, known as a resident, in Kabul in the person of Sir Pierre Louis Napoleon

Cavagnari with a small protection force. But things went no better for the British than they had in the First Anglo-Afghan War. No sooner had the British army withdrawn than the Afghans killed Cavagnari, along with his guards. Once again, Britain sent a retribution force from India and installed another Afghan prince as the amir.

Gladstone, who was back as prime minister for his second term (1880–1885), decided that it was not wise to maintain British personnel in the rebellious country and withdrew all British forces by 1881. Britain's second humiliation in Afghanistan reinforced the fear of stationing troops in the mountainous region far from bases in India.

Throughout much of the later nineteenth century, the Russian threat was a source of bitter discord between Disraeli and Gladstone. Their legendary rivalry was sharpened by the failure of the second British invasion of Afghanistan. The Russian advance in Central Asia was viewed with great concern in Britain. In 1881, a member of parliament declared: 'India, I affirm, is the goal, the ultimate end, not only of all Russian progress in Central Asia, but of the military aspirations of the great bulk of the Russian Army.'[15] The following year, he noted Russia's progress in attaining this objective: 'By the conquest of the Turcomans, Russia has put the coping stone to her steady approach to the Indian Frontier.'[16]

Britain's fear of Russia grew as its insecurity over India's defence deepened. It had been unable to conquer Afghanistan and establish a presence in Tibet. The Russian advance sent it into a frenzy. According to the historian K. W. B. Middleton, by then the spectre of a Russian attack on India had grown 'to full stature'.[17] Not everyone in Britain was as suspicious of Russia's motives. Lord Lawrence, Viceroy of India, in the 1860s, wrote: 'Russia might prove a safer neighbour than the wild tribes of Central Asia.'[18] But the dominant perception of Russia was one of fear, accentuated by Disraeli, who was prime minister in 1868 and again between 1874 and 1880. Russia became a deeply emotional issue in Britain. The Russian Tsar was referred to as the sanguinary despot of

St Petersburg and the monster Nicholas. Both sides of the political spectrum in Britain – the Liberals and the Conservatives – were anti-Russian.

Britain's connection to India became an amusing additional point of discord with Russia in the Russia–Turkey war. Its defeat was humiliating enough, but it was compounded by the presence of Indian soldiers in the British army. Russia protested against Britain bringing Indian troops to Europe.

Gladstone's second term, coinciding with the defeat in the Second Afghan War, proved to be significant for Afghanistan. He reverted to the policy of non-interference in the region, which Russia took full advantage of. Its military engineers started constructing a railway line from the eastern shore of the Caspian Sea into Central Asia. General Mikhail Skobelev overran the territory – up to what is now the northern border of Afghanistan – with surprising ease, causing great alarm in London. Turkmenistan fell in 1881, with the collapse of Merv three years later completing Russia's conquest of the region.

When Merv fell, Britain advised Afghanistan to resist any further incursions by Russia. This led to a series of skirmishes between Russian and Afghan forces, culminating in an 1885 encounter at Panjdeh – an outpost on the road to Herat that Britain considered to be in Afghanistan and the gateway to India – in which the Afghans suffered heavy casualties.[19] The incident caused fright among the British in India, reinforcing their conviction that Russia was preparing to invade India.

Reserves in England were called out, and it was decided to extend the railway line from Quetta to Kandahar. Britain provided money and arms to the amir and sent its experts to Herat to bolster its defences. British officials also tried to convince Afghan tribes that Russia was a threat to their independence. They reached out to the Ghilzai tribe, who inhabited the land between Kabul and Kandahar. The Afridis, another Pashtun tribe, were offered inducements to keep the passes in the Suleiman Mountains, such as the Khyber Pass, open.

The Panjdeh incident, however, did not escalate into a wider conflagration. Britain confined its response to lodging a protest with Russia. Gladstone once again started talks with Russia to demarcate the northern border of Afghanistan and create a politically safe buffer zone between the two empires. He also accepted Russia's proposal to set up a joint commission to define the border of Afghanistan.

Another fortuitous development facilitated the successful culmination of the joint commission's work. Lord Salisbury became the British prime minister in 1886. He had played an important role in shaping relations with Russia, having participated in the Congress of Berlin (1878), which brought the Russia–Turkey war to an end. Although a Conservative, he believed that bolstering Turkey against Russia was a mistake. The joint commission met, partly in secret, and after two years most of the Russia–Afghanistan border was demarcated in 1887. Only the north-eastern region, in the Pamirs, was left undefined.

But even so, the agreement failed to alleviate the fears of the big powers or curb their urge to expand their spheres of influence elsewhere. Middleton wrote about this intense period:

> In the nineties, the imperialist pace became feverish. The Powers snarled and elbowed in competition for points of strategic and economic advantage all over the world. It was the age of Cecil Rhodes, Rudyard Kipling, Joseph Chamberlain and their counterparts in Russia, in France, in Germany, in Italy, and even in small countries like Belgium.[20]

Much to Britain's alarm, the venue of the Great Game shifted closer to India's borders – to the Pamirs, East Turkestan and Tibet. As it looked around for options to counter the Russian threat, it saw an unexpected but tantalizing prospect in the tottering Manchu empire.

Chinese Turkestan and British India, 1892. No boundaries shown.

5

British Empire in China: Power to Trade

Britain's relations with China in the nineteenth century were largely driven by its interests in the subcontinent and the overriding objective of ensuring India's security. Managing such a vast empire left Britain with little appetite for acquiring more territory in China. Moreover, its military requirements in India limited its involvement in the region. Consequently, India became the staging post for all of Britain's operations, particularly the opium trade with China, on which it concentrated, making it the hub of its supply chain.

The First *Firangis* Arrive in the Pacific

The Portuguese were the first Europeans to reach China by sea. With their colonization of Goa in 1510, they were in a position to exploit trade routes to the east – and soon, they were joined by the Spanish. The Chinese called the Portuguese '*Fo-Lang-Chi*' (Sinicization of 'Firangi', the Arabic name for Europeans).[1]

Christian missionaries played an important role in Portuguese and Spanish colonization. The Society of Jesus, or the Jesuits, had been formally established by Pope Paul III in 1540, and it eventually became China's most active Christian organization. The Jesuits were also known for introducing European gadgets, such as watches, that greatly fascinated the Chinese.

Towards the end of the sixteenth century, an Italian priest named Matteo Ricci prepared a world map for the Ming ruler. Unfortunately, his first map placed Europe in the centre and China in the far east, infuriating the ruler of the Middle Kingdom. However, Ricci swiftly rectified the situation by drawing one with China in the centre. This revised map won wide acclaim and was proudly circulated by the emperor to showcase the extent of his empire.

A century later, the Jesuits undertook a more ambitious project after exploring a greater portion of the country. Their map, the first of China with longitudes and latitudes, was completed in 1716, during the reign of the Kangxi emperor.

But by the end of the sixteenth century, the Dutch had dislodged both Portugal and Spain in the region. The Dutch East India Company, based in Indonesia, came to control the spice trade in the Indian and Pacific oceans for most of the seventeenth century. They kept the Ming and the Manchu rulers in good humour – in part by accepting their demand for kowtowing. The Chinese listed them in their records as a tributary state.

Eventually, Britain set up its 'factory' – as trade centres were called – in 1699 in Canton (Guangzhou), the port designated for foreign trade in China since medieval times. Foreigners were permitted to trade only in Canton, under what was called the Canton system. But Britain desired greater access to the market, so, in 1793, it sent the Anglo-Irish nobleman Earl George Macartney to the court of the ageing Qianlong emperor, who was basking in the glory of his long, prosperous reign in Beijing. The emperor gave audience to Macartney at his summer palace but refused to grant trade presence beyond Canton.[2]

Britain made another attempt, through Lord Amherst in 1816, but the Jiaqing (Chia-ch'ing) emperor was no more willing than his father to grant any more concessions than he had to other European traders. Thus, Britain remained handicapped in China. Its access was from its bases in India, where there was a greater requirement for its troops. At the turn of the eighteenth century,

China was at its imperial peak. In India, Britain had been able to subdue all its European rivals, but in China it had no option but to cooperate with them – France, Portugal, Spain, the Netherlands and, above all, Russia.

The decline of the Manchu dynasty started in the latter part of Qianlong's reign as he rested in contentment after demolishing the Mongols. It accelerated after his abdication. In contrast, European powers were on the ascendant. The industrial revolution was rapidly enhancing their military capacity and, after defeating Napoleon together, Russia and Britain had emerged as the leaders in the European imperial race.

But how could European traders find goods to sell in China that would cover their purchases? The Portuguese had started selling opium, which was used at the time as a painkiller. The East India Company, whose shareholders often questioned the economic benefits of military adventures in India, decided that one solution was joining the opium trade in China. It established a monopoly on opium cultivation in India, switched vast tracts of agricultural land from food crops to opium cultivation and perfected a low-cost technique of growing it. The product was then shipped to China.

The conquest of India, and trade with China, became mutually complementary and highly profitable. The opium business grew by leaps and bounds; opium was traded for tea in China, which was then exported to Britain. The availability of cheap opium quickly increased its use, exacerbating addiction in both India and China. By diverting agricultural land, the opium trade devastated India's food security. It was equally disastrous for China.[3] In 1796, China banned the import of opium – though, unsurprisingly, this did not deter European traders, who resorted to smuggling and bribing Chinese officials.

European traders reaped rich profits from trade with China, which they conducted both privately and openly through their companies. Scuffles erupted frequently in the charged atmosphere of private trade and smuggling. Hsü describes the impact of this change thus:

By 1820 the complexion of the Canton trade had changed: private trade had surpassed the company trade, and opium had superseded regular articles as the chief item of import. These two developments contributed to the breakdown of the outworn Canton system and precipitated the long-delayed clash between Britain and China.[4]

According to Bradley, by 1850, the drug 'accounted for a staggering 15 to 20 per cent of the British Empire's revenue'.[5]

In 1833, the British government ended the East India Company's monopoly of trade with China, opening it to other British companies. It appointed government superintendents in Canton to manage dealings with Chinese authorities, altering the character of British representation there. The trade disputes and violent incidents that frequently occurred between European opium smugglers and Chinese officials also took on a more diplomatic tone.

The Opium War of 1839–1842 marked the first major conflict between Britain and China. It was ignited by a demand from Britain for an apology and reparations related to a perceived act of injustice against a British trader. British troops captured Canton before moving north and threatening Nanjing. The Chinese were no match; they accepted all British terms. Under the Treaty of Nanjing in 1842, China paid a hefty indemnity and agreed to open the ports of Amoy (Xiamen), Foochow (Fuzhou), Ningpo (Ningbo) and Shanghai – adding vast opportunities for foreigners to trade in ports other than Canton. It also ceded the island of Hong Kong to Britain, which resulted in yet another 'unequal' treaty coming into being for China.

Taiping Rebellion (1850–1864)

Defeat at the hands of the British severely weakened the authority of the Manchu rulers, particularly in southern China, where the Han Chinese formed the majority. Within eight years, a revolt broke out among them. The Taiping Rebellion, as the fourteen-year national uprising of the Han Chinese against Manchu rule is called, became one of the worst civil wars in human history.

The rebellion started among the impoverished Han Chinese of the Guangxi and Guangdong provinces under the leadership of Hong Xiuquan (Hung Hsiu-ch'üan), who lived near Canton. Frustrated at having failed the civil service examination four times, he formed a 'Society of God-Worshippers', drawing supporters mainly from his nomadic Hakka community. The Society was inspired by the Christian teachings that Hong Xiuquan had picked up from European missionaries.

He questioned the practices and beliefs of Confucianism and Buddhism, which formed the curriculum of the civil service examination. His ire was directed against the Manchus, who used these religious doctrines to uphold their authority. Once government officials started persecuting the sect, tensions escalated. In an incident in 1850, imperial forces were outnumbered by the locals, who seized control of their small town. Their ranks swelled rapidly as poor peasants joined them.

By 1851, Hong Xiuquan had set up the Taiping Tianguo (Heavenly Kingdom of Great Peace) and declared himself emperor. Over the next two years, his control spread to the interior of southern China. Early in 1853, the Taipings conquered Wuchang and, soon after that, Nanjing, massacring the Manchus living in the city. They renamed the city 'Tianjing' – the heavenly capital. The rebellion became the biggest threat to Manchu rule in China in two centuries.

Britain Invades Beijing

Meanwhile, the trade issues between Britain and China persisted. In 1856, in the 'Arrow Incident', a Chinese-owned ship, registered with the British, was boarded by Chinese officials searching for pirates. In the scuffle, the British flag was pulled down. Britain demanded an apology and shelled Canton when one was not forthcoming. The Chinese reciprocated by burning down European factories in Canton. In London, while William Gladstone, then in the opposition, criticized the actions of the local British officials, Prime Minister Palmerston took a tough line and despatched Lord Elgin to punish the Chinese.

Elgin's invasion was delayed as his army had to be diverted to India to help the British suppress the 'Sepoy Mutiny'. Once this was accomplished, Elgin proceeded to China. He occupied Canton and sent its governor to die as a prisoner in Kolkata. Then he sailed north and seized the port town of Tianjin, where he compelled the Chinese to sign the Treaty of Tientsin (Tianjin) in 1858, opening new ports, permitting travel by foreigners in China and stationing a resident mission in Beijing. The treaty also stated that when the instruments of ratification were ready, they would be exchanged in Beijing. Britain appointed Elgin's brother, Frederick Bruce, as its first minister in Beijing. But the following year, when Bruce tried to go to Tianjin with the instruments of ratification, he was repulsed at Taku, with heavy casualties. In Britain, Bruce's humiliating withdrawal was likened to the rout in Kabul in 1842.

Elgin recommended invading Beijing. Palmerston and Foreign Secretary John Russell were both keen to avenge the humiliation and persuaded Napoleon III of France to jump onto the bandwagon. Thus, Britain and France – long-term enemies but recent allies in the Crimean War against Russia – joined forces to invade Beijing. Baron Gros led the French troops while Britain entrusted the task to Elgin.

The British and French troops seized Tianjin. Beijing sent negotiators but without the instrument of ratification. Elgin decided that the only solution was to confront the emperor directly. He was accompanied by a journalist, Thomas Bowlby, who sent a report to the *London Times* explaining his decision to march on the Chinese capital: 'By arms alone can China be opened to trade. An ambassador must negotiate with an army by his side, ready to act at a moment's notice.'[6] Elgin sent Bowlby and Harry Parkes, a diplomat, to Beijing to negotiate with the Chinese. Both were taken prisoner; Parkes survived, but Bowlby succumbed to the torture. This was the final provocation for the British. London approved the invasion and the British and French forces marched on Beijing. The Xianfeng (Hsien-feng) emperor fled to Jehol, Manchuria, the homeland of his ancestors, with many of his xenophobic court officials in tow. He left behind his half-brother, Prince Gong (Kung), to deal with the British.

The Manchu empire lay at Elgin's feet. He toyed with the idea of destroying the royal palace – but settled for burning Yuanmingyuan, the exquisite summer palace built by the Qianlong emperor. He also considered replacing the Manchu dynasty with a Chinese one, but there was no obvious choice and, conveniently, Prince Gong readily accepted all his conditions. Under the Convention of Peking, China ceded the Kowloon Peninsula, north of Hong Kong, and agreed to a British mission in Beijing. Britain and France imposed an indemnity of 16 million taels (approximately 5 million pounds sterling) to be shared equally. Given this amount was well beyond China's paying capacity – several times the amount of silver in the imperial treasury – Prince Gong agreed that the payment would be made over time using the customs duty on foreign trade.

Russia was not a party to the invasion of Beijing. Its ambassador, General Nikolai Ignatiev, instead took advantage of the situation to present himself as a benefactor to the Chinese. He persuaded Gong to make concessions in order to prevent the British from overthrowing the Qing dynasty and advised the British to withdraw to Tianjin before the onset of Beijing's harsh winter. The general convinced Elgin that the British forces would be vulnerable to Chinese reprisals during winter, when the rivers would freeze and no longer be navigable.

Ignatiev also offered to help the Manchus in suppressing the Taiping rebellion by providing 10,000 rifles and eight cannons.[7] Prince Gong reversed China's long-standing policy towards foreigners by citing the internal rebellion, arguing that engaging in a conflict with foreigners was inadvisable until the Taipings were suppressed. The disease within was more serious and needed to be dealt with first.

The following year, the Xianfeng emperor died in exile in Manchuria. His six-year-old son, Tongzhi (T'ung-chih), succeeded him. But Tongzhi's mother, Cixi (Tz'u-hsi), was unhappy with the court elders who had appointed themselves regents. So, she teamed up with another wife of the emperor and hurried back to Beijing with the child-emperor and the royal seal ahead of the elders, extending a hand of friendship to Prince Gong. When the regents reached Beijing, they were charged with misguiding the deceased emperor into adopting a policy of confrontation with the foreigners. Ultimately, they were all exiled or executed.

Britain's invasion of Beijing, and the concessions it extracted from Prince Gong, also benefitted France and the United States, which received the same trade benefits under the most-favoured-nation principle imposed on China. However, the biggest beneficiary was Russia.

Two years earlier, Russia had extracted concessions in Manchuria using the Treaty of Aigun. Ambassador Ignatiev had also persuaded Prince Gong to allow opening Russian consulates in Urga (modern Ulaanbaatar) and Kashgar to start trading operations. It now made China sign a new agreement, the Treaty of Tarbagatai, and four years later, a supplementary protocol that realigned the border (fixed earlier by the Treaty of Nerchinsk in Manchuria) in Russia's favour. Russia strengthened its hold in Central Asia by expanding south into Kyrgyz and Kazakh territory, occupying large tracts of rich cotton-growing land and extracting trade concessions in East Turkestan. Russia was now a little too close for comfort to Britain's empire in India.

Meanwhile, China's civil war intensified. The myth of the Manchu's invincibility – and their unquestioned authority over the Chinese people – had already been shattered. Taipings took full advantage of their difficulties to expand their territory. They shifted the civil war narrative away from religion (Christianity versus Confucianism) and towards nationalism (Chinese versus Manchus). They occupied Suzhou, the capital of the Jiangsu province, which included Shanghai and Anqing, the capital of the Anhui province. In August 1860, they threatened Shanghai but were pushed back by the British and French troops. By December 1861, they had managed to capture Hangzhou, the capital of the Zhejiang province, and proceeded to take Ningbo. Stephen R. Platt, a historian of modern China, describes this pivotal turn: 'In the dawn of the year 1862, China stood at the edge of the unknown. The upper ranks of government in Beijing and Nanjing were both in a state of metamorphosis, re-forming themselves for the next stage in a war whose end none could divine.'[8]

Restoring China, Rescuing Trade

After ceding additional trading rights to Britain and allowing a resident mission (called a legation) to be set up, Prince Gong asked for assistance against the Taiping rebels. Britain was not as confident as it was in India about removing the dynasty and running the country itself. The once-impenetrable Manchu empire was falling apart but there were fears that Russia would be the biggest beneficiary of its collapse. Many erstwhile colonies and tributary states had broken away – Thailand had thrown off the Chinese yoke and Vietnam had been taken by the French and Myanmar by the British themselves. East Turkestan and the outlying provinces were also in rebellion. Russia had already occupied Kulja in the Ili Valley in Zungaria and was threatening Manchuria.

China proper was in turmoil. In addition to the Taiping Rebellion, three other revolts had turned particularly intense: the Nian (Nien) Rebellion in northern China, the Panthay Rebellion in Yunnan and the Dungan Rebellion in the north-west. A local leader in the Sichuan province was also up in arms. The long-serving British diplomat Thomas Wade dreaded the possibility of China succumbing to a foreign power 'out of sheer backwardness and inertia'.[9]

The Taipings were not unaware of the value of courting foreigners. They sought Britain's friendship, but the British traders in Shanghai and Hong Kong were unwilling to oblige. Their interests lay with these cities' wealthy Chinese traders, anathema to the Taipings. Disdain for the emaciated and fractious Taipings was strong, even among the British representatives stationed in China.

Both Wade and Frederick Bruce firmly believed that the Manchus were the legitimate rulers of the country and the Taipings were merely a bunch of rapacious rebels. Elgin shared this opinion. As the Taipings' hold over the interior regions expanded, wealthier Chinese fled to the coastal cities, swelling the ranks of those opposed to cooperating with the British.

Britain decided that it would be prudent to keep China united under the Manchus and set about the task of resurrecting it. A stable government in Beijing would better serve its interests. Middleton explains this diplomatic turnaround:

> Britain's concern with China was commercial, not territorial. She held Hong Kong but would not incur the military responsibility of any except insular possessions. India, her one continental dominion in Asia, constituted a serious enough burden. It suited her that the Chinese Empire, like the Ottoman, should be kept as far as possible intact, provided it was open to British trade.[10]

Now that the British, the French and the Americans had 'a big stake in the continued existence of the Manchu rule', they unanimously extended their support.[11] This became the 'cooperative policy' of the Western powers in China, based on the principle that their interests in China were commercial, not territorial. The 'remarkable comeback' of the Manchus in the 1870s and 1880s, despite expectations of collapse, has been noted by other historians as well.[12]

The cordial relations built by Prince Gong with the British officials in Beijing ensured close cooperation between the countries. Britain started actively assisting the Manchu government in suppressing the Taiping Rebellion. Frederick T. Ward, an American mercenary, 'trained a small Chinese force of about four thousand men, whose Western arms and use of amphibious tactics of manoeuvre on the waterways of the Yangtze delta won more than a hundred engagements and brought them the name of "Ever-Victorious Army".'[13] Ward was killed in January 1862 while leading Manchu troops during a siege of Shanghai by the Taiping rebels.

Britain now placed a regular officer of its army, Major Charles Gordon, in the service of the Manchu emperor.[14] Gordon, who took command of the Chinese forces, crushed the rebellion within a year. He became a British icon for his military skills and was nicknamed 'Chinese Gordon' for his achievements in restoring order. His appointment to the Chinese army was made possible by an 1862 British government decision to waive a century-old law that prohibited British subjects from serving in foreign military forces. Two other officers, Horatio Lay and Sherard Osborn, were also permitted to serve in the Chinese military.

Lay can be called the founder of modern China's navy. He commissioned eight ships that carried forty modern British guns and 'European officers and seamen, of the very best character'. These warships were state of the art as British shipbuilders were 'delighted to have the Qing dynasty's business, and they put their best work on display'. He also designed a new navy-green-and-yellow ensign with a dragon in the centre for the Chinese navy.[15]

With British assistance, and, occasionally, France and the United States, China also started modernizing its army. It formed a 'New Army' trained by Europeans. Army drill books were translated from English to Chinese, and an armament factory was established at Foochow under a French naval officer named Giguel. This was followed by one in Nanjing, under Sir Halliday Macartney*, and another in Shanghai.[16] And because the Chinese could not operate the new equipment at first, Westerners (mainly British) were hired.

Two Han Chinese, Zeng Guofan and Zuo Zongtang, quickly acquired enough skills, as well as the trust of the British, to be given charge of the new troops. Armament factories were set up using European help. In 1864, Zeng Guofan obtained an entire factory's worth of steam-powered industrial machinery from the US, while a French force assisted Zuo Zongtang in liberating Hangzhou – the capital of Zhejiang province – from the Taipings.

---

* He belonged to the same family as a George Macartney who had visited the Qianlong emperor in 1793. His son George Macartney from his Chinese wife would later become Britain's representative in Kashgar.

Another Englishman who served the Chinese government was Sir Robert Hart, who established the Chinese Maritime Customs Administration and then served for fifty years as its inspector-general from 1863 to 1908.[17] Described as 'one of the most striking monuments ever produced by the genius and labour of an individual Englishman',[18] this department helped the government deal with the foreigners preying upon the country and enforce terms of the trade treaties it was being made to sign. It also managed China's port facilities. By 1875, the office had 252 British and 156 other western employees. When Hart died in 1911, he was given the rare honour of being bestowed the title of 'Senior Guardian of the Heir Apparent' by China.

The customs office remained under a British inspector-general until the Chinese Communist Party seized power. The last inspector-general, the American Lester Knox Little, was part of the entourage that fled to Taiwan with Chiang Kai-shek in 1949.

Britain also helped China build diplomatic relations with other countries. In 1866, Hart organized a Chinese mission to Europe. Though not a diplomatic mission, it was still the first foray of its kind and its senior-most Chinese official, Pin Chun, was given official rank. He visited London, Copenhagen, Stockholm, St Petersburg, Berlin, Brussels and Paris. In 1868, China sent a mission to the US.

These missions were designed to transform China's image from one of a disintegrating empire to a state deserving equal treatment as a member of the contemporary circle of power. In 1869, when the trade treaties of the European powers came up for revision, negotiations took place for the first time in an atmosphere free of military threats and intimidation. In 1877, China set up its first resident embassy in London. This was followed by legations in Paris, Berlin, Madrid, Washington, Tokyo and St Petersburg.

Britain went to great lengths to ensure that its employees did not behave as arrogant rulers, but rather as employees of the Chinese government. In a circular dated 21 June 1864, Hart spelt out a code of behaviour for foreign employees:

> It is to be distinctly and constantly kept in mind that the
> Inspectorate of Customs is a Chinese and not a Foreign
> Service, and that, as such, it is the duty of each of its members
> to conduct himself towards the Chinese, people as well as
> officials, in such a way as to avoid all cause of offence and
> ill feeling.[19]

Despite actively helping the Manchu regime, Britain maintained that it was pursuing 'strict *bonâ fide* neutrality' in the Chinese civil war. Its policy of supporting an 'Asiatic' ruler instead of annexing his kingdom was hotly debated within Britain, drawing sharp divides among officials in Kolkata, Beijing and London. The British government had a difficult time explaining the new policy to its bewildered and sceptical parliament. British commanders fighting alongside Chinese troops to suppress the Taiping rebels was confounding. Among its critics was Benjamin Disraeli, the leader of the opposition, who attacked Palmerston for supporting the 'Tartar dynasty'. He contrasted Britain's neutrality in the American Civil War to its support for the 'Tartars' in China: '25 years have elapsed, and the noble Lord who made war against the Tartar dynasty is now supporting the Tartar dynasty and making war against these rebellious subjects of Emperor of China. We have completely changed our position. We are making war against the Taeping insurrection.'[20] Oxford professor Goldwin Smith was also critical of British soldiers and seamen being made to serve a 'barbarian Prince' as mercenaries.

Britain's China hands who supported the Manchu rulers were also chastised. British historian Robert Bickers writes that some people maintained that Britain had lost its moment to conquer China due to the 'treason' of these officials: 'Robert Hart, and the British ministers Sir Rutherford Alcock and Sir Thomas Wade in particular assisted the self-strengthening moves of the Tongzhi restoration.'[21] There was also no shortage of voices within Britain urging the country to extend its empire to China. They advocated for the Indian model, which involved keeping the nominal presence of the king while dealing directly with the provincial governors and other princes.

The British government, however, relied on the policy recommended by its China hands. Alcock argued that by supporting the Manchu rulers, Britain could rescue China and gain more trading rights.[22] Prime Minister Palmerston admitted that it was unusual for British subjects to be so employed. Still, since their indemnity was 'to be paid out of the produce of these Customs', he believed they had 'a direct interest in seeing that they are fairly levied and completely paid'.[23] He cited the concurrence of France and Russia to Britain's policy, saying they all agreed that if peace could be restored to China's interior, the ensuing commercial intercourse would become an important source of wealth and national prosperity.

Palmerston declared in the British parliament that the 'Tartars' had been in power for 'five hundred years' and should not be called foreigners. When corrected by another member that the duration of 'Tartar rule' was '250 or 260 years', Palmerston insisted that it was nevertheless 'well rooted' and had a good hold on the country's population. In any event, the alternative to it was 'extensive anarchy'.[24]

Palmerston told parliament, 'our object in China is simply trade. We do not want conquest – we want trade'.[25] He went on to express confidence that given friendly relations with China, commerce would increase yearly. Then he cited trade benefits to convince the parliament:

> It was long felt that trade with China would open a vast field
> of commercial enterprise to us, and there can be no doubt
> that, among other things, the great expansion of commerce
> with that empire has contributed to enable us to meet without
> disaster the unfortunate obstructions to our commerce and
> manufactures occasioned by events still going on in America.[26]

He claimed that the intervention in China had become necessary because Britain's treaty rights were endangered, and national interests were at stake. Britain could benefit from trade concessions in China only if the Qing dynasty remained in power, adding that this policy was vindicated by the tripling of trade revenues since Britain joined the war against the Taiping rebels.

Foreign Secretary John Russell argued that it was important for Britain to repel the Taipings from Shanghai because it was an open port through which Chinese merchants traded with foreigners. Business interests in both nations would suffer a severe blow if the city were to fall into the hands of the rebels.

This was further bolstered by Austen Layard, the under-secretary for foreign affairs, who explained Britain's policy towards the Manchu dynasty in the parliament: 'Our policy had in view two objects – to strengthen the Chinese Government as far as we could legitimately do so, as the best means of preserving tranquillity in China, and to secure the observance of treaties.'[27] He said that the Treaty of Tianjin had completely changed Britain's relations with China. Britain now treated China as a 'civilized' country, and its government had also started to understand the importance of maintaining good international relations. Issues that would earlier have led to war were now handled through diplomacy. The British and other foreign officials who had been allowed to serve under the Chinese and train Chinese troops, starting with the defence of Shanghai against the Taiping rebels, had earned the trust of the Chinese officials.

Layard disavowed any intention to turn China into a protectorate, declaring that Britain could not contemplate such action even if it wanted to because 'the representatives in China of France, Russia, the United States, and other Powers, would exercise a vigilant control to defeat them'.[28] He added that the collective consensus among the European powers in China was to ensure China's stability and support whoever could best maintain order and secure the treaty ports. Such a policy, Layard emphasized, had the full support of the British officials in China – best demonstrated by the fact that the Chinese government had purchased several war steamers and staffed them 'temporarily' with foreigners under British command.

Britain's support enabled the Manchus to suppress the Taiping Rebellion and survive another half a century. As Platt discernibly concludes: 'Without the British intervention, it is far more likely that the rebels would have won.'[29]

But Britain did not stop there. It was keen to help China recover its continental possessions in order to keep Russia at bay. Once the Taipings had been defeated, it began to help China quell other rebellions. The Nien gangs in northern China and the Panthay Muslims in Yunnan were crushed. Next came the turn of the Dungan Muslims, whose rebellion had cut China off from East Turkestan. After subjugating the Dungans, China turned its attention to East Turkestan, where Yakub Beg, a soldier from Khokand, had seized power and Russia had occupied the Ili Valley. Britain now decided to support China in its mission to reclaim Central Asia.

Reconquest of East Turkestan

This was one of Britain's most significant successes in China's recovery of Central Asia. Despite its size, the region of East Turkestan yielded little revenue and fell far short of covering Russia's expenses to maintain control over it. Given the long distances, Russia concentrated its resources on building a railway line to it. But Britain was convinced that Russia wanted to use Central Asia as a base to invade India, as a regional power vacuum would give it easy access across the Kunlun Mountains.

Since the conquest a century ago, the Manchu hold on Zungaria and Kashgaria – the northern and southern halves of East Turkestan – had been stormy. In 1825, the Khoja ruler of Kashgaria, Jahangir, had led a revolt that the Chinese put down brutally, capturing Jahangir and sending him to Beijing, where his body was cut to pieces and fed to dogs. In 1847, another band of Khojas living in exile in Khokand had attacked the Chinese.

In 1861, when the Muslim Dungans of the adjoining Chinese provinces of Qinghai and Gansu revolted, the Chinese position in East Turkestan became truly untenable. Within a short time, all of Kashgaria erupted in rebellion. By 1864, Yakub Beg emerged as a strong army commander, conquering nearly the entire province and proclaiming himself the ruler of 'Yettishahr', meaning 'Seven Cities'.[30]

Beg tried to stabilize his rule by strengthening his army and establishing relations with neighbouring countries. He employed an Indian, who had fought the British in Punjab and later migrated to Kashgaria, and appointed him the commander of his artillery. In 1867, the year the British stationed a representative in Ladakh to keep an eye on the frontier, he sent an envoy to the maharaja of Kashmir.[31] Three years later, he sent another man to Kolkata to establish ties with the British.

Britain was reluctant to recognize the rebel ruler, but, in 1870, it sent Thomas Douglas Forsyth, an officer of the Indian Civil Service, with a delegation. Beg was supplied with some rifles and encouraged to continue sending envoys to India, and through it to Constantinople. By 1873, the Ottoman sultan, the self-styled Caliph of the Islamic world, conferred the title of '*amir-ul-Momineen*', the ruler of the faithful, on Beg. He also sent some weapons via India.

Both Russia and Britain were convinced that the other side was aiding Beg. General Kuropatkin, the Russian military officer and explorer, wrote that the British encouraged the independence of Yakub Beg, citing Forsyth's 1870 mission. Russia believed that Britain wanted Kashgaria to emerge as a neutral zone between India and Russia. Both countries established contact with Beg, despite their concerns about his stability.

Yakub Beg, eager for international recognition, sent an emissary, Mirza Shadi, to St Petersburg. Russia wanted to protect the earlier trading rights granted by China, and although Beg was willing to accept them, Russia was hesitant to recognize him as a sovereign ruler, viewing him as an insurgent. As soon as Mirza Shadi returned, Beg sent him to Kolkata. This prompted Russia to send a diplomatic mission led by Alexander Kaulbars, a military officer and explorer of Central Asia, to Kashgar in 1872. Kaulbars signed a trade treaty acquiring free trade rights in Kashgaria. The following year, Russia established its trade mission in East Turkestan, thus fulfilling its 'long-cherished wish' to set up a presence in the region.[32]

In 1871, during the regional unrest, Russia had occupied Kulja, displacing a local Muslim chieftain who had earlier seized power from the Chinese. The Russian minister in Beijing assured China that his country 'would withdraw from Ili whenever Ch'ing control should be re-established'.[33] Britain, however, was alarmed by the Russian encroachment and decided to pursue a two-pronged strategy: explore the possibility of establishing friendly relations with Beg and prod China to reconquer the region. In 1874, it sent Forsyth back to Kashgar. This time, he signed a trade treaty with Beg, securing for Britain free trade rights, settlement rights, most-favoured nation status and extra-territoriality in Kashgaria (meaning that British nationals would not be subject to the local jurisdiction).

The second strategy, persuading China to send a military expedition to Turkestan, proved to be more difficult. In July 1871, the British *chargé d'affaires* in Beijing, Thomas Wade, wrote that while he did not expect Yakub Beg to last long in Turkestan or weave its rebellious people into a nation, the Chinese were doing practically nothing to recover Turkestan. He believed that Russia was keen to help China reconquer East Turkestan, but warned that if China did not do so, Russia would annex it. Russia was unhappy with Beg because of his overtures to Britain, so he cautioned his government against annexing East Turkestan, as this would not be worth the expense.[34]

Wade had assessed, correctly, that Yakub Beg's relations with Russia were tense. Although Beg had allowed Russia to open a trade mission in Kashgar, British exports had started flooding the market following their trade treaty. In 1874, Russia amassed 20,000 troops to invade Kashgar, but unfortunately, a revolt in Khokand compelled it to redeploy its forces. This created an urgency in Britain, which decided to concentrate on the second strategy – persuading China to reoccupy the region.

Yet China was in no position to send a military expedition to East Turkestan. Its coffers were empty, and the barren Central

Asian steppes offered no financial rewards. Besides, Japan's invasion of Taiwan in 1874 called for pressing action. China was unable to decide which front to tackle first. China's Grand Secretary Li Hongzhang (Li Hung-chang) saw the loss of East Turkestan as a blessing and preferred to concentrate on coastal areas. He ascribed Britain's advice to reconquer it to its Russophobia, not concern for China. Britain, too, was unsure of China's capacity to wage this war. Wade was asked to mediate an agreement between Beg and China in which Beg would accept Chinese suzerainty while maintaining an autonomous status. But Beg was unwilling to do so and, therefore, Britain turned to a trusted Chinese general to reconquer East Turkestan.

Zuo Zongtang (Tso Tsung-T'ang)[35] is lesser-known than his more illustrious contemporaries, Li Hongzhang and Zeng Guofan. He was a Han Chinese who had failed his civil service exam. In 1860, he joined the staff of Zeng Guofan, one of the most powerful leaders during the minority of the Tongzhi Emperor. Making his mark in the war against the Taiping rebels, he drew the attention of the British army commanders. He played a key part in suppressing the Muslim Nian rebellion in 1868, which involved several Western soldiers. Following these successes, he was appointed the governor general of the Fujian and Zhejiang provinces and the commissioner of the naval industries.

Zuo, firmly believing in the need to acquire Western technology, both for the military and the economy, set up China's first modern arms factory in Foochow. This facility was equipped with both a shipyard and naval academy. With French help, the Foochow Naval Yard built sixteen gunboats and trained a Chinese crew in naval construction, marine engineering, navigation and how to command the small squadron by 1874.[36] Zuo also established a woollen mill in Lanzhou in 1880 with German assistance.

His first task was to persuade his government to reconquer east Turkestan, although many government officials were reluctant to expend money on it. The Chinese viceroy of Canton told the British that the country was more anxious to recover territories seized by Russia in Manchuria than East Turkestan. For the Manchus, Manchuria held a revered status, as their native country and the birthplace of their most famous emperors. On the other hand, East Turkestan was a more recent conquest without any traditional value. The viceroy also said that in 1871 – when Russia occupied the Kulja region – it did so because of the rebellious nature of the province and had used it as a penal settlement. Russia, too, was concerned about East Turkestan as a source of disturbance and wanted China to maintain order there, which it was unable to do.

Zuo persuaded the Manchu rulers by appealing to their dynastic pride, arguing that the western lands had been conquered by their legendary forefathers, Kangxi and Qianlong. It was their family duty to recover them. Zuo carried the day and was appointed governor general of Shanxi and Gansu provinces and authorized to build an army to recover East Turkestan. He was the first Han Chinese to head a province beyond the Great Wall, which had so far been reserved for Manchu and Mongol noblemen.

The Manchus were uncomfortable with Zuo commanding such a large army, but being adept at European military tactics, he enjoyed the confidence of the British. His army displayed far more discipline and military acumen than Yakub Beg's. Zuo received an initial loan of 1.6 million pounds sterling from Britain's Hong Kong and Shanghai Banking Corporation (HSBC), which was considered enough to fund the expedition.[37] China pledged the customs revenue from four ports as surety for the loan.[38] He procured Berdan rifles and Krupp cannon, giving him overwhelming superiority over Yakub Beg's forces. Later, as expenses mounted, Zuo took additional loans. 'During the whole period of military operations in Sinkiang,' Hsü describes, 'Tso miraculously managed never to run short of money, in spite of all the financial troubles of the state.'[39]

Zuo's army of 60,000 marched into Xinjiang in 1876. It defeated Beg near Turfan and, in the following year, at Urumqi. When Zuo's forces captured Zungaria, Yakub Beg sought Britain's mediation. The Chinese minister in London, Kuo Sung-Tao, demanded that

Beg cede certain Chinese towns he had seized and assist China in reconquering all of East Turkestan. However, the lightning military successes of Zuo's army, along with the internal dissensions within Yakub Beg's ranks, led to his rapid collapse. With neither Britain nor Russia coming to his rescue, Beg committed suicide in May 1877 – though it is speculated that he might have been poisoned by rivals. Still, it took almost a year for the Chinese army to recover all of East Turkestan. In Turfan, the Chinese massacred the inhabitants and destroyed the city. In Kashgar, the leaders were cut in pieces and several hundred decapitated. Some people fled to Ladakh, others to Russian Turkestan.

Hsü calls this reconquest of East Turkestan an epic event for modern China, due to both its significance and the extreme circumstances that made it possible:

> Rare is the historical event that has won the acclaim of traditional Chinese chroniclers, nationalistic writers and Marxist scholars alike. The Ch'ing recovery of Sinkiang from the Moslem rebels in the 1870's ranks among the few occurrences that have received such widespread support. It was a remarkable achievement given the sharp decline of the dynasty, the financial stringency of the court and the military weakness of the country.[40]

In 1884, China established East Turkestan as a province and named it Xinjiang, meaning 'new province'. It was placed under a governor subordinate to the governor general of the Shanxi and Gansu provinces.

Getting Russia Out of Kulja

Although Zuo Zongtang had recovered East Turkestan, he could not make Russia leave Kulja. Having promised to vacate the region when the Chinese returned, Russia now refused to do so, insisting on negotiations taking place in St Petersburg to hammer out withdrawal terms. These negotiations ended disastrously for China as Russia kept its ambassador, Chunghow (Ch'ung-hou), waiting for an extended period and then compelled him to make significant territorial concessions in Manchuria, along with 5 million roubles as indemnity in return for withdrawing from northern Kulja. Russia would retain control of southern Kulja, including the passes over the Tianshan Mountains, giving it access to Kashgaria.

This 1879 Treaty of Levadia created outrage in Beijing and was rejected. Chunghow was arrested upon his return and sentenced to death. Russia criticized China for reneging on the treaty and despatched a naval fleet, with Britain coming to China's rescue at once. Hart recalled Charles Gordon ('Chinese Gordon'), then serving as a secretary to the viceroy in India. He returned swiftly to China, where he took on the challenge of reorganizing China's defences. He also later wrote to the British governor of Hong Kong, pithily summarizing Britain's China policy during this period: 'Were China not threatened by Russia, she had better be left weak. As she is threatened, it is better she was strong, even if we have to put up with her airs.'[41]

Britain also secured reprieve for the hapless Chunghow. It appealed to Russia not to press China too hard, since this would lead to the collapse of its ruling dynasty, 'which would be neither in the interest of Russia nor of Europe'. A chastened Russia agreed to renegotiate the treaty, asserting that it did not want to retain control of Kulja and had no 'intention of pushing things to the extremity'. Its primary objective was to prompt China to settle the indemnity once and for all.[42]

The negotiations were once again held in St Petersburg. This time, China's Minister to Britain and France, Zeng Jize (Tseng Chi-tse), son of Zeng Guofan, led its delegation. Before leaving London, Zeng requested that Foreign Secretary Earl Granville instruct the British ambassador in St Petersburg to give him 'unofficial assistance and advice'. Sir Halliday Macartney, his assistant, accompanied him on this mission and the British foreign office extended their full support.[43] The British ambassador in St Petersburg became Zeng's 'secret adviser',[44] and Britain persuaded France and Germany to put pressure on Russia.

The terms of the new agreement, the 1881 Treaty of St Petersburg, were far more favourable to China. Russia agreed to withdraw completely from Ili and reduce the number of its missions in the region to two. It also agreed to pay compensation to China. The new treaty was celebrated in China as a diplomatic victory, and Zeng thanked Britain for its assistance.[45]

There is a common misconception that Britain supported Yakub Beg and the independence of East Turkestan. Britain's support to Beg was, at best, a tactic to keep Russia at bay. Once it realized Beg could not be trusted, it threw its weight behind China, energetically supporting its demand that Russia withdraw from Kulja. This is also acknowledged by Hsü, who supports the conventional view: 'Wade counselled the court in Peking, Colonel Gordon came from India to help with defence, and Lord Dufferin, Britain's ambassador in St Petersburg, offered confidential advice to the Chinese negotiator in Russia, Marquis Tseng'.[46]

China followed its conquest by flooding East Turkestan with Han Chinese people. It overhauled its administration and divided the new province into four administrative segments – each overseen by a lieutenant governor (*taotai*) who reported to a governor stationed in Urumqi. Chinese bureaucrats were now permitted to work there – and many did. The Uyghur inhabitants were not treated as Chinese citizens, and learning the Chinese language was made mandatory. Fenby writes that the 'Han Chinese moved in to solidify the imperial presence, taking official posts, opening Confucian schools, establishing walled garrisons, and putting up Chinese names on the gates of their sections of racially segregated towns'.[47]

The Kulja incident also helped China regain its confidence after the chaos of the Taiping rebellion and the British invasion of Beijing. Wade, whom the Chinese considered a friend to be consulted on matters of importance, wrote to London during the crisis about this change:

When we were first installed in Peking, nineteen years ago,
it was my lot, as Sir Frederick Bruce's Chinese Secretary,

to be constantly in communication with the Prince and the Ministers of the Tsung-li Yamên, a new and very unpopular institution, and in those days, there was no subject hardly upon which we did not talk most unreservedly.

Over the years, this relationship changed, and the ministers met Wade less frequently. When they did, a secretary recorded the proceedings.[48]

Negotiating for Kulja: Trade vs Territory

The Kulja talks revealed a striking aspect of China's boundary negotiations. As a safety measure, Zeng Jize sent a detailed memorandum to Beijing outlining his proposed strategy to negotiate. He discounted the military option by cautioning that there was no certainty of victory and that the warmongering generals were oblivious to the troubles that would follow. China, having just recovered from a succession of severe calamities, was quite unprepared to go to war. Russia, too, faced internal problems, and other European nations could be expected to curb its ambitious designs. Also, if China requested their assistance with military action, wouldn't there be a price to pay? After all, Britain had helped Turkey fight its war against Russia, but, in exchange, it had taken Cyprus.

Zeng recommended that China follow the strategy of Western countries in negotiating such treaties – being firm on territory and flexible on trade. He assured Beijing that he would not cede territory but would make trade concessions, which were temporary in nature: 'Territory being a question to be settled once and for ever, it is expedient to pursue a fixed policy on the subject, from which there must be no deviation.'[49]

Even after Russia withdrew from Kulja, Britain was still afraid of an invasion of India. Chinese control over the province was weak and there were reports that Russia had made a deal with it to not block expeditions in the Pamirs. These reports were supported by news of the rapid progress in the construction of a railway line, which had already reached Ashkabad in January 1886 and was due to reach Merv by April. The fear of China losing control continued to haunt Britain.

So, it started strengthening China's claim to East Turkestan by calling it Chinese Turkestan and treating it like it had always been a historical part of China. Boulger, who was one of the first Britons to write a history of the region soon after it was reconquered by China, was fulsome in his praise for Chinese rule:

> China's rule in Eastern Turkestan and Jungaria is one of the most instructive pages in the history of modern Asia, yet it may freely be admitted that the brief career of Yakoob Beg gave an interest to the consideration of the Chinese in Central Asia that that theme might otherwise have failed to supply.[50]

He wrote that the Chinese were thoughtful and considerate rulers – as opposed to the 'thoughtless and improvident' rule of Russia in West Turkestan.[51]

Boulger declared that the frontiers of China's empire had historically extended to Central Asia and even to India: 'For a considerable number of years anterior to the ninth century, the Chinese Empire extended to the borders of Khokand and Cashmere.'[52] As for why Chinese rule had disappeared from East Turkestan from the ninth to the early eighteenth century, Boulger attributed it to 'a series of misfortunes'.[53]

Courting Foreigners: China's Strengths and Weaknesses

British assistance led to a period of relative calm and progress in China known as the Tongzhi Restoration, inaptly named after a ruler too young to claim credit for it. His uncle, Prince Gong, was its real architect. With British help, one of his administrative reforms was setting up the Tsungli Yamen (the Office for General Management), which also served as a foreign office and dealt with the leading foreign powers in China – Russia, Britain, France and the US. There were separate bureaus to deal with each foreign power and one to look after coastal defence. Britain's under-secretary for foreign affairs, Austen

Layard, took credit for the formation of the office, claiming that the Chinese government had for the first time admitted the rights of foreigners and consented to treat them as equals.

The key to Prince Gong's success was maintaining good relations with the British. This enabled him to survive in power despite frequent confrontations with Cixi, Tongzhi's mother. Robert Hart and Wade were his key advisers, and while they often got carried away by their enthusiasm for modernizing the country, Hsü writes that Lord Stanley, the British foreign secretary, advised restraint: 'We must not expect the Chinese, either the Government or the people, at once to see things in the same light as we see them; we must bear in mind that we have obtained our knowledge by experience extending over many years, and we must lead and not force the Chinese to the adoption of a better system.'[54]

As the most influential figure in China in the second half of the nineteenth century, Prince Gong forestalled the Qing dynasty's inevitable collapse and prevented the empire's disintegration. His diplomacy helped China survive as an independent country – a rare achievement for an Asian country in the era of European imperialism. Although Japan soon eclipsed China as the pre-eminent Asian power, Prince Gong successfully imprinted his country on the British mind as a friendly imperial power and one to turn to in Asia for promoting British interests. However, he fell victim to the relentless advance of the Europeans and could not survive the French invasion of China through Vietnam in 1884 and the concessions extracted by it. Eventually, he withdrew from state affairs and disappeared into oblivion.

Britain succeeded in maintaining close relations with Chinese officials by developing a corps of experts, its China hands, who acquired local expertise and enjoyed access to the Chinese government that was unavailable to other European powers. Frederick Bruce took up residence in Beijing in 1861 as a minister and Wade joined him as the secretary of the legation. Prince Gong was their main interlocutor as head of the Tsungli Yamen. They were followed by others like Alcock and Harry Parkes. Three of them were promoted from the China Service to Britain's main diplomatic service: Alcock, Wade and Parkes. All three spoke Chinese.[55]

Alcock advised the Chinese government regarding its relations with Western powers. Westad notes the importance of these offices:

> Foreign advisers were part of China's weakness and part of China's strength. Some Chinese resented their presence … But other Chinese lauded those among the foreign advisers who were incorrupt and hardworking, and who made a contribution to building state institutions while introducing new forms of administrative and economic skills.[56]

Another key figure in the nascent diplomatic corps in Beijing was Anson Burlingame, the American minister in Beijing from 1861. He presented a book on international law to Prince Gong to help him protect Chinese interests against foreign powers, which the grateful prince had translated into Chinese. He retired in 1867 and became an accredited representative of the Chinese government to eleven European countries. In his role, Burlingame negotiated treaties with the US, England, Denmark, Sweden and Holland on behalf of China. Unfortunately, he died in St Petersburg in 1870 on one of his missions. According to the contemporary American historian S. Wells Williams, the services of Burlingame and Ward were 'not likely to be soon forgotten' in their home countries.[57]

Russia also took credit for helping China recover from the crisis during the Taiping Rebellion and successfully restoring its empire. In 1886, the Russian army officer and explorer Nikolai Przhevalsky wrote *From Kiakhta to the Sources of the Yellow River*, a book in which he compared China's policy of dealing with the more powerful European powers to Ottoman Turkey's – both survived by skilfully playing one against others – and cited China taking Russian assistance to suppress the Turkic rebellion in Xinjiang.

Understandably, Przhevalsky was less supportive of Chinese rule in Central Asia. He advocated a policy of liberating the Turks and the Mongols:

It is clear that the inhabitants of Chinese Turkestan who are related to our Turkestanians by their origin, language, and religion and suffer from severe Chinese oppression also have good grounds for seeking a better fate. Then the Mongols, especially northern Mongols, who have known Russians across the Siberian border for a long time are attracted toward Russia as a result of the lawlessness and arbitrariness of the Chinese rule. Finally, the Dungans, who are dispersed sporadically about the oasis of Central Asia and who not very long ago experienced all the mercilessness of the Chinese atrocities and still find themselves under severe oppression are awaiting Russians as their liberators from the Chinese.[58]

The Taiping Rebellion was crushed, but it continued to inspire Han China. Sun Yat-sen, the first provisional president of the Republic of China and the founding leader of the Nationalist Party of China, saw it as the precursor to the anti-Manchu struggle. Mao Zedong and the communists viewed it as the forerunner to the peasant revolution.

Once China reconquered East Turkestan, Britain started the process of demarcating its border with its empire in India to secure it against Russian predation. The task was assigned to the Intelligence Branch in Simla.

6

British Empire in India

The East India Company was established in London in 1600, receiving exclusive trading rights in India and other eastern countries from the Crown. In 1618, Sir Thomas Roe made his way to the court of Mughal emperor Jahangir in Agra, where he was granted permission to set up a trading centre in Surat.

More than a century later, as the Mughal empire collapsed, Britain joined the ensuing power struggle. Its first victory came in the land battle at Plassey in Bengal in 1757, marking a key moment in their ascent. The EIC soon discovered that its commercial interests could be significantly amplified by seizing political control. Over the next ninety years, it ultimately conquered all of India.

The Ladakh Frontier

Punjab became the last major province to be annexed by Britain in India. Its conquest in 1849 extended the British empire to the Central Asian frontier. The ruler of Punjab, Ranjit Singh, had conquered Jammu in 1808, followed by Kashmir in 1819, with Gulab Singh being appointed as the governor of the combined province of Jammu–Kashmir. Gulab Singh added Ladakh to the province in 1834 and Baltistan five years later. Mehta Mangal, the wazir (governor) of Ladakh, built a fort in Shahidulla (spelt Xaidulla now by the Chinese) on the Karakash River, south of the Kunlun Mountains.

Ten years after Ranjit Singh's death, Britain annexed his kingdom. They allowed Gulab Singh to proclaim himself its 'maharaja', or king and retain the province of Jammu–Kashmir, which joined the ranks of the Indian princely states enjoying internal autonomy under British 'paramountcy'. Ladakh abutted Tibet to the east and East Turkestan to the north. This brought the British empire, through India, within invading distance of Russia's Central Asian empire, with only the formidable Pamirs and barren plateaus separating them. In addition to sending the customary resident to Kashmir's capital, Srinagar, Britain stationed a joint commissioner in Ladakh.

The term *pamir* means valley, characterized in the region by an average elevation of 13,000 to 14,000 feet. Towards the east, these valleys become lower and more accessible. To better understand the terrain and climate of the Pamirs, both Britain and Russia sent explorers. The Trigonometrical Survey of India began in Ladakh in 1855, with initial surveys conducted in 1865 by a civil sub-assistant, W. H. Johnson. The next year, Johnson crossed the Karakoram Pass and travelled to Shahidulla, where he recorded the construction of the fort by the maharaja of Kashmir. His survey also took him east into Aksai Chin, a high plateau spanning about 7,000 square miles (18,000 square kilometres) at an elevation of 15,500 to 17,500 feet, situated between Ladakh and Tibet's Changthang region. Johnson's expedition yielded a map in 1865. He was followed by G. W. Hayward in 1868. These surveys resulted in a more detailed version prepared by Frederic Drew, a geologist stationed in Ladakh between 1869 and 1871. Another survey of the frontier followed – by T. D. Forsyth in 1874.

East Turkestan emerged as an archaeologist's delight upon the discovery of its ancient ruins. Several renowned travellers, including the Swedish geographer Sven Anders Hedin, Britain's Marc Aurel Stein and Russia's Nikolai Przhevalsky, also undertook explorations.

Russia laid claim to the Pamirs on the basis of its inhabitants – Kyrgyz nomads with ties to Khokand, which Russia had annexed in 1876. In the late 1880s, Russia intensified its efforts to explore the

Pamir region, dispatching expeditions under Colonel Grombchevsky and Captain Yonoff.

Russia's approach to the border question in the Pamirs can be gleaned from an article published in the *Moscow Gazette* in 1892, which argued that since Russia had no natural boundaries like mountains, seas or broad rivers, it had to expand control over territory to protect itself from robber bands: 'The history of the last thirty years proves that our advance into the heart of Asia was not made in a spirit of conquest, but solely with the object of securing our possessions against the irruptions of marauding bands.' The article also asserted Russia's claim to the Pamirs: 'But we hear no protest from China, nor yet of any dissatisfaction on the part of the Amirs of Bokhara and Afghanistan. England alone raises her voice but her protest we can estimate at its real worth.'[1]

Britain's earliest contact with Kashgaria occurred during Yakub Beg's rule. Robert B. Shaw, a tea planter serving as the British agent in Leh, was the first Englishman to visit Kashgar in 1868. Forsyth went twice – in 1870 and 1873. In 1887, after China reconquered East Turkestan, the British military officer Colonel Mark Bell travelled from China to Kashgar and commented on the power dynamics between China and Russia there: '[It] must be considered an unnatural dependency of China, impossible to defend against Russia so long as the Chinese troops are not trained and led by European officers, and without communication by rail between it and Shense [Shanxi]'.[2]

Britain identified the passes in the Hindukush Mountains – spanning from Wakhan and Badakhshan and leading up to Kabul, Gilgit, Chitral and Kashmir – as possible routes for a Russian invasion. It conducted surveys of these regions and started defensive works, including railways, roads and bridges. General Maclean was stationed at Meshed on the Afghan–Iran border to monitor Russian movements and advise the amir. South of the Pamirs, Britain occupied Hunza, Gilgit, Nagar and Chitral. Lord Dufferin also wanted to acquire the territory north of the Hindukush in order to control the passes. Consequently, the Indian rulers in Punjab were urged to offer men and money to strengthen the British army, leading to the formation of a force – the Imperial Service troops – which was commanded by Indians but trained by British officers.

The route across the Karakoram Pass from Ladakh to Yarkand was considerably more difficult than the Hindukush routes. Nevertheless, in order to remind his country not to neglect this route, Colonel Lumsden underscored the successful invasion and conquest of Kashmir in 1543 by Mirza Hyder and Sikandar Hayat Khan of Kashgar by this route.[3]

Once China had reconquered East Turkestan, Britain decided to conduct a joint survey of the frontier. But China's control over the restive province was tenuous, and lacked any presence in the Pamir area. With the Manchu dynasty in disarray, Britain failed to elicit a response from China and carried out surveys on its own.

The Pamir region posed a formidable challenge for all three empires. Both Britain and Russia felt the need to define the limits of the three Central Asian empires. These negotiations were conducted exclusively between Britain and Russia, with Afghanistan and China merely kept informed as needed. Britain took on the task of strengthening China in response to Russia's territorial claims, though the Chinese were unwilling to move out of the safety of the towns in Kashgaria and had to be pushed to extend their territorial control. Britain pressed China to expand its empire to make it conterminous with India, thus leaving no gap for Russia to penetrate. This was based on an assessment that it would be easier to persuade Russia to accept Chinese control of the region than Britain annexing it. In any event, Britain was reluctant to send forces to remote areas that were difficult to defend. China was the weakest of the three empires, and Britain and Russia were willing to compromise by assigning it the barren areas.

At the same time, Britain was anxious to ensure that China would not enter into an agreement with Russia that could harm its interests. Its mission in Beijing was to reassure the Chinese that Britain would always act in the common interests of both countries and never leave it 'in the lurch'.[4]

Contrary to the case with China, Britain had to keep the rulers of Afghanistan and Kashmir on a tight leash. Russia viewed the Afghans as British proxies who, due to their aggressive political culture, needed to be treated with suspicion. Kashmir, too, was keen to recover lost ground beyond Ladakh. When China overthrew Yakub Beg, the wazir of Ladakh, Radha Kishen, wanted to reoccupy Shahidulla. But Ney Elias, the joint commissioner of Ladakh, dissuaded him from venturing beyond the Karakoram Pass. Britain instructed the maharaja of Kashmir to accept the Indus watershed as his kingdom's boundary.[5]

Britain and Russia had to define the eastern limit of Afghanistan in the Pamirs, as well as the southern border of Chinese Turkestan. It is evident from British records that at this time China considered the Kunlun Mountains the southern frontier of Xinjiang. There was no Chinese presence in the Pamir region or the plateau between the Kunlun and Karakoram Mountains. The critical question for Britain was whether to fix the northern border of Ladakh along the Karakoram Mountains or further north along the Kunlun range. The territory between the two mountain ranges was a barren plateau inhabited by a handful of Kyrgyz herdsmen. The fort at Shahidulla on the Karakash River was the only settlement, and no ruler maintained a permanent presence there.

When Forsyth travelled to Kashgaria in 1870, he found Shahidulla in Yakub Beg's control – but not the territory south of it. He advised treating the Kunlun range as the border. In 1879, Britain published a map of Turkestan captioned 'Turkestan: The British and the Russian Dominions in Asia' based on surveys carried out by British and Russian officers prior to 1878. With Forsyth's assessment in mind, the northern border of Kashmir on the map was drawn north of the Karakoram Pass, passing through Aktagh, midway between Shahidulla and the Karakoram Pass. The Soda Plains and Lingzithang Plains of Aksai Chin were included in Kashmir.[6]

The same year, Britain sent Ney Elias to East Turkestan, or Chinese Turkestan as it had started calling it, a year after China's reconquest of the region. Elias did not find any Chinese presence in Shahidulla nor in Kilian, north of the Kunlun Mountains, which he referred to as the border village. The local elder in Kilian (the 'Beg') told him that no Chinese official had visited the village, despite the fact that ever since they had taken over in Yarkand, everything had fallen into disarray.

Elias then travelled to Yarkand, where he met the Chinese amban. He discovered that the Chinese were annoyed with the Russians for harbouring Kashgarian rebels active on the border. Elias was also astounded by the Chinese officials' ignorance of the region. They were unaware of the proximity of places like Kashmir and Kabul, even though he used their Chinese names:

> But one of the most remarkable features of the Chinese rule … is the contemptible ignorance of the responsible authorities regarding everything outside their own borders. It is doubtless this ignorance that leads them to seek safety in exclusiveness, that prompts them to suspect the motives of every foreigner, and gives birth to the idea that they are surrounded by a chain of enemies, all leagued together, from Ili round to Ladakh … The fact is scarcely to be believed, that officials who have ruled over Yarkand for a year and a half should be unaware of the existence of places so near their frontiers as Ladakh, Kashmir and Gilgit, or of countries so important as India and Afghanistan, though there are hundreds of traders, Hajis and others living at the very doors of their Yamens, who could give every information if called on to do so.[7]

Elias gave a map to the amban and explained the geography of the region, including why Britain was concerned about Russia's movements. The Chinese had little knowledge of what lay south of the Kunlun Mountains, regarding its passes – such as Kugiar, Kilian, Sanju and Kiria – as the southern limits of their territory. They had no presence near any of these passes. Elias also met a Chinese general who wanted to learn about the road to Ladakh and the people living there. Elias was eager to proceed to Kashgar to meet the taotai, the senior-most Chinese official in Kashgaria, but was dissuaded from it because of local disturbances.

In 1885, Elias was sent back to Kashgaria and Badakhshan 'to watch the movements of the Russians in and around the regions'. He emphasized the threat that Russian occupation of the Pamirs would pose to the passes leading into Chitral and recommended that the Karakoram Mountains be retained as the northern border. But he was so overawed by the looming Russian threat that he urged Britain to tread cautiously, advocating for China to expand its authority there:

> Chinese authority definitely asserted up to the Karakoram Mountains, and to the limits of Afghan territory on the Pamirs, so that no gap may be left through which any third power may push its way ... All our policy requires is a one-sided assertion of dominion by China – not an agreed frontier between China and Afghanistan; and the less our Government mix themselves up in any measure of delimitation, the less likely they are to arouse any Russian or Afghan jealousy.[8]

Britain was alarmed when it learnt that a Russian army contingent under Captain Grombchevsky had entered the Pamirs.

Britain Prods China

In 1889, Britain sent a young officer, Captain Francis Younghusband, to explore the territory and report on Russian activities there. Younghusband's copious reports on the Pamirs became the basis of Britain's subsequent boundary policy in the region.

He described the land north of the Karakoram Pass as a 'dreary waste of barren gravel hills'. At Aktagh, a route joined from Hunza that was used by robbers to attack traders. Suget, a tiny habitation 9 miles south of Shahidulla, was the next stop, which, according to Younghusband, was the first sight of bushes and trees in a 160-mile journey. Both Suget and Shahidulla were inhabited by a small number of Kyrgyz. Younghusband wrote that the fort at Shahidulla was 20 yards by 15 yards and had seven-foot walls made of mud and stones. The wazir of Ladakh had abandoned it after construction and, later, Yakub Beg stationed troops to protect the trade route. Under his protection, the place was well fortified and the inhabitants grew crops.

Younghusband learnt that a year earlier, the Kanjutis from Hunza had raided Suget and Shahidulla. Some Kyrgyz elders had travelled to Yarkand to appeal to the Chinese amban for protection. But the amban informed them that Shahidulla was beyond the Chinese frontier and in British territory. The elders asked Younghusband to protect them from the Hunza raiders.[9]

Initially, Younghusband believed that Britain should occupy Shahidulla and treat the Kunlun Mountains as the border. However, he changed his mind on realizing that his government was unwilling to station troops north of the Karakoram Pass. On his visit the following year, he met the amban in Yarkand and told him that that Britain did not want a no-man's land, and if China could protect the trade route, Britain would not extend its frontier beyond the Karakoram Mountains. This encouraged the amban to claim that the Chinese had always considered the Indus watershed as a natural boundary between Kashmir and Yarkand, and that they were prepared to protect the trade route as far as the Karakoram Mountains.[10]

During his visit, Younghusband ran into Grombchevsky, who had been appointed the governor of Fergana (now in eastern Uzbekistan). Grombchevsky wanted to travel to Tibet via Ladakh and asked Britain for permission. The permission was denied, but his presence in the area and the request made the British realize the urgency of settling the border issue.

Younghusband also reported that the Chinese had sent a force to build a fort in Suget, adding that they had erected a boundary pillar at the Karakoram Pass, and the Indus watershed could now be treated as the border between Kashmir and Chinese Turkestan.[11] He recommended that since the Chinese were willing to occupy the land between the Kunlun and Karakoram mountains, Britain should treat the Karakoram range as the northern border of Kashmir. He wrote that in Britain's official maps of Kashmir, the northern border followed the course of the Yarkand River, north of the Karakoram Pass. This line was impractical because the river was fordable and the road crossed it frequently from side to side, thus making it an ineffective border. He proposed keeping the mountain crests as the border. To the east, it would run from the Karakoram Pass north-east through the Karatagh Pass to the bend of the Karakash River. This would bring the Lingzithang Plains up to the eastern Kunlun Mountains and under the control of the maharaja of Kashmir. Although uninhabitable, it would please him because it was a large territory. Younghusband justified his recommendation by asserting that defending Ladakh would be easier from south of the Karakoram Pass.[12] While a Russian invasion across the Karakoram could embarrass the British, sustaining supply lines for a large Russian force across the barren land would be much more difficult.

Therefore, the British government in India advised London to persuade the Chinese government to assert its authority all the way up to the Karakoram Mountains and the borders with Afghanistan in the Pamirs, leaving no openings for Russia to push through. This was formulated in a joint letter sent by Lord Lansdowne, the viceroy of India, and all six members of his council to the India Office in London. The letter also acknowledged that the Chinese had never formally gained possession of Shahidulla; the maharaja of Kashmir, on the other hand, had built a fort and kept troops there for a while. Younghusband's report that China had taken measures to occupy the location meant it was to Britain's advantage 'that the tract of country intervening between the Karakorum and Kuenlun Mountains should be definitely held by a friendly Power like China'.

The viceroy's advice was endorsed by the India Office in London. In a note to the British Foreign Office, it sent its recommendation:

In order to check any further advance of Russia towards India in this direction, the Government of Lord Lansdowne suggest, for the consideration of Her Majesty's Government, that the Chinese should be invited to extend their authority up to the limits of the Afghan territory on the Pamirs. They are encouraged in making this recommendation by the recent action of the Chinese authorities, who, it is believed, are now in effectual possession of Shahidula, a post on the trade route from Leh to Yarkand, and situated to the north of the Karakorum Pass ... The Government of India point out that, on the north of Cashmere, between Karakorum and Kuen-Lun Mountains, there is a strip of land which they are not disposed to bring under their control as they would gain little by extending their responsibilities to the further side of a great natural barrier like the Karakorum Mountains and that it is evidently to their advantage that this tract of the country should be definitely held by a friendly power like China.[13]

In Ladakh, Elias' successor, H. Ramsay, questioned Younghusband's assertions about China's ability and willingness to control the plateau between the Karakoram and Kunlun Mountains. He wrote that while the Chinese had started work in Suget, they had withdrawn very quickly. Younghusband's advice, he argued, would make sense only if China was interested in occupying the region, which it was not. Also, unless China's control was effective, it would not serve the objective of keeping Russia out. He did not expect China to retain its soldiers in Suget, and it meant that the local fort would suffer the same fate as the Kashmir fort in Shahidulla – regularly plundered by local people.[14]

Ramsay's scepticism was not unfounded. Despite agreeing to claim the plateau south of the Kunlun Mountains, China remained unwilling to occupy it. Prince Ch'ing, the head of the Tsungli Yamen, told the British minister in Beijing, Sir John Walsham, that 'a large belt of country inhabited by Mohammedan tribes was wedged in between the boundaries of the two Empires' and they could not be considered to be conterminous.[15] This point was repeated a year later to Walsham, who reported that 'the Yamen have always declined, in my discussions with them as to a British

Agency at Kashgar, to admit that China and India are conterminous in this region, holding that there was a belt of Mohammedan tribes which separated them'.[16]

Thus, China's presence in Shahidulla and the plateau to its south remained notional. Although another report in 1892 claimed it had built a border pillar at the Karakoram Pass, a map published the same year in London showed Killian, north of the Kunlun Mountains, as the last Chinese outpost.[17] In 1907, when the British army officer Major G. P. T. Feilding crossed the pass, he found the boundary pillar to be no more than a 'cairn of stones'. He also found the fort at Shahidulla deserted.[18]

Younghusband was accompanied by George Macartney, the son of Sir Halliday Macartney, as his interpreter. Macartney stayed behind in Kashgar as Britain's representative for twenty-eight years, until 1918. He was designated 'Special Assistant to Resident in Kashmir' after Russia refused to let China accept him as a consul. It was only after the 1907 Convention with Britain that Russia relented. The consulate continued to operate until 1948. Like Elias, Macartney was unwilling to ruffle Russia and even suggested a neutral state in Kashgar to allay its suspicions, which was rejected by his government.

While the maharaja of Kashmir does not appear to have raised any objection to Shahidulla being ceded to China, Britain's decision to treat the Indus watershed as the border upset the Mir of Hunza (the title of the region's leader), who controlled the Taghdumbash and Raskam valleys across the Karakoram Range and collected revenue from them. Since the reign of the Qianlong emperor, he had also been annually sending an ounce and a half of gold dust as a gift to the Chinese taotai in Kashgar in exchange for Chinese silk. To China, this made Hunza a vassal state in perpetuity, even though it had been in no position to assist when the maharaja of Kashmir invaded it. When the Mir of Hunza protested against the loss of revenue from Taghdumbash and Raskam, the British offered him monetary compensation.

The Pamir Frontier

Britain had greater difficulty fixing the frontier between Chinese Turkestan and Afghanistan in the Pamirs, because the Afghans were keen to expand their frontier against both Russia and China. The post in dispute here was Somatash (now Sumantash), located near Yeshil-kul. Chinese forces had occupied it following their reconquest of Kashgaria, but were driven out by the Afghans, who also controlled Shignan and Roshan, both across the Oxus River, which Britain and Russia had agreed would be the northern limit of Afghanistan. The taotai in Kashgar urged Younghusband to deploy British troops and drive the Afghans out of Somatash. He wrote: 'I have now to beg that you will force these Afghans who with arms in their hands have crossed the boundary, to return within their own frontier, and that you will not leave them at liberty to make mischief.'[19]

According to Younghusband, Britain had considered pushing forward Afghanistan's claim eastwards but ultimately refrained, fearing that 'such a step might disturb [the] friendship with China'. He supported the Chinese claim and recommended it to his government.[20] In 1891, Younghusband encountered a Russian force led by Colonel Yonoff at Bozai Gumbaz. Younghusband thought he was in Afghan territory, as defined by the 1873 agreement between Britain and Russia. However, Yonoff showed Younghusband a map of Russia which included most of the Pamirs. Since he had the stronger force, his argument prevailed, and Younghusband beat a hasty retreat.

Younghusband suggested threatening Russia with military action in Manchuria or diplomatic pressure, similar to what was done in Kulja a decade earlier.[21] But Russia was determined to punish the Afghans. In 1892, Colonel Yonoff led a small contingent to the area, claiming to respond to appeals from the local Kyrgyz for protection against the Afghans. This led to a skirmish between the Russian and Afghan forces in which some Afghan soldiers were killed.

London continued to press China to extend its territory. Secretary of State Lord Salisbury 'confidentially' gave the Chinese ambassador in London a map featuring Chinese names, emphasizing 'the expediency of periodical tours [by] Chinese officials along the frontier'.[22] He then instructed the minister in Beijing, J. Walsham, to impress upon the Chinese government the importance of occupying Alichur Pamir. In 1892, the Chinese ambassador in London told Lord Salisbury that even though Alichur Pamir had been assigned to China, it was unwilling to station troops there due its remoteness and the difficulty of defending it against the Afghans. He proposed making it neutral territory, recognized by Britain, China and Russia, acknowledging that China did not wish to retain the territory. Since Britain was unwilling to cross the Hindukush, turning the area into a neutral territory with joint administration was the best option.[23]

In 1893, Britain and Russia began talks to settle the borders in the Pamirs. They agreed to expand Afghan areas through the Pamirs up to Chinese Turkestan. This narrow territory, which came to be called the Wakhan Corridor, served as a buffer between the British empire in India and the Russian empire in Kyrgyzstan. Although Afghanistan was not happy with its frontiers being defined by two European powers, Britain was determined to reach an agreement. Boundary pillars were erected in 1895 by a joint Pamir Boundary Commission of Britain and Russia. Afghanistan sent a representative but not China. George Macartney joined the exercise to facilitate the supply of provisions from Kashgar and liaise with the Chinese border posts, staffed by Kyrgyz locals.

The settlement of the Afghanistan frontier in the Pamirs and persuading China to extend its claim up to the Karakoram Pass would have led to some respite for Britain, except a new threat emerged for China in the east. Britain's efforts to build China as a buffer against Russia received a jolt when Japan gave China a drubbing in 1895.[24] Some British officials in India once again expressed doubt about China being an effective counter to Russia.

In 1897, Director of Military Intelligence John Ardagh prepared a memorandum, *The Northern Frontier of India from the Pamirs to Tibet*, which declared that China was useless as a buffer. Ardagh, who had served as private secretary to two viceroys in India, was aware of China's ineffective control over Kashgaria. It had only a single line of communication – the road between Kashgar and Beijing – passing through rebellious Muslim populations disaffected by unruly Chinese soldiers stationed to control them. In August 1901, the intelligence department of the British War Office estimated that the Indian army was in no position to defend itself against a Russian attack. But the view in London remained steadfast.

Border Proposals Fall on Deaf Ears

Britain's continued efforts to affirm China's hold over East Turkestan with a border agreement in Ladakh met with indifference. In 1899, through its ambassador in Beijing, Sir Claude MacDonald, it proposed a border settlement to China – its first proposal in this sector. The plan suggested dividing Aksai Chin into two equal parts – the Lingzithang Plains to go to India, and the area northeast of the Laktsang range designated for China. A critical part of the proposal was China giving up its claim to Hunza in return for Hunza relinquishing its claim to Taghdumbash and Raskam. However, China never responded to the proposal, as its rulers were busy conspiring with the Boxer rebels to expel Europeans from Beijing. According to a British embassy despatch, China had verbally informed them that the proposal had been sent to the governor of Chinese Turkestan for consideration.

In 1906, Curzon repeated the proposal, suggesting ceding Raskam and Taghdumbash to China in exchange for it relinquishing its claim of suzerainty over Hunza, which conflicted with the local mir's rights over the valleys. The complex web of claims and relations were common in these inaccessible regions, so Curzon was prompted to place them on a clearer footing. Yet, the British mission in Beijing cautioned against it. John Jordan wrote:

> We know with what tenacity they [the Chinese] clung to similar claims in the case of Corea, Burmah, and Tonquin, and although the tie with Kanjut is much weaker, the annual

tribute forms the subject of a memorial in the Peking Gazette, and represents, with the quinquennial mission from Nepaul, the only remnant of China's once extended suzerainty over distant regions on the frontiers of the Empire.[25]

This concern to avoid offending China and protect its imperial possessions and pride remained the defining refrain of Britain's policy.

The collapse of the Manchu Qing dynasty in 1912 once again threw the future of the Chinese empire into turmoil, further complicating matters for Britain. As the empire disintegrated, Britain's support of it lay in tatters. Once again Britain considered, and abandoned, Ardagh's idea of occupying territories north of the Karakoram. The same year, Viceroy Lord Hardinge proposed an 'advanced line' for negotiations with Russia on the Ladakh–Turkestan border. This line proposed bringing Taghdumbash, Raskam and Shahidulla under British control. Endorsed by the India Office in London, it recommended that Britain concede Chinese Turkestan to Russia in exchange for Tibet and recognize the claim of the mir of Hunza to Raskam and Taghdumbash Pamir. However, negotiations with Russia failed to materialize, and the forward line proposal was abandoned.

But it was even earlier – by the turn of the twentieth century – that Britain had also become concerned about Russian designs on Tibet and the threat to India's security through this route. Now, Tibet had become the focus of their rivalry.

7

Britain and Tibet: Forcing Trade

After conquering Bengal in 1757, following the Battle of Plassey, Britain soon found itself entangled in disputes with Tibet. Skirmishes erupted between the British troops and the Bhutanese along Bengal's northern border. Tibet claimed that Bhutan was a tributary state, leading the Sixth Panchen Lama, based in Shigatse, to write to British governor-general Warren Hastings in Calcutta in 1774. With the Dalai Lama still a minor, the Panchen Lama was the highest-ranking monk in Tibet. He urged Hastings to stop hostile acts against Tibet, dispatching some gifts alongside the letter.

The British had little knowledge of Tibet, and Hastings was bemused by the gifts – which included sheets of gilt leather stamped with the Russian eagle. He saw the prospect for trade and sent his young Scottish private secretary, George Bogle, to Tibet.

Bogle travelled to Shigatse and met the Panchen Lama, who told him that China had prohibited Tibet from dealing directly with other countries. However, the Panchen Lama promised to convey the proposal to the emperor in Beijing, where he had been invited to attend the Qianlong emperor's seventieth birthday celebrations. Bogle spent approximately six months in Tibet, fostering a warm friendship with the Panchen Lama, conversing in Hindi.

In 1780, the Panchen Lama went to Beijing as scheduled, choosing not to inform the Chinese amban in Lhasa about Bogle's visit. As there was no Chinese official in Shigatse, the amban did not hear about it from any other sources either. It is unclear if he raised the British request with the emperor. Tragically, his visit came to an end as he succumbed to smallpox. His body was sent back by the grief-stricken Qianlong emperor with an abundance of gifts. There was new strife in Tibet when one of the brothers of the Panchen Lama, Shamar, quarrelled with the monastery lamas over their ownership. Shamar fled to Nepal thereafter, where he persuaded the king to invade Tibet.

Nepal's Invasions of Tibet

A kingdom in the central Himalaya, Nepal had come under the control of the Gurkhas, who lived in the region's western hills. In 1769, they seized Kathmandu and extended their kingdom to the border of Tibet. Tempted by Shamar's tales of the precious gifts lying in the Tashilhunpo monastery in Shigatse, Nepal invaded Tibet. In 1788, their army marched into Shigatse. Tibet sought the help of both the British and the Chinese in vain. Neither responded. The Nepalese forces plundered the gifts and compelled Tibet to pay tribute.

The raid whetted Nepal's appetite, and its army returned three years later, once again plundering the Tashilhunpo monastery. Again, Tibet appealed to China for help. This time, the Qianlong emperor sent an army of 15,000 led by his formidable Manchu general, Fuk'anggan (Fukang'an in pinyin). He chased away Nepal's army and claimed to reach the outskirts of Kathmandu in 1793. Whatever the truth of his claim, both sides were willing to come to an amicable settlement. Fuk'anggan was keen to return early to China after brokering an agreement that would enable him return home victoriously. Nepal's interest in Tibet was mainly financial. Fuk'anggan persuaded Nepal to pay a small tribute to the Chinese emperor every five years in return for a substantial indemnity to be paid by Tibet. This was a very gratifying outcome for the Qianlong emperor, whose earlier ventures into Burma and Vietnam had ended disastrously. He listed the Nepal campaign as the tenth and last of the great campaigns of his reign. The tribute from Nepal was largely ceremonial and even after its victory over Tibet in 1856, it continued to pay it. According to Chinese sources, it did so until 1908, even though China's rulers never exercised control over the kingdom.

The Qianlong emperor took this opportunity to reorganize Tibet's administrative structure. He issued an order of twenty articles, the most elaborate governance system imposed by China since its conquest of Tibet earlier in the century. It remained in force until Tibet broke away from China a century later. The order prescribed using a golden urn to draw lots from a shortlist of three candidates to select the Dalai Lama and other high lamas. In addition, it defined the administrative position of the ambans, who were given a status equal to that of the Dalai Lama and the Panchen Lama, and were authorized to handle government affairs in consultation with them. Relations with the neighbouring states of Nepal, Bhutan and Sikkim were entrusted to the ambans. An army of 3,000 soldiers was placed at their disposal.

Nepal had hoped that its tribute to China would ensure its support against the British. It repeatedly proposed joint action against them to the Chinese amban in Lhasa. In 1812, alongside its tribute, Nepal appealed for China's help in tackling the British. Two years later, when a British invasion appeared imminent, Nepal cautioned the Chinese that the real target was Tibet, through which it wanted to attack China. However, the amban did not take these concerns seriously, counselling the emperor that there was no reason for the 'Pileng' tribe – as he called the English – to invade Tibet, and that Nepal should avoid petty quarrels with its neighbours. The Chinese emperor agreed. Nepal, which believed China to be a strategic ally, was deeply disappointed.

Despite Nepal's efforts, Britain kept trying to open Tibet to trade. In 1782, Samuel Turner spent nearly a year in Shigatse as an envoy, though he couldn't visit Lhasa or negotiate a trade agreement. His reports reveal a minimal presence of the Chinese in Shigatse. The Tibetans considered the Chinese a 'gross and impure race of men' but respected their role in keeping other foreigners out. They were also aware of the Russian interest in trading with them.[1]

In 1811, Britain sent Thomas Manning – an early Chinese studies scholar – to Tibet, hoping to make contact with the local Chinese official. Manning, who was accompanied by a Chinese interpreter, met an official at Phari in the Chumbi Valley, where he gained permission to proceed to Lhasa – among the first Europeans to do so. He confirmed Bogle and Turner's observations that the Tibetans feared and loathed the Chinese. Despite his success in getting to Lhasa, he couldn't advance trade negotiations. No other Englishman would venture into Tibet until Younghusband in 1904.

Britain invaded Nepal in 1814. Progress in the mountainous terrain was slow, taking two years to subdue the kingdom. The Treaty of Sugauli, which defined Nepal's border with India, was signed in 1816. One of its sticking points was that the British wanted to station a resident in Kathmandu. Nepal was wary as experience in India had shown that the British residents interfered in local governance and deposed the ruler if he opposed Britain's interests. It pleaded the same case as Tibet, that the Chinese emperor would not permit a British resident. Britain agreed to drop its demand if China posted its agent in Kathmandu to mediate future disputes. Consequently, Nepal asked the amban in Lhasa to post a Chinese resident in Kathmandu. But the amban, without refuting China's authority over Nepal, replied that his emperor did not post agents in all his subject tribes, thus ending the possibility of China stationing an amban-like official in Nepal.

This episode, as Mosca noted, underscored that 'the Qing government felt no moral or strategic need to defend the Gurkha regime by force'.[2] It also showed that the British were still unfamiliar with Tibet and the extent of China's empire. They were feeling their way in the mountains, unwilling to take undue risk. Besides, in the wake of the Napoleonic Wars, Britain was still preoccupied with events in Europe.

Nepal continued to look for allies against the British, sending envoys to Burma, Afghanistan and Tibet. When news of the Opium War reached Nepal, initial reports suggested the defeat of British 'traders' against the Chinese. This prompted the Nepalese king,

Rajendra Bikram Shah, to congratulate the Manchu emperor on his victory, reminding him that Nepal stood ready to attack the British in India if China supported it. But on learning of China's defeat, Nepal stopped seeking its help.

In 1855, Jung Bahadur Rana – the de facto Gurkha ruler of Nepal – took advantage of China's internal troubles to invade Tibet. He occupied Lhasa and forced the government to sign the Treaty of Thapathali, granting Nepal several trade privileges and the right to station a legation in Lhasa. The treaty also included a clause related to Kashmir at the request of its ruler, Gulab Singh, providing for the release of prisoners taken during Zorawar Singh's invasion. Both sides offered ritualistic respect to the Manchu emperor in the treaty. Furthermore, Tibet agreed to pay Nepal an annual tribute of 10,000 rupees – a practice that continued until 1952.

The 1856 treaty also obligated Nepal to come to Tibet's assistance, should it come under threat from another country. This was an empty assurance, though, as Nepal was in no position to aid it against the three imperial powers that could possibly threaten it. Nevertheless, it exposes the spasmodic nature of China's control over Tibet. Nepal's privileges in Tibet continued until the China–Nepal Treaty in 1956.

Chinese Perceptions of British Threat

Few people in China understood the magnitude of Britain's threat to their vast empire. Nor was the country able to craft a strategy to deal with it. One notable exception was the Chinese geographer Wei Yuan, who, in 1844, soon after the Opium War, wrote *Haiguo Tuzhi*, in which he outlined the threat and offered a radical solution. As he had learnt from his European friends that Britain's strength came from its control over India's resources, he suggested inciting Indians to revolt and joining forces through Tibet to oust the British from India. He lamented that 'when the Gurkhas obediently requested to attack India, this was rejected, and when the French and Americans were willing to aid us with their warships and discuss terms on our behalf they were doubted'.[3]

Similar advice came from the Manchu general Jalafuntai in Ili, Xinjiang. In 1860, shortly before Britain's invasion of Beijing, he wrote to his emperor that a Russian envoy had warned him of French and British plans to attack Beijing, adding that the best course of action for China would be to instigate a rebellion in India and then send forces via Yunnan and Tibet to invade India. Needless to say, the emperor paid no heed to it, and after Britain's occupation of Beijing, the subsequent events were out of his control.

The Manchu court's indifference to these suggestions stemmed not only from a lack of interest in Tibet, but also from a failure to identify the Yingjili people in Canton with the Pileng, about whom the ambans reported from Lhasa. Only after their defeat in the Opium War did the Manchus start piecing together their fragmented knowledge of the neighbouring kingdoms and peoples to better understand the magnitude of the threat posed by European powers – particularly the British, of whom there was no mention in their historical chronicles. Following the Opium War, the Manchus finally realized that the Yingjili and the Pileng were 'hairy barbarians' from the same tribe.

Tibet–China Relationship

While the Manchu rulers were basking in the glory of their heavenly empire, the British in Canton were agog with rumours of Russian conspiracies. Local British newspapers speculated about the possibility of an alliance between China and Russia during the First Afghan War. One article published in the *Canton Press* on 25 July 1840 alleged that a Russian delegation was travelling to Beijing to offer support in its struggle against Britain and 'to organise Eastern Asia against us, through means of its Lord Paramount, the Emperor of China ... The Russians have studied the affairs of India to little purpose, if they have not learned, that the most effectual mode of bringing down the Nepaulese on our plains, is by a mandate from Pekin.'[4]

The British were keen to trade with Tibet and settle the boundary issue; however, they were confounded by its stubborn

The Remnants of an Army, 1879. Elizabeth Butler
represents the defeat of the British in the
First Anglo-Afghan War (1839–1842).

resistance. They were unsure whether the opposition came from them or China. They wanted to understand the mysterious country and find a safe way to enter it. The complex relationship between Tibet and China was also enigma to them. A contemporary French writer Fernand Grenard wrote:

> The question has sometimes been mooted whether it is the Tibetans who wish to close their door or the Chinese who force them to close it. This is an idle question. The Chinese and the Tibetans sometimes quarrel with each other, but they are quite at one against the foreigners.

He went on to say that the Chinese controlled the country with the help of the lamas and a small army of around 1,500 soldiers, though they were highly circumspect about their presence. All senior officials were Manchus, and they were not allowed to keep their families in Tibet because Tibetans disliked foreigners – a trait encouraged by the Manchus to maintain their hold. The lamas did not want new ideas brought to the country by foreigners. Senior lamas and monasteries were on China's payroll.[5] Grenard wrote that, in Britain's perception, the threat to Tibet came from Russia, not China:

The Indian Government is in not so great a hurry to extend its territory in the direction of Tibet as in that of Afghanistan, because it has not, on that side, to fear the progress of so ambitious and formidable a Power as Russia. It has, I know, up to the present, been a fundamental axiom of Indian policy to keep China as far as possible; but China has only just enough power in Tibet to prevent herself from being driven out by the natives, she is not capable of taking the offensive and asks only to be left in peace and to leave her neighbours in peace in their turn. Only, should the day come when England would be unable to defend Turkestan against Russian conquest, then it would seem to her necessary to enforce her protectorate on Tibet, not only by way of compensation, but especially in order to establish on her northern frontier a border-state similar to that of Afghanistan and serving to keep at arm's length a disagreeable and dangerous neighbour.[6]

China's control over the Tibetan lamas was not solely rooted in security but also in mutually profitable trade arrangements. China gave protection against aggressive neighbours, such as the Mongols and Nepal, while making clever use of the tea trade, thus affording the lamas exclusive privilege of importing it from China. This import monopoly was a rich source of revenue for the monasteries and kept them indebted to China.

Another indication of the tenuous, intermittent nature of Chinese control over Tibet became apparent in 1863, when a British education inspector stationed in Almora in India, Captain E. Smyth, wished to visit Lhasa. Tibetan officials informed him that he could proceed only with permission from Lhasa or Beijing. Through the British mission in Beijing, Kolkata raised the issue with the Chinese government. The following reply of the British head of mission in Beijing to the British viceroy of India is indicative of the relationship between China and Tibet:

Thibet is not formally subject to China, but the former looks up to China on account of her proximity and of the material advantages derived from her wealth, and the latter maintains a connection otherwise onerous to her, because of the additional hold it gives to her over the Mongolian tribes to recognize the religious supremacy of the Grand Lama at Lassa. The Chinese Government is, therefore, careful not to take any steps that may be disagreeable to the religious prejudices of the country.[7]

British officials remained confounded. The position of the amban seemed as enigmatic as the country itself. In 1870, the British resident in Nepal, Colonel R. C. Lawrence, forwarded the English translation of a letter written by the head of a Nepalese delegation that had visited Lhasa in 1866. The delegate had provided a detailed account of the Tibetan government and its people, and the position of the Chinese amban:

> All measures of importance are submitted to the Chinese Umba [Amban] or representative, and must be confirmed by him. Thibet being under the protection of China, the Umba is greatly deferred to, and has a powerful voice in the Councils of the State ... Vacancies in office are filled up from among the presidents of the monasteries of Lhassa and Digurtcha, subject to the approval of the Umba.[8]

In 1873, Britain's minister in Beijing made a similar assessment of the position of the ambans in Tibet:

> Theoretically, two Residents or Commissioners always, either Manchu or Mongol by race, who are stationed in Lassa, exercise control in all but religious questions over the Dalai Lama in the eastern division of the country known to the Chinese as Exterior Thibet, and the Peshu Lama or Banchin Erdeni in Western or Ulterior Thibet. The former Lama resides at Lassa, the latter at Zhikassé. The representatives of China further superintend all questions of tribute or revenue due to China and of Chinese trade. They are also supreme over the native military force organized, *á la Chinoise*, in *ying* or cantonment battalions, and a small Chinese contingent supplied from the garrison of Szechuen.

The report went on to state that the Chinese also asserted jurisdiction over Ladakh, a territory included by the Chinese statistical geographers under the emperor of China's realm.[9] But the British discovered that despite the evident dominance of the Chinese, the Tibetans could be very stubborn even with the ambans.

First Britain–China Treaty on Tibet

In 1874, Britain decided to send a mission from Myanmar to explore the Chinese provinces of Sichuan, Guizhou and Yunnan, which had recently faced a rebellion by Muslim inhabitants and were struggling to recover. Wade, by now Britain's minister in Beijing, secured clearance for a 200-member delegation to visit Yunnan. But China's authority in the province was nominal, and local authorities turned back the delegation. A British interpreter travelling separately, Augustus Margary, was killed before he could join the delegation. The incident was resolved in 1876 with the signing of an agreement at Yantai (then called Chefoo), in which China agreed to permit the exploration of Tibet and Britain proposed an exploratory mission, which China agreed to facilitate.[10] The Chefoo Convention marked the first treaty relating to Tibet signed by the British with China.

But this misadventure was not looked upon kindly by the Chinese, who felt that the British should have considered the expedition as passing through hostile territory. Britain used the incident to extract further commercial concessions from China, including permission for a consulate in Chongqing – although it would take another fifteen years for it to open due to challenges navigating the Yangtse River.

In 1886, Britain entered into an agreement with China to set up a Delimitation Commission tasked with demarcating the border between Myanmar and China. It also addressed Tibet, with China agreeing 'to adopt measures to exhort and encourage the people with a view to the promotion and development of trade'. China also pledged to consider trade regulations, but stipulated that if there were 'insuperable obstacles', the British government would not 'press the matter unduly'.[11]

When Britain annexed the kingdom of Ava in Myanmar, it allowed the tradition of exchanging gifts every ten years with China, which claimed sovereignty based on this practice, to continue. In exchange, Britain agreed not to insist on sending a trade mission to Lhasa. This was a relief to China, since it was in no position to stop Britain from sending a mission, nor to persuade the Tibetan lamas not to accept it. This was yet another episode, like others involving Tibet, that underscored the largely exaggerated and ceremonial nature of China's claims to these distant lands.

Skirmish Between Britain and Tibet

The first military clash between Britain and Tibet occurred on the Sikkim border. In the 1860s, Britain had annexed some territories from Sikkim and Bhutan into Bengal, turning both kingdoms into protectorates. By 1886, Britain proposed sending a delegation to Tibet led by Colman Macaulay, the financial secretary of Bengal, but the Tibetan government refused permission and the delegation was called off. Subsequently, in 1887, Britain installed a political officer in Gangtok, Sikkim. Tibet, which regarded Sikkim as its protectorate, protested, sparking skirmishes on the border.

The tensions escalated in 1888, when Britain asked Tibet to remove some fortifications in Lungthur, claiming the area as Sikkimese territory. Despite Tibetan resistance, British forces pushed forward. The Tibetan government moved aggressively on Gnatong (now Gnathang) in Sikkim, believing China would support it. Although the Chinese amban tried to dissuade them, they refused to listen. The lamas in particular remained aggressive in their stance and assured the army that they would come to its assistance. A Tibetan force of around 2,000 attacked a British camp at Gnatong. The British repulsed the attack, inflicting nineteen casualties. In response, Britain protested to the Chinese government in Beijing, which itself was unhappy that its amban in Lhasa had not restrained the Tibetans and recalled him.

Britain decided to settle the Sikkim border issue directly with China, instructing troops in Gnatong not to invade Tibet. Sir

Robert Hart was to proceed to Lhasa with the new Chinese amban, Sheng Tai, to assist in border negotiations. But the Tibetans refused to take orders from the new amban or accept the boundary of Sikkim as claimed by Britain.

Bir Shamshir, the king of Nepal, who had developed a better understanding of Britain's strength, advised the Tibetans to show deference. In a letter to the Tibetan Council, he suggested that more responsible, trustworthy officers should be dispatched to the border to negotiate an amicable settlement. He counselled the lamas: 'The British Government is great and enlightened, such a Government, I do not apprehend, will do an injustice to any one.'[12] Nepal's representative in Lhasa informed the Chinese amban that it was his responsibility to prevent the Tibetans from waging war against the British. He warned that if the amban did not keep the Tibetans in check, he would be removed by his emperor.[13] The Tibetans remained unmoved.

The Sikkim Convention

Britain decided to bypass Lhasa and summoned Sheng Tai to Kolkata, where negotiations for the 'Convention in 1890 between Britain and China Relating to Sikkim and Tibet', signed by the viceroy Lord Lansdowne and the amban, took place. The preambular section of the convention expressed the desire to 'maintain and perpetuate the relations of friendship and good understanding which now exist between their respective Empires'.[14]

The convention did not define the status of Tibet; rather, it established China's right to negotiate on its behalf. It set the Sikkim–Tibet border as the watershed between the Teesta River in Sikkim and the Mochu River in Tibet. It also recognized Sikkim as a British protectorate, granting Britain control over its internal affairs and foreign relations. Notably, representatives of Sikkim and Tibet were neither present in the negotiations nor kept informed. The method of official communication between India and Tibet remained unresolved, left to future discussion.[15]

Britain was now confronted with the task of implementing the convention, which Tibet outright rejected. China could not persuade it to permit the import of tea from India or force its herdsmen to respect the border. With no Chinese officials at the border, clashes between Tibetan and British officials occurred frequently. The British grew increasingly frustrated by Tibet's stubbornness, which the Chinese amban attributed to the Tibetans' 'ignorance and stupidity'.[16]

Chinese historians Wang and Gyaincain offer a broadly similar take on these events, arguing that the crisis was perpetrated by the British, who laid claim to a place called Mount Lungdo in Tibet. Against the advice of the amban – Wen Shu – the Tibetan kashag despatched 900 troops. On 20 March 1888, during the attack on Tibetan troops, 100 of Britain's own soldiers were killed. Subsequently, however, the British inflicted heavy losses on the Tibetan force and compelled them to retreat. China recalled Wen Shu and replaced him with Sheng Tai. But this did not alleviate tensions, since Tibet insisted on sending more troops to the border. They were no match for the British, who occupied the Chumbi Valley. In the face of weak Qing rulers, China sued for peace and ultimately signed an 'unequal treaty'.

It took Britain and China three years to finalize the 'Regulations regarding Trade, Official Communications and Pasturage' to put the convention into effect, which was signed in Darjeeling in December 1893 by A. W. Paul, the British commissioner, and Ho Chang-jung and James H. Hart, the Chinese counterparts. The Regulations provided duty-free access to Indian tea in Tibet and permitted Britain to open a trade market at Yatung in Tibet.

Tibet Refuses to Bend to Britain's Will

The implementation of the regulations also ran into trouble. Tibetans refused to lift the import duty on Indian tea, and the market in Yatung could not be operationalized because of the Tibetan government's reluctance to act – despite the new amban's efforts. John Claude White, an exasperated British political officer in Sikkim, reported to his government: 'The Chinese have no authority whatever here. The Tibetans will not obey them, and the

Chinese are afraid to give any orders. China is suzerain over Tibet only in name.'[17]

In 1895, British and Chinese officials erected three boundary pillars at Jelap La. These were almost immediately destroyed by the Tibetans, who resumed grazing in the pastures south of the location. Plans to build more pillars at Donchuk La were made, but neither Tibetans nor the Chinese officials visited the demarcation site.

White wrote that Chinese officials hated the Tibetans and repeatedly subjected them to humiliation. During receptions, Tibetan officials were relegated to lower-level seating positions than the Chinese. A Chinese military officer stationed in Tibet informed the British that he was unable to travel from Lhasa to the Sikkim border because the Tibetan government had not provided him with transport.

Although the British took up this matter with the amban, they were told that he had been able to get the Tibetan Council's consent, 'but the Lamas of the three great monasteries are still full of suspicion and are pressing certain matters upon me which makes it necessary for me to further enlighten them. Under the circumstances I am compelled to request that you will kindly postpone commencing work for a time, in order to avoid trouble on this point.'[18]

When a commissioner from Darjeeling met Tibetan officials in Yatung, they told him that they were not bound by the 1890 convention as they had not signed it. The British official conveyed to his government that the Chinese appeared sincere about implementing the convention and that the real opposition came from the Tibetans.

Britain was reluctant to ascribe any blame to China for the destruction of the border pillars, because of Japan's emergence as the new, infinitely more serious threat to China than the Europeans. Determined not to exacerbate its problems, British executives and the political officer in Gangtok were advised not to take any action. Instead, the matter was raised with the Chinese government through their diplomatic mission in Beijing.

The British minister, Sir N. R. O'Conor, asked the Chinese government to either instruct the amban in Lhasa on how to better manage the Tibetans or replace him with a more capable official. Chief Secretary to the Government of Bengal H. J. S. Cotton summed up Britain's struggle to enforce China's suzerainty over Tibet in a letter to the secretary to the Government of British India:

> The affair is complicated by the relations of Government with China and our desire to uphold the feeble and tottering authority of the Chinese in Lhasa, the result of which is that the people who are in real power are not those we deal with, and that the people we deal with have no powers to carry out their engagements with us.[19]

He went on to recommend that the British, with the consent of the Chinese government, occupy the Chumbi Valley in Tibet to establish its authority more firmly in Lhasa.

In 1895, five years after signing the border agreement, the Chinese amban pleaded with the British to postpone the demarcation of the border for another five years as the three prominent lamas still wanted to retain the 'ancient boundary'.[20] Three years later, White wrote: 'This boundary has been in dispute ever since, the Tibetans asserting that the Chinese had no authority to make a treaty in their name without first consulting them.'[21]

Both Jiawei and Gyaincain, presenting the Chinese government's official viewpoint, concede that the Anglo-Chinese agreements were against Tibet's interests, and Beijing could not persuade the Tibetans to accept them:

> [T]he Qing Dynasty court negotiated with the British government and reached an agreement that was detrimental to the state and Tibetan interests (such as the 1890 and 1893 treaties), while the local government of Tibet refused to implement these treaties.[22]

Even in this narrative, it is clear that China's authority over Tibet was nominal at best. Furthermore, it exposes the sentiments within

China that the Manchus worked against the interests of Tibet as well as China.

Curzon's Forward Policy

The British officials in India harboured reservations about Britain reliance on China as an ally against Russia and its policy of bolstering it, often at India's expense. These concerns received a shot in the arm with the arrival of George Nathaniel Curzon, who assumed the role of Governor-General of India in 1899. Curzon came with impressive credentials – and an ego to match, based partly on his distinction as a rare British leader who had travelled across Asia. In the 1880s and 1890s, he visited several countries and wrote a book on Russian expansion in Asia. From his experiences, Curzon concluded that Russia's ultimate ambition was to snatch India, the 'most splendid appanage of the Imperial Crown', from Britain, and emphasized that protecting India remained Britain's main responsibility.[23] Ascending to the position of under-secretary in the foreign office in 1895, four years later, he became Britain's youngest viceroy of India.

Curzon was dismissive of his compatriots who believed that a Russian invasion of India was implausible. He was also determined to exorcise the ghost of the British defeats in Afghanistan from the collective consciousness. Convinced that the security of the Indian empire depended on Britain appearing to the Afghans as their saviour, rather than their enemy, he perceived Russia as the intruder in Central Asia, not Britain or China. He refused to accept that China could effectively counter Russia.

In 1874, General Rawlinson had argued that Russia would face the same difficulty controlling Bukhara that Britain had with Afghanistan. Curzon dismissed this concern: 'The analogy to Afghanistan is a faulty one, for the Bokhariots are not a turbulent or a fanatical people; and, though composed of several nationalities, present a fairly homogenous whole.'[24] Instead, he declared that the amir of Bukhara would be as subservient to Russia as the khan of Kalat or the maharaja of Kashmir to the British.

Curzon made a facetious distinction between Russian and Chinese colonization of Central Asia: 'The Chinese colonists are Chinamen, while the Russian colonists are to be Russian, or, in other words, that the one are indigenous, while the other will be aliens.'[25] He also did not see the contradiction in calling the Chinese 'indigenous' and 'colonists' in the same sentence.

While Curzon advocated for a forward policy in Tibet, in Ladakh and Afghanistan he acknowledged that the mountains formed the natural boundary, and that Britain should not cross them: 'The limits to British dominions in Central Asia are fixed by natural conditions, which we should be insane to ignore or overleap, and which sever us, as by oceans, from Tartar prairies or Turkoman steppes.'[26] He envisioned three possible routes for a Russian invasion of India: across the Pamirs to Chitral and Kashmir, from Samarkand to Balkh and Kabul and from Merv to Herat. With the exception of the months from June to September, he regarded the Pamir route impassable, but noted that Russian forces would encounter no opposition on this route until they reached Kashmir, since the independent tribes north of it would not oppose them. Curzon concluded that the Merv–Herat route was the most vulnerable and that since Russia was on the verge of seizing Herat, it would thus 'without an effort, win the first hand in the great game that is destined to be played for the empire in the East'.[27] He contrasted Russia's rapid advance with Britain's withdrawal from Herat to Quetta.

Curzon believed that India's most critical border was with Tibet, followed by Hunza–Kashgar and Myanmar. He told Britain's minister in Beijing, Ernest Satow – who met him in Kolkata on his way to China – that the Chinese amban in Lhasa was an ineffective interlocutor. He wanted to deal with the Tibetan government directly and instructed Satow to convey this to the Chinese government. Curzon also shared with Satow that he was against the mir of Hunza asserting his revenue rights in Raskam. He did not want any dependency in the Trans-Karakoram region, nor did he want China to cede Kashgaria to any other country.[28]

Curzon's warnings had enthusiastic recipients in London due to Russia's continuing strategic alliances. In 1894, France and Russia established an understanding directed against Germany, but Britain was suspicious of its intent. In 1901, the British War Office prepared a report on *Military Needs of the Empire in a War with France and Russia* that concluded that an Indian army was in no position to defend the empire against an invasion.[29]

To keep an eye on Russian movements, Curzon was eager to establish relations with Tibet. He persuaded Prime Minister Salisbury to authorize direct negotiations with the Tibetans. In August 1900, he wrote to the Dalai Lama, inviting him to depute a responsible official to India for discussions on commercial and political ties. However, the letter ended up in the hands of a Tibetan official in Gartok, who held on to it for six months before returning it undelivered. Infuriated, Curzon sent another letter to the Dalai Lama in June 1901, this time warning that his government reserved the right to take steps 'to enforce the terms of the treaty and to ensure that the trade regulations are observed'.[30]

But the Tibetans were resolutely opposed to negotiating with the British. They ignored the viceroy's second missive as well. Outraged by this effrontery, Curzon complained bitterly to London:

> It is, indeed, the most extraordinary anachronism of the twentieth century that there should exist within less than 300 miles of the borders of British India a State and a Government with whom political relations do not so much as exist, and with whom it is impossible even to exchange a written communication. Such a situation cannot, in any case, be lasting.[31]

He proposed that the political officer in Sikkim be permitted to proceed with military force to eject the Tibetans from any illegally occupied territory and to stop them from levying the import duty on British tea.

The British foreign office expressed unease with what came to be called Curzon's 'forward policy' on Tibet. In London, Tibet was perceived as distinct from Afghanistan. Russia treated it as part of the Chinese empire and conceded Afghanistan as within Britain's sphere of influence. London was focused on the impact of any move in Tibet on relations with Russia. Additionally, the forbidding prospect of a military operation in Tibet's inhospitable terrain acted as a deterrent.

In a letter to Curzon, the Secretary of State for India George Hamilton cautioned:

> [A]ny such movement on the part of India would be viewed with much disquietude and suspicion; and it must be remembered that Tibet is politically subordinate to China. The character of the country, rugged and sparsely inhabited, is against the conduct of important military operations in that region, and diplomatic pressure for closer relations with your Government would be likely to increase distrust of our intentions.[32]

Hamilton advised Curzon to consult London before undertaking any action in Tibet and to keep the British embassy in St Petersburg informed.

Tibet's Dalliance with Russia

At this juncture, the Tibetan government made a tactical error by opening negotiations with Russia. The Thirteenth Dalai Lama, Thubten Gyatso, sent his close adviser, Agvan Lobsang Dorjiev, as his special envoy. Dorjiev, a Buryat Mongol from the Transbaikal province and a Russian subject, had acquired immense respect in the region for his scholarship and erudition. At the age of twenty-six in 1880, he had arrived in Lhasa – where he soon became a teacher, or 'debating partner', to the young Thirteenth Dalai Lama. In 1901, Dorjiev travelled to St Petersburg via Odessa, receiving a ceremonial welcome from the tsar. Both the British consulate in Odessa and the embassy in St Petersburg monitored his visit, which also got generous coverage in the British press. This sparked deep concerns in Britain regarding Russian designs on Tibet.

The Russian press declared that the object of the mission was to obtain religious liberties for Buddhist subjects of the tsar.[33] Odessa's local publication, *Odessika Novosti*, reported that the eight-member Tibetan delegation was visiting Russia to strengthen bilateral relations. While acknowledging Tibet's status 'at the present time' as a protectorate of China, the article highlighted its wars with China in the past and extolled the Dalai Lama's significance among the Mongols and other Buddhists, including those in Russia. It said about the Dalai Lama – 'He rules the whole Buddhist world from his mysterious palace, or rather monastery, in Lhasa' – and speculated that the visit might lead to a permanent Tibetan mission being set up in St Petersburg.[34] However, the Russian government tried to allay British fears by stating that the visit held no political or diplomatic undertone.

For Curzon, this was a vindication of his long-held view that Russia had imperial ambitions in Tibet. Refusing to accept Tibet's innocence, he insisted on confrontation. Initially, he used a senior Bhutanese official, Ugyen Kazi, to inform the Dalai Lama that failure to implement the 1890 convention would compel Britain to take practical measures. But the Dalai Lama

Thubten Gyatso,
the Thirteenth Dalai Lama

deflected Kazi's letter, pleading that the Chinese amban had forbidden him from corresponding directly with any other government.

Curzon's suspicions were aggravated by reports that China and Russia had entered into an agreement to keep any third country out of Tibet. Rumours circulated in Britain that Russia was conspiring to use Tibet as a base to stir trouble in Sikkim and Bhutan, with Dorjiev's visits to St Petersburg cited as evidence. Matters worsened when, in July 1902, the *China Times* published what it claimed was the text of a twelve-clause secret agreement between China and Russia. According to the alleged agreement, given its weakening position in Tibet, China had agreed to transfer it to Russia in exchange for protection of its commercial rights. China was to relinquish its privileges in Tibet, other than the right to appoint consuls and continue normal trade. All other Chinese interests would be ceded to Russia, including constructing railway lines and mining. In exchange, Russia agreed to suppress all disturbances in the interior, which China was unable to cope with, and help maintain the integrity of the Manchu empire in China.[35]

Britain immediately raised concerns with Beijing and St Petersburg. Both governments denied the report, but Britain remained suspicious that it was a trial balloon. It cautioned the Russian government that 'the Indian Government would certainly not be indifferent to any alteration in the present status and relations of a country so near to their frontiers as Tibet'.[36]

This episode made Curzon even more determined to deal with Tibet directly, bypassing Beijing. He sent another letter to London, declaring that China's suzerainty over Tibet was a 'constitutional fiction – a political affectation which has only been maintained because of its convenience to both parties'.[37] He continued to press for local action on the border, compelling Tibet to implement the 1890 convention.

Around this time, White conducted a tour of the border region and met with Tibetan officials. Not encountering any Chinese officials, he observed the harsh Tibetan terrain but noted that military movement would not be overly difficult once the Himalayan passes had been crossed. Moscow perceived White's visit as a prelude to Britain's occupation of the Chumbi Valley and protested to Britain, warning that such action was likely 'to produce a situation of considerable gravity, and that it might be compelled in such case to take steps to safeguard the interests of Russia in those regions'.[38] Britain assured Russia of having no intention of occupying Tibet. Still, since this region was only a short distance from India's northern border, 'any sudden display of Russian interest or activity' would cause concern in Britain. It reiterated that Tibet was 'altogether outside of her [Russia's] sphere of influence'.[39]

The Russian ambassador to London continued to protest about Britain's aggressive designs in Tibet. In 1903, he told the British foreign office that Russia regarded Tibet as a part of the Chinese empire and wanted to maintain its integrity. Britain repeatedly assured Russia that it had no desire to annex Tibet and merely sought to exercise its trade rights. However, it added that since Tibet was adjacent to India, it was inevitable that it 'should exercise a certain amount of local pre-dominance ... But it did not follow from this that we had any designs upon the independence of the country'.[40] Lansdowne, the British secretary of state who wrote the letter, saw no dichotomy in referring to Tibet as an independent country while calling it a part of the Chinese empire. He warned the Russian ambassador that any Russian move in Tibet would trigger a strong response from Britain. He told him that Britain was talking to Tibet directly because China was using 'dilatory methods' and its influence was slender there.[41]

In September 1903, Curzon relayed to London intelligence reports from Lhasa that Tibet, determined not to negotiate, was mobilizing troops. He complained that Britain's authority was not being taken seriously by either China or Tibet and cited an incident from July that same year when Tibetan authorities had captured two Sikkimese men at Shigatse, where they had gone to trade. Curzon wrote to the secretary of state for India in London:

> There has been a complete failure of the policy pursued for the last 25 years by the Government of India towards Tibet; the only result being that the Tibetans mistake our patience for weakness, reject our overtures with scorn, and despise our strength. In Colonel Younghusband's opinion, since we retired in 1888, both Tibetans and Chinese confidently expect our retirement, refusing to believe we shall do anything.[42]

He declared that Chumbi Valley, lying south of the watershed, should not be considered part of Tibet and emphasized that the people of Tibet were amicable towards fostering relations with British India, with opposition stemming only from the lamas. He recommended occupying the Chumbi Valley and marching up to Gyantse, about 130 kilometres north of Sikkim, to convince the Tibetans of their seriousness.

Curzon demanded that both the Chinese and Tibetans show their sincerity by sending the amban and Tibetan councillors for talks. The amban was willing, but the Dalai Lama refused to send a state councillor. A frustrated Curzon despatched an irate letter to the amban, rebuking his failure to persuade Tibet towards a more reasonable attitude, and warning of measures to safeguard his delegation in Tibet. The Chinese pleaded that the arrogance of the Tibetans was due to their reliance on promised support from Russia to Dorjiev. The amban went on to declare that 'obstinacy is engrained in the character of the Tibetan barbarians'.[43]

Next, Curzon proposed for a mission to be sent to Tibet in order to negotiate with the Chinese and Tibetan officials on the border or in Shigatse or Gyantse. Dorjiev's visit to Russia had caused London to become more willing to listen to Curzon's warnings. Secretary of State for India Hamilton wrote: 'The importance of excluding the establishment of Russian influence in Tibet, and the inconveniences and intrigues which might be occasioned by it along the frontier between Tibet, India and Nepal, is fully appreciated by His Majesty's Government.'[44] But a week later, he advised caution: 'The position of China, in its relations to the Powers of Europe, has been so modified in recent years that it is necessary to take into account those altered conditions in deciding on action affecting what must still be regarded as a province of China.' He added that any armed intervention would encounter international opposition and questions would be raised about 'the status of a portion of the Chinese empire'.[45]

Ruling out precipitate military action, Hamilton suggested a warning to Russia that Britain would counter any Russian action in Tibet and take further actions based on Russia's response. Britain had to consider the views of other European powers, especially Russia, when dealing with China. The Boxer Rebellion in Beijing

(1899–1901), which required an alliance of eight powers, including Russia, to be crushed, exposed once again Britain's need to bring other European countries along with it in its dealings with China.

Younghusband's Invasion of Tibet

Curzon proposed sending a force to Tibet to address all aspects of British relations with the region and posting a British resident in Lhasa. But this was turned down by the British cabinet, which was still not willing to deal with Tibet except through Beijing. Curzon was authorized to send a mission with the limited objective of implementing the 1890 convention and the 1893 trade regulations. The mission was not to proceed beyond Khamba Dzong, north of Sikkim, and was cautioned against advancing to Lhasa. However 'if complete rupture of negotiations prove[d] inevitable', they were permitted to occupy the Chumbi Valley and proceed up to Gyantse, as safely as possible. The British mission in Beijing was also directed to convey this warning to the Chinese government, with London once again advising Curzon to exercise restraint.[46]

This was enough for him to spring into action. He appointed Francis Younghusband, the British resident in the princely state of Indore, to lead the delegation to Tibet, with J. C. White as the joint commissioner. Younghusband shared Curzon's views on the need to civilize the world through British dominance:

> In cases of this kind, where an uncivilized country adjoined the positions of a civilized Power, it was inevitable that the latter should exercise a certain amount of local pre-dominance. Such a pre-dominance belonged to us in Tibet. But it did not follow from this that we had any designs on the independence of the country.[47]

For Younghusband, London's reluctance to give him a free hand proved to be the main hurdle. Field officials were frequently admonished for peddling local concerns over the broader considerations that the headquarters had to keep in mind. Questioning the efficacy of this approach, Younghusband wrote:

> Local officers are often told that they are too impatient, and
> that they too frequently want to settle a matter by local action,
> when it might be so much better disposed of by correspondence
> from headquarters; by negotiations, for instance, between
> London and Peking, or London and St Petersburg. They are
> urged to take a wider view, and to display a calmer spirit,
> and greater confidence in the wisdom and sagacity of their
> London rulers.[48]

But after thirty years of pursuing such a policy, Younghusband felt
that when the British government was still asking the Chinese why
they had not implemented the agreement, 'the local officer's faith
in the superior efficacy of headquarters treatment [was] somewhat
shaken'.[49] Curzon proposed to Yu Kang, the Chinese amban,
sending a delegation to meet the British mission in the Chumbi
Valley and to include a fully empowered Tibetan representative so
that Tibet would also be bound by any agreement reached. He also
sent this message to the Chinese foreign office in Beijing, asking it
to issue instructions to its amban in Lhasa. Despite these efforts,
the amban remained unable to persuade the Tibetans to cooperate.
In exasperation, the Chinese foreign office – to demonstrate its
sincerity – published the amban's letter to the Tibetan Council in
a gazette.

This letter offers insights into the Chinese attitude towards the
Tibetans and the relationship dynamics between the amban and
the Tibetan government. The amban advised the Tibetan Council
not to heed the lamas or try to stop the British by force, warning
of the potential for war and catastrophe for Tibet. He cautioned
that such actions would hinder his ability to mediate, ending the
letter with a plea to the council urging 'not to repeat [their] former
error'. Additionally, he sent a copy of the letter to Beijing with
a contemptuous comment on Tibetans stating that 'obstinacy is
engrained in the character of the Tibetan barbarians'.[50]

In July 1903, White proceeded to Khamba Dzong in Tibet
with 200 troops, joined by Younghusband later with another 300.
The amban designated two Chinese and two Tibetan officials to

talk to the British; however, the Tibetans refused to meet with the British and reacted to the presence of the British on their soil with extraordinary stubbornness. They declared that they would not negotiate until the British had withdrawn, closing all border trade, blocking mountain passes and insisting on the talks taking place in Sikkim. The Chinese pleaded with Younghusband not to advance beyond Khamba Dzong.

Five months passed in this stalemate. In November, after persistent requests by Curzon, London agreed to let the mission advance to Gyantse. It took the precaution of keeping Russia informed, reassuring it, yet again, that it had no intention of annexing Tibet or permanently occupying it. Russia protested against the invasion, remarking that it would cause 'a grave disturbance to the Central Asian situation' at a time when the two countries were trying to resolve their differences amicably. Britain insisted that it had the right to enforce its treaty obligations and that its action did not threaten Russia's interests in Asia, citing Russia's encroachments in Manchuria, Chinese Turkestan and Iran to justify its own action in Tibet.[51]

As soon as winter receded, Younghusband started his march. A Tibetan army detachment tried to stop him near Guru in April 1904 but was pushed back with heavy casualties. Emboldened, Younghusband decided to advance to Lhasa. He proceeded cautiously, reaching the city in August. By then, the Thirteenth Dalai Lama, appointing the head of the Gaden monastery as regent, had fled to Mongolia.

Younghusband imposed a harsh treaty on Tibet, forcing it to respect the 1890 convention and the 1893 regulations. Tibet would have to erect boundary pillars, permit British trade markets in Gyantse and Gartok (in addition to Yatung) and pay an indemnity of 7.5 million rupees in instalments. Britain would occupy the Chumbi Valley for three years or until the trade markets were established. Tibet committed to not ceding territory to a foreign power or grant it any concessions for railways, telegraphy, mining or other rights. It also agreed not to allow any 'Foreign Power' to intervene in its affairs or station a representative there.

The Dalai Lama's seal was affixed to the treaty by Losang Gyaltsen, the head of the Gaden monastery. The seals of all three powerful monasteries – Sera, Drepung and Gaden – were affixed, as were those of the council and the national assembly. Thus, the entire top leadership was brought to heel, binding Tibet to the agreement in the Dalai Lama's absence.

China remained astonishingly stoic during Britain's invasion. The Chinese publication *Shenpao* expressed concern about an invader profaning China's 'sacred dynasty's feudatory State' but cautioned against using Russia or Japan to counter Britain. Instead, it argued that Tibet was strategically crucial for Britain's defence of its empire in India, and that appealing to its good sense would be the most prudent approach. This was sound advice, given that China was in no position to defend Tibet. Allowing Britain to protect its interests, as reassured, was its best bet.[52] As events unfolded, China was rewarded because it was able to make a powerful comeback in Tibet by riding on Britain's back, despite internal turmoil and a disintegrating government in Beijing.

It was with Russia that Britain struggled the most. Russia warned the British ambassador, Sir Charles Hardinge, that it was deeply disturbed by the action. Hardinge countered by pointing out that Britain had been equally upset by Dorjiev's visit.[53]

The Undoing of Curzon's Policy

Curzon had tried hard to convince London that China lacked the capability to defend Tibet against Russia, writing that '[t]o talk of a Chinese army marching by fixed stages across Asia, or even of confining itself to … recovering the adjoining countries which once acknowledged the sovereignty of Peking, appears to me the wildest freak of fantasy'.[54] He wanted to bring Tibet under British control but, as Alastair Lamb observed, the British in India could not convince their superiors in London that Tibet was not a part of the 'Chinese world'.[55]

Curzon's 'forward policy' forced Britain to clarify its stand to other European powers on Tibet's status. It pleaded that its 'political mission' to Tibet was with the 'concurrence of the Chinese Government' and was intended to secure observance of the Convention of 1890.[56] When questioned about China's concurrence, the secretary of state for India, John Brodrick, explained that the Chinese government had 'accepted' Khamba Dzong and Yatung as the meeting places for the mission with Chinese and Tibetan officials. As for the mission's further advance to Gyantse, Brodrick stated that China had been informed that Britain was 'unable to consent to stop the further advance of the Mission into Tibet' and had been instructed to resort to force only when met with resistance.[57]

Britain went to great lengths to reassure Russia and critics at home that it had no intention of annexing Tibet. It downplayed its occupation of the Chumbi Valley as a temporary measure to ensure payment of the indemnity. Dismissing arguments that Tibet was an isolationist country seeking to be left alone, Britain cited the Dorjiev mission to St Petersburg as evidence that Tibet was conspiring with Russia against British interests.

Britain pleaded in vain with Russia and other European powers that it respected China's integrity and independence, including its suzerainty over Tibet. Ambassador Hardinge reported that Britain's invasion was a 'disagreeable pill' for Russia to swallow. Even France was disturbed by Britain's aggression. Lansdowne tried to reassure Hardinge by stating that 'we shall not leave an Agent there, and our retirement will probably have begun before you read these lines'.[58] This did little to calm suspicions, with Hardinge writing back saying that Russia was suspicious of Britain's treaty with Tibet and regarded the occupation of the Chumbi Valley as an annexation. Lansdowne could not agree more, acknowledging that Younghusband's actions had placed Britain in a very embarrassing position, deeming his occupation of the valley 'mischievous' and emphasizing that they needed 'to avoid even an apparent deviation from the assurances given to the Russian Government'. He added that although Britain enjoyed geographical dominance over Tibet, all its lawful trade with other countries would continue.[59]

However, the reality of China's hold on Tibet was not lost on Britain. While disputing Curzon's characterization of it as mere 'constitutional fiction', London declared that China was 'powerless to bring about a more satisfactory condition of affairs between ourselves and Tibet'. Despite this recognition, Britain tied itself in knots on the issue of Tibet's independence and Chinese suzerainty. In a lengthy debate in the House of Lords, Lord Lansdowne asserted both positions, stating:

> [W]e have throughout these long negotiations constantly leant on the suzerainty of China, and spared no pains to carry the Chinese Government with us at every step … Our view is that the independence of Tibet should be recognised but that if any other Power is to exercise a preponderance in that country, that Power can only be Great Britain.[60]

The same duality prevailed in later debates. In one instance, Brodrick refused to answer a pointed question put to him whether Tibet was an independent kingdom or a part of the Chinese empire. In another debate, he said that Britain would not attempt to annex Tibet, nor establish a protectorate over it or control its internal administration 'so long as no other Power endeavoured to intervene in the affairs of Tibet'.[61]

In February 1904, Lord Hardwicke, undersecretary of state for India, said in the House of Lords:

> I can only say that so far as the policy of His Majesty's Government is concerned, we have always recognised the suzerainty that China has over Tibet; and in all the negotiations that have taken place the noble Marquess the Foreign Secretary has been in close communication with the Chinese Minister and with the Government of Peking.[62]

He also argued that Tibet had been emboldened by Russia's support, and Britain could not remain indifferent to the internal affairs of a country adjacent to India. He denied any intention of establishing a political agent in Lhasa or Gyantse.

In the course of the same debate, Lord Ripon, Leader of the House of Lords and former viceroy of India, elaborated on Britain's attitude towards China: 'I suppose it is our policy to maintain the integrity and independence of China and to set ourselves, so far as we can, against any step on the part of any Power to interfere with that independence or threaten that integrity.'[63]

How true were Curzon's allegations about Russia's designs on Tibet? Russia did make diplomatic contact with Tibet during the Tsarist era, mainly due to Dorjiev's efforts. He had visited St Petersburg between 1898 and 1901 to get Russian protection against the British. But like Britain, Russia did not wish to start a race to dismantle the Chinese empire, especially since the threat from Japan was more immediate than Britain. The tsar merely assured Dorjiev that 'under the friendly and benevolent favour of Russia no harm may come to Tibet'.[64]

During the 1901 visit, Dorjiev carried a message from the Dalai Lama describing the British as 'enemies and oppressors' and seeking the tsar's help. Whether Russia supplied any arms to Tibet remains unclear. Accounts from a Japanese monk in Lhasa, Ekai Kawaguchi, mention that he saw two large Russian caravans carrying rifles and ammunition soon after Dorjiev's visit.[65] Some British sources refer to old American rifles allegedly being sent through Russia. However, no such weapons were found by Younghusband on reaching Lhasa.

Russia set up a small consulate in Tachienlu (now Kangding) on the eastern border of Tibet to monitor the activities of the French and the British. But the office lasted only about a year until 1904.

When Younghusband's invasion of Tibet became imminent, Russia decided to send an expeditionary force under Naran Ulanov to assess British designs. But the outbreak of the Russia–Japan war diverted its attention. Ulanov didn't reach Lhasa until 1905, by which time the British had withdrawn. He advised the lamas to trust China and Russia but not the English, because they were hostile to Buddhism.

Meanwhile, Dorjiev – who had fled to Russia – continued his efforts to procure military aid for Tibet. In 1912, when the Manchu dynasty collapsed, he organized for three Mongol military trainers to be sent to Tibet. By this time, though, the Romanov dynasty in Russia was itself in turmoil and unable to help Tibet against Britain.

Curzon's foray into Tibet was widely opposed in England. London did not view Younghusband's expedition, or the treaty, with favour. Secretary of State for India John Brodrick, who had replaced Hamilton in October 1903, launched a campaign against Younghusband, publishing a blue book that presented his expedition in a bad light. But the invasion was popular among the public and media, leading the government to issue a mild reprimand and expeditiously proceed to address the international fallout.[66]

China emerged as the unlikely beneficiary of Britain's invasion of Tibet. Taking full advantage of the flight of the Dalai Lama to assert its authority, it confiscated his rank. It was also aware that other European powers were against the invasion, which Britain could not afford to ignore. Prince Ch'ing informed the British minister in Beijing that the United States, Germany, France and Italy had expressed their opposition to China granting exclusive privileges to Britain in Tibet.[67]

Britain–China Convention on Tibet

Britain realized that it could absolve itself of the charge of annexing Tibet only by securing China's endorsement of the 1904 agreement. Britain's diplomats in Beijing were also unhappy with Younghusband's invasion. Ernest Satow, the minister in Beijing, persuaded London that the treaty was not 'worth the paper it is written on'.[68] Other diplomats in Beijing and St Petersburg underscored the need to sign an agreement with China to assuage other European powers.

Tang Shao-yi, the vice president of the Board of Foreign Affairs and China's ambassador-designate to London, was asked to come to Kolkata for negotiations in 1905. He was accompanied by a Briton working for the Chinese government, Henderson of the customs service, who acted as his adviser. Given his close relations with the British officials in Beijing, Tang was not short on self-confidence. He presented a draft agreement on behalf of his government, stipulating recognition of Chinese sovereignty over Tibet and restricting Britain's trading rights there. This was, however, rejected by Curzon with London's support.

Tang argued that China bore responsibility for Tibet's security. But the British officials dissuaded him from pressing the point because it would make China liable to pay indemnity for the murder of a French missionary in Tachienlu by Tibetan lamas.[69] The resulting Adhesion Agreement, as it was called, 'The Convention between Great Britain and China Respecting Tibet', was signed in April 1906. Britain explicitly recognized China's suzerainty over Tibet while retaining the commercial rights it had acquired. Notably, the 1904 agreement had made no reference to Chinese suzerainty over Tibet, even though a Chinese version had been signed. The China connection was reinstated in 1906.

The preamble to the treaty stressed the desire of the two 'Empires' to maintain friendship and good understanding. It stated that Tibet had refused to 'recognise the validity of or to carry into full effect the provisions of the Anglo-Chinese Convention of March 17, 1890', necessitating British intervention to secure its rights and interests. Consequently, China admitted, implicitly, that it had been unable to enforce its treaty on Tibet and that it was an 'empirc'.

The 1904 treaty was reaffirmed, subject to subsequent modifications, and affixed to the convention. Britain agreed to not annex Tibetan territory or interfere in its administration. To counter any Russian designs, Britain compelled China 'not to permit any other foreign state to interfere with the territory or internal administration of Tibet'.[70] Furthermore, the indemnity stipulated in the 1904 treaty was reduced to a third – 2.5 million rupees – and Britain assured that it would withdraw from the Chumbi Valley upon payment.

Anglo-Russian Convention of 1907

A year after Britain signed the convention, it also came to an agreement with Russia on the three countries lying between their empires in Asia – Iran, Afghanistan and Tibet. This was the momentous 'Convention Between Great Britain and Russia Relating to Persia, Afghanistan and Tibet', signed in St Petersburg in August 1907.

The agreement was facilitated by the British ambassador to Russia, Arthur Nicolson, who had started his diplomatic career in Tehran. He was convinced that the solution to the problems of Central Asia lay in St Petersburg and was willing to share the region with Russia rather than fight for sole supremacy. Despite serving in Iran, his attitude towards Russia was opposite to Curzon's. The convention was signed by Nicolson and Alexander Isvolsky, Russia's foreign minister.

Russia, too, did not want to overstretch itself in Tibet, realizing that it would be best to leave it to China. Explaining this decision, Count Sergei Witte, the Russian prime minister from 1905 to 1906, wrote in his memoirs: 'I clearly saw that it was to Russia's best interests to have as its neighbour a strong but passive China, and that therein lay the assurance of Russia's safety in the East.'[71] He wanted Russia to uphold the integrity of the Chinese empire and ensure that no power was allowed to increase its territorial possessions at China's expense.

Resolving Tibet proved the easiest of the three countries in the convention, which assigned 'suzerain' rights to China. Article 11 of the Tibetan Section of the agreement stated: 'In conformity with the admitted principle of the suzerainty of China over Tibet, Great Britain and Russia engage not to enter into negotiations with Tibet except through the intermediary of the Chinese government.' Both countries pledged to respect Tibet's territorial integrity and refrain from interfering in its internal affairs. They would conduct their dealings with the Tibetan government through China's intermediary and agreed not to station a representative in Lhasa. But British commercial agents were permitted to stay in Gyantse and Gartok. Article 2 of the convention recognized the Britain–China Convention of 1906, with Russia accepting that Britain had a 'special interest in the maintenance of the status quo in the external relations of Tibet'.

The main sticking point was Britain's occupation of the Chumbi Valley and its insistence on prohibiting scientific missions. To allay this concern, Britain agreed to withdraw as soon as the indemnity was paid. While it remained firm on the ban on scientific missions, it agreed to let Russian Buddhists visit Tibet for religious purposes, acknowledging that Russia had an interest in Tibet on account of its Buddhist population, many of whom lived in or wanted to visit Lhasa.

Although Britain were satisfied that Russia had recognized China's suzerainty over Tibet and accepted Britain's special interest in the region due to its geographical proximity to India, the agreement had whittled down some of the concessions extracted by Curzon. It disavowed Curzon's forward policy and agreed not to interfere in Tibet's internal affairs in return for a similar commitment by Russia. Curzon had forced Tibet not to award any concession relating to railways, roads, telegraphs, mining or other rights to any foreign power without Britain's previous consent. Now, both countries agreed not to take such concessions or other rights in Tibet.

The agreement also included an annex in which Britain repeated its declaration to withdraw from the Chumbi Valley on payment of the indemnity. It stated: 'It is clearly understood that if the occupation of Chumbi Valley by the British forces has for any reason, not been terminated at the time anticipated in the above Declaration, the British and Russian Government will enter upon friendly exchange of views on this subject.'[72]

Russia wanted the territory of Tibet to be defined, but Britain argued that doing so would unnecessarily delay the negotiations. Still, it asked its legation in Beijing to conduct an unofficial check with the Chinese. When John Jordan asked a Chinese minister, Tong Shoa-yi, about Tibet's borders with China, the latter replied that he was not sure about the north and east.[73] The treaty described Tibet as the country south of the Kunlun and Nanshan mountains, extending in the east up to Tsaidam. Even seven years later, at the Simla Conference, an agreement on the Tibet–China border would remain elusive.

Although Mongolia was not part of the agreement, Russia was able to persuade Britain that it had a special interest in the country – thereby gaining a foothold there. It wanted to preserve the status quo, arguing that China was trying to replace the traditional power structure with a centralized Chinese administration, which was causing discontent among the Mongolians.

Britain and Russia also agreed not to facilitate the Dalai Lama's return to Tibet. They felt it was undesirable because he would stir up trouble there.

Ironically, neither China (the 'suzerain') nor Tibet was party to the treaty. Following its signing, the British and Russian ministers in Beijing gave a copy of the convention to the Chinese government and instructed it to ensure that foreigners did not enter Tibet through China. Jordan reported that China had a policy against foreigners doing so, but its enforcement was lax.

China was quite pleased with the agreement, since it recognized its sovereignty over Tibet and left it free to manage affairs as it saw fit. An editorial in a Chinese paper, the *Shen Pao*, astutely remarked that the Russia–Britain rivalry had allowed China an opportunity to strengthen its hold on Tibet, which had weakened over the years due to apathy. It emphasized that this was a critical time for China to consolidate its empire – not only in Tibet but also in Yunnan and Manchuria.[74]

Afghanistan posed no problem either. In exchange for a commitment not to annex it, Britain obtained Russia's consent to keep it within its sphere of influence.

But what about Iran? Russia claimed that the country fell within Russia's sphere of influence and refused to accept its presence as a threat to India. A compromise was reached whereby Iran was divided into three zones: a Russian sphere in the north, which included Tehran; a British sphere along the Indian border in Baluchistan; and a neutral sphere in the south.

The British government had a torrid time defending the treaty at home. It argued that the agreement was 'animated by the sincere desire to settle by mutual agreement certain questions concerning the interests of Great Britain and Russia on the continent of Asia'.[75] Defending the deal, it stated that it remained within the bounds of assurances given by Lord Lansdowne in 1904 to Russia. Moreover, Russia had consented to Britain's 'preferential position' in Tibet 'over all other foreign countries in regard to frontier and commercial matters'. In return, Britain had guaranteed it would not annex any part of Tibet nor establish a permanent mission in Lhasa.[76]

Curzon, then an opposition member, voiced strong criticisms of the provisions relating to Tibet. He accused the government of appeasing Russia by mutually committing to non-interference. Several other British officials in India shared these objections, particularly against the assurance of non-interference, surrendering mining and other concessions and permitting Russian Buddhists to travel to Tibet. Grey overruled their objections and moved ahead without consulting them. He did not see any harm in permitting Buddhist subjects from Russia to visit Lhasa, as this was in line with the treatment of the Dalai Lama as a religious leader. He highlighted that Russia's genuine interest in Tibet because of its significant Buddhist community.

The under-secretary of state, Lord Fitzmaurice, rebutted Curzon's critique by reminding him that he, too, had assured Russia in 1904 that as long as there was no foreign intervention, Britain would not annex or establish a protectorate over Tibet. Fitzmaurice specified that Tibet was remote even from the British Empire in India, advocating that their 'policy ought to be a minimizing policy, a policy of reducing our engagements to a minimum and, if anything, of drawing back from any policy of adventure that may have been contemplated'. He likened the Dalai Lama to the Pope of Rome, asserting that as the head of a religious community, he should be allowed to receive pilgrims from all over, including Russia.[77]

The convention proved to be a triumph for Britain. It brought to a close its rivalry with Russia in Central Asia. By keeping Russia out of India's periphery, Britain's empire was secured. Moreover, it brought the Iranian province adjoining Baluchistan, and Afghanistan, under Britain's sphere of influence and consigned Tibet to China – thereby out of Russia's reach. Earlier, both powers had recognized East Turkestan as part of the Chinese empire. Britain also disengaged itself from the fate of Mongolia and northern Manchuria. Grey wrote: 'In its primary and cardinal object, the security of the Indian frontier, the agreement was completely successful.'[78] Nicolson reassured his government that Russia was no longer instigating the Dalai Lama. Previously, there were considerations of escorting him to Lhasa and facilitating his reinstatement, but attention had now shifted to Mongolia due to suspicions of Chinese and Japanese interference.

The agreement brought the Great Game to a close for Russia too. It turned its focus to the new threat that had emerged in continental Europe: Germany. And by the time Russia recovered from the two world wars, Britain had ceased to be an Asian power.

For Tibet, the convention was an unmitigated tragedy, sealing its fate during the dying days of Manchu rule in China. Once dubbed a 'broken reed' by former Prime Minister A. J. Balfour, China subsequently descended into revolution and civil war. But the two big powers, Britain and Russia, would not let Tibet escape its clutches.

China blames its Tibet dilemma on foreign conspiracies, primarily implicating Britain and India, while viewing Russia as a benign influence. Professor Bai Shouyi's historical account of China for the government's Foreign Language Press describes the struggle between Britain and Russia for control over Tibet:

Since the latter half of the 19th century, Britain and Russia had been engaged in fierce contention over Tibet. At the end of 1903, taking advantage of Russian preoccupation in the northeast, Britain launched an invasion of Tibet. The local Tibetan army and people resisted British aggression, putting up a particularly heroic defence at the battle of Gyangze (Gyantse) in southern Tibet. The British army occupied and looted Lhasa in August 1905, and in 1906 Britain forced the Qing Court to sign an unequal treaty (Convention between

Great Britain and China respecting Tibet, 1906) opening Gyantse and Gartok as trading towns.[79]

But this simplistic narrative ignores the fact that even though Britain could have easily annexed Tibet into its empire at that time, it chose not to do so, instead reaffirming China's suzerainty over Tibet in treaties with China and Russia in 1906 and 1907 respectively.

How did the momentous 1907 convention come about with such ease? How did the two mighty empires – Britain and Russia – come to a compromise in Central Asia? The resurgence of the Liberals in Britain had certainly fostered a more conducive environment. Lord Salisbury, previously critical of propping up the Ottoman empire against Russia, was reluctant to repeat this stance with China. Thus, he acquiesced to giving Russia a free hand in northern China in exchange for limiting its expansion in the south.

But it was a more dramatic development to the east of mainland Asia that brought about a sea change in the balance of power in the region: the rise of Japan. Russia's defeat at its hands was a humiliation of epic proportions. To understand its full impact, one must turn to China again, where the Manchu dynasty was breathing its last.

8

Fall of the Manchus

Russia's expansion in Asia encountered a formidable blockage not from China, but from Japan, which emerged as a major military power by the late nineteenth century and briefly entered the imperial game in Central Asia. In 1894, Japan attacked Korea – a territory China regarded as a tributary state and moved to defend – but Japan won spectacular victories over China on land and sea. The following year, it conquered Taiwan and the Liaodong peninsula. China expected Russia's support but found itself disappointed when Russia excused itself by claiming that its intervention would draw Britain to Japan's aid.

China's attitude towards the Japanese people was far more hostile and contemptuous than towards Europeans. The Chinese referred to them as *wojen* – dwarves – and saw them an inferior race that owed its culture to China.[1] The defeat to Japan had a devastating effect on its morale. Robert Hart wrote: 'China's collapse has been terrible, and the comical and tragical have dovetailed … in the most heart-breaking, side-bursting fashion.' Chinese scholar Yu Tsan lamented that China had never been poorer or weaker in its history.[2]

Japan's success took Britain's China hands by surprise. After China had recovered its empire – with their help – they had developed a deep trust in the country and its people. The historian James L. Hevia, citing contemporary sources, concludes that 'on the eve of the Sino-Japanese War, some of these experts thought that China was ahead of Japan and even predicted a victory for the former if the two ever went to war.' British diplomats in Beijing had come to believe that 'Qing interests and their own were fundamentally the same' and that Manchu China was the kind of ally they needed in that part of the world.[3]

The Boxer Rebellion (1899–1901)

Despite their defeat to Japan, the Manchus – still left with some fight in them – changed targets by trying to expel Europeans from China. This signalled the last flicker of a dying flame.

The spark for the Boxer Rebellion came from Empress Dowager Cixi, who had crushed a series of administrative changes, the Hundred Day Reform, introduced by the Guangxu emperor to break out of her control. But Cixi, through a calculated palace coup, got rid of his advisers and confined him. Leveraging anti-foreigner sentiment and fears of losing control to outsiders, she mobilized the Manchu nationalists to her cause.

Empress Cixi bolstered a secret society of Manchus, the Yi He Tuan (called the 'Boxers' by Europeans) to attack foreigners in Beijing. Two senior diplomats – one Japanese and one German – were killed. Beijing's large diplomatic corps, including 475 civilians and 2,300 Chinese Christians, sought refuge in the Legation Quarter, with only their guards to protect them from the marauding Boxer gangs. Sensing an opportunity, the court declared war on the foreign powers. Boxer gangs rampaged through Beijing, destroying churches and killing Chinese Christians.

The foreign powers in Tianjin hurriedly put together an eight-nation force of 18,000 to rescue their beleaguered compatriots from Beijing. Made up of forces from Japan, Russia, Britain, France, Austria, Italy, Germany and the US, it stormed Beijing in August 1901, prompting Cixi and her court to flee to Xian in Central China. Once again, the Manchu empire lay at the mercy of foreign invaders, with historical rivalries among the major powers shaping its outcome.

As soon as the Boxer Rebellion was put down, the Europeans began arguing over what concessions they could extract from China. Britain was disgruntled about having to share China's indemnity with others, especially the smaller powers whose contribution was negligible. But this paled in comparison to its contempt for Russia, which was rumoured to have secured secret concessions in return for military assistance to China.

Russian foreign policy experts advised against dismantling the Manchu empire. They shared Britain's fear – that it would lose control of the vast empire and other European powers would seize most of it. In 1900, during the peak of the Boxer Rebellion, Fedor Martens, who was a professor at the University of St Petersburg and member of Russia's foreign ministry, had written a memorandum entitled *Europe and China*. He advised against Russia, or any other power, annexing territories of the Chinese empire, suggesting that it was in Russia's fundamental interest to support 'the principle of the absolute inviolability of China'.[4]

Although eager to push its railway line to Vladivostok through Manchuria, Russia realized the need for caution. Japan's rise and its interest in Manchuria raised concerns, yet as an Asian country, Russia was confident it could manage Japan. Britain remained its main concern, and gaining China's consent would pre-empt British objections. Russia offered to help China against Japan while trying to convince it that allowing the railway line in Manchuria served its best interests. With China in no position to defend Manchuria against Japan, a Russian railway line seemed a small price to pay for the survival of the empire. In 1896, the two countries came to a clandestine agreement, permitting Russia to construct its railway line in return for assisting China in its defence against any external threat.

In the context of Sino-Russian relations at the turn of the century, Alexander Lukin, a Russian diplomat and writer, observed, that 'the idea that the Chinese should be indebted to Russia for supposedly being especially supportive of China in its relations with other European powers was very popular at the end of the nineteenth century and the beginning of the twentieth century'.[5] Russians reminded the Chinese that even after the Taiping and other rebellions, they had not exploited the weakness of the Manchu dynasty to acquire territory.

During the Boxer Rebellion, Russia had occupied Manchuria on the pretext of suppressing rioters. It now put pressure on China to cede the territory – a move that was opposed by Japan and Britain, who warned China against such action. Faced with resistance, Russia found it prudent to withdraw.

The Anglo-Japanese Alliance, 1902

China's defeat to Japan and the Boxer Rebellion once again revived Britain's quest for an ally to counter Russia. Hevia summed up Britain's dilemma:

> [T]he British objective of assimilating the Qing as allies for their own geopolitical concerns in Asia lay in disarray. Indeed, after 1895, the British acted like any other predator, and thoughts of Qing-British partnership were eclipsed by great power politics. China was now the sick man of Asia and 'informed' opinion wondered what would stand in the way of the Russian tsar's ascending the throne in Beijing and mobilizing the largest military force the world had ever seen.[6]

Britain decided to end its splendid isolation in the Far East and seek new allies to protect its own interests and the unity of the Manchu empire. France was ruled out as a possible ally because it had aligned itself with Russia in 1894.[7] In 1900, Britain turned to Germany, signing an agreement to ensure free and open trade access to the ports and rivers of China. Germany also committed to maintain the integrity of the Chinese empire, pledging military intervention 'in case the integrity of China was threatened by the aggressive action of any other power or by internal Chinese trouble'.[8] The German chancellor, Bernhard von Bülow, told the Reichstag that Germany's interest in China was purely commercial and that the agreement was meant to preserve China's integrity for as long as possible. But very soon, Britain realized that Germany was unwilling to antagonize Russia.

So, Britain turned to Japan – even though it was also acquiring Chinese territory – as Japan shared Britain's animosity towards Russia. Secretary of State for the Colonies Joseph Chamberlain was among the first British leaders to advocate such an alliance to counter Russia in the Far East. When Russia attacked Port Arthur in China in 1897, he made the same suggestion to Prime Minister Salisbury. In 1902, Britain entered into a formal alliance with Japan, which viewed Russia's expansion into southern Manchuria as a threat to its interests in Korea. Despite their divergent interests in China, Britain did not let this stand in the way of cooperation. The Anglo-Japanese treaty paradoxically also recognized the independence and integrity of China.[9] Britain began to assist Japan in strengthening its navy.

Russia responded by resurrecting the threat of marching on India. A Russian journal published an article by its minister of war, General Kuropatkin, calling on his forces to be ready to fight Afghan and English troops. He also revived plans to improve rail connectivity to the Afghan frontier. Lord Kitchener estimated that more than 200,000 troops would be required to defend India from a Russian invasion.[10]

Japan's acquisitions sparked a fresh scramble for China. Germany seized the port of Jiaozhou, while Russia took control of two ports in the Liaodong peninsula. Although they were presented as long-term leases, these were virtual annexations. Britain viewed this with concern, fearing it would lead to China's disintegration, and started to advocate for an open-door policy allowing the special interests of these countries to be retained in the ports and keeping them open to other countries as well. The US supported this policy of equal commercial opportunity for all in China.

Russia offered to help China by paying the indemnity demanded by Japan for the two ports it had seized. This gesture ingratiated China, prompting a strong lobby within the Manchu court to advocate for an alliance with Russia. Tsar Alexander III, keen to build the railway line to Vladivostok, saw this as the best solution for reaching this distant part of his empire. By going through

Manchuria instead of around it, the distance of the 2,000-kilometre line could be reduced by a quarter.

Emboldened by its alliance with Britain, in 1904 Japan declared war on Russia after negotiations over its presence in Manchuria and Korea failed. Britain welcomed the war as it diverted Russia's focus to Manchuria and eased the pressure on India. Consequently, Britain closed its ports to Russia's Baltic fleet, blocking their access to the Pacific Ocean. The war culminated with Russia being routed by Japan.

Russia's defeat was devastating and had a defining impact on its foreign policy. It was the first time an Asian country had defeated a European power. Russian authorities were furious with Britain. General Kuropatkin, himself involved in the defeat, blamed Britain for aligning with an Asian country against a European power: 'Because of the fear of a mythical Russian invasion of India [Britain] with its own hands [had] created not a mythical, but a real, threat for the very same India.'[11] But he realized that Russia could do little to threaten Britain and advocated maintaining solidarity among European powers to preserve their possessions in Asia, suggesting an agreement 'of all European states aimed at securing the dominant position on Asian and African continents and suppression of armed struggle among various states – members of a future "European union"'.[12]

Russia's imperial ambitions were decisively halted for half a century. As Ernest Satow, Britain's minister in Japan reported, it 'seemed to knock on the head all Russian schemes of territorial acquisition'.[13] It triggered a series of revolts against the Russian monarchy that compelled it to come to terms with Britain in Asia as fears of an invasion of India subsided. The outcome was the Convention of St Petersburg of August 1907.

The 'Sick Man' of Asia

The Manchu dynasty survived the Boxer Rebellion, but its days were numbered. It had never recovered from the humiliation of 1860, despite receiving both British and Russian assistance. The reigns of the child emperors, Tongzhi and Guangxu (Kuang-hsü), were marred by intense palace intrigues, conspiracies and even murders. Tongzhi's death at the age of nineteen in 1875, amidst rumours of poisoning by his mother, Cixi, for trying to assert his independence, marked a tumultuous period. She replaced him with the four-year-old son of her sister, who was married to Prince Chun, Tongzhi's uncle. When the new emperor came of age, he too fell afoul of Cixi, eventually being placed under house arrest.

The Boxer Rebellion further exposed the weakness of the dynasty, as its resort to violence against civilians and the humiliating surrender foretold its demise. Many Chinese leaders, such as Sun Yat-sen, were convinced that political change in the country could only be achieved by its overthrow.

The dynasty declined precipitously after its defeat to Japan. The ageing Cixi and the sidelined Guangxu emperor were in no position to rule the country. Things took a turn for the worse in 1908, when Cixi and Guangxu died within days of each other. Rumours circulated that Cixi had arranged the poisoning of the emperor before her death to nominate another of her grand-nephews, the three-year-old Pu Yi, who succeeded as the Xuantong (Hsüan-t'ung) emperor – the twelfth and last Manchu ruler of China. His reign lasted merely four years. By now, the country was beyond control, with numerous revolts breaking out all over, especially in the Han-dominated south. Between 1906 and 1911 alone, ten serious revolts erupted.

The Manchu dynasty had survived half a century at the mercy of foreign powers, chiefly Britain and Russia. Historian John Fairbank observes that these imperialist nations supported the conservative Ch'ing dynasty to maintain their special privileges, preferring stability over significant changes that might disrupt their interests. He remarks that 'great changes seldom seemed to the foreigners to be in their interest. They preferred to prop up the old order'.[14]

Echoing the sentiments of his peers, historian Stuart Fe remarks, 'Only the support of Western powers that profited from China's infirmity prevented the collapse of the dynasty.'[15] Expanding upon this theme, Odd Arne Westad delves deeper into this exploitative relationship, highlighting how the foreign presence both weakened and preserved the Qing state: 'The Western powers made use of the Qing's weakness to extract privileges from it, but supported it so that it did not collapse entirely, only then to be exploited a little bit more.'[16]

Massacre of the Manchus

As the Manchu dynasty weakened, it faced growing vilification by the Han Chinese for its foreign origin and dependence on Europeans for survival. The anti-Manchu sentiment was particularly strong in the Han-dominated south, and, unsurprisingly, the 1911 revolution was a culmination of this animosity.

In *Brotherhood of the Five Races*, Sun Yat-sen describes the Manchus thus: 'Our ancestors refused to submit to the Manchus. Close your eyes and imagine the picture of the bitter battles, when rivers of blood flowed, and the bodies of the fallen covered the fields, and you will realise that the conscience of our ancestors is clear.'[17] In four essential points, he outlines the Revolutionary Alliance's agenda – the first two of which proposed the expulsion of the Manchus and the restoration of 'Chinese' rule:

> The Manchus are a foreign, barbarian people, who had entered China 260 years ago and have oppressed and enslaved the Chinese. It is time to liberate China from this yoke. Those who surrender, when the revolution takes place, are to be spared; those who resist are to be disposed of without scruple.[18]

This treatment was to apply not only to the Manchus but also to their Chinese collaborators.

In 1911, as China's nationalist revolution started against the Qing dynasty, the Manchu people faced massacres in various locations. Thousands were hunted down and killed. Among the most gruesome incidents was the November 1911 massacre in Xian, where nearly 20,000 individuals were trapped without supplies and brutally slaughtered. Some Manchus managed to escape to Manchuria in the north, while others concealed their Manchu identity even from their own children, living in hiding within China.

Revolution and Counter-revolution in China

During the twilight of Manchu rule, two contrasting figures, Yuan Shikai and Sun Yat-sen, emerged as prominent players. Yuan, from a military background in Henan, swiftly ascended the ranks. His tenure as imperial resident in Seoul in 1885 and subsequent leadership of the New Army bolstered his influence in Beijing. Skilful manoeuvring in court power struggles further propelled his rise, as he notably sided with Empress Dowager Cixi in 1898 and aided foreigners against the Boxer rebels two years later. However, Yuan's fall from grace after Cixi's demise led to his dismissal in 1909.

In contrast, Sun Yat-sen, born into a peasant family near Canton, pursued scholarly interests and studied science and medicine. His conversion to Christianity spurred his involvement in revolutionary activities aimed at overthrowing Manchu rule. Forced to flee China following a failed revolution in Canton in 1895, Sun sought support from the US and Britain to limited avail. Yet, the Manchus' harsh actions during the Boxer Rebellion swayed foreign powers against the ruling dynasty, fostering sympathy for the revolutionaries.

In October 1911, a revolt erupted in Hankou, Hubei province, with the rallying cry 'Away with the Manchus'. Sun Yat-sen, in the US for fundraising, journeyed to Britain seeking support before returning to China. Initially, Britain refrained from aiding the Manchu rulers and preventing Japanese intervention. By December, the revolutionaries established a provisional government in Nanjing, inviting Sun to assume the presidency. In response, the Manchus, guided by British advice, turned to Yuan Shikai, who returned as the prime minister in Beijing.

Britain persuaded Yuan Shikai to hold talks with the southern revolutionaries instead of resorting to military action against them. British Minister John Jordan instructed the British Consul at Hankow to mediate. Yuan accepted the truce but broke off negotiations when Sun assumed the presidency. China found itself with two governments – one led by Yuan in the north and the other by Sun in the south – both beset with internal dissension.

The chaos in China during this period has been succinctly captured by Fenby: 'In the first month of 1912, China was in an extraordinary situation. A republican president sat in Nanjing. Yuan was prime minister and in command in Beijing. An infant emperor, Puyi, was in the Forbidden City, with no regent.'[19]

Yuan pressured Pu Yi's mother to declare the abdication of the Manchu dynasty, despite opposition from the Manchu and Mongol princes, making it a condition for sparing their family members' lives. The abdication was finally announced in February 1912, allowing Yuan to instal himself as the president in Beijing, appointing Li Yuanhong as vice president. Sun Yat-sen, however, found no place in the new government, relegated to the role of director of railway construction.

Yuan faced two key challenges: restoring Beijing's control over the provinces and securing funds to meet the government's financial needs. Although Russia arranged a loan of £1 million through a Belgian bank, Western countries blocked the deal. Subsequently, a six-nation consortium arranged a £10 million loan – at an exorbitant rate of interest.

In April 1912, Sun Yat-sen promulgated a Provisional Constitution in Nanjing, gaining recognition by the US and a few others, though not Britain. Tensions between Yuan Shikai and Sun Yat-sen continued to escalate. Sun formed the nationalist Kuomintang Party (KMT) to contest the elections held at the end of 1912. However, instead of running himself, he had a young revolutionary, Song Jiaoren, lead the party. Despite the Nationalists' handsome victory, Yuan Shikai responded by having Song assassinated.

This election remains the only one in China's history, although its conduct remains unclear. Yuan Shikai swiftly subverted the newly established national assembly and, in October 1913, secured his presidency through intimidation and bribery, outlawing the KMT.

He consolidated control, employing the army to quell rebellious governors in the south. Sun Yat-sen fled to Japan during this period, known as the Second Revolution. Russia and Britain recognized Yuan Shikai's government in November 1913.

Warlord Era

Yuan's hold on the south remained weak. Once again, the south adopted a constitution with a parliamentary form of government, which infuriated him. In May 1914, he called a national conference in Beijing, where he promulgated his own constitution. However, he overreached when he declared himself the emperor at the end of 1915. This action aroused such opposition among military officers that he was compelled to back down within three months.

By then, the First World War had broken out in Europe. European powers ceased devoting much attention to China – and it started falling apart. The Yunnan province declared itself independent, soon followed by all seven provinces of South China revolting against Beijing. Yuan, significantly weakened and ill, asked to leave China under foreign protection, but Britain persuaded him to stay, fearing the chaos that would ensue. Nevertheless, even the British could not keep their favourite general around for long. He succumbed to illness in June 1916.

Yuan had named his war minister, Duan Qirui, his successor, but it was Vice President Li Yuanhong who took over with the help of a general backed by Germany. Meanwhile, another general tried to restore the young emperor Pu Yi to the throne, while Duan marched into Beijing alongside Japanese forces. This was the beginning of China's Warlord Era, spanning three decades. The peripheries of the empire, Tibet and Xinjiang, broke away, and Manchuria fell under the control of a Japan-dominated warlord who frequently threatened his counterpart in Beijing. In Nanjing and neighbouring areas of the south, the Nationalists remained strong, but the Shanghai area succumbed to another warlord. The south had its parliament in Canton and the support of the Guangxi, Guangdong and Yunnan provinces. Neither the revolutionaries in

Nanjing nor the army in Beijing could unify the country, as old rivals Britain and Russia kept an eye on one another to prevent the other from grabbing more territory than mutually agreed upon.

Although Tibet and Mongolia declared independence, Britain and Russia adhered to their 1907 convention, recognizing them as under Chinese suzerainty. In light of the Manchu empire's collapse, however, they expanded their spheres of influence into these regions, adopting a stance of 'Chinese suzerainty and Outer Mongolian autonomy (which permitted actual Russian domination)' and 'Chinese suzerainty and Tibetan autonomy (allowing a British permanent interest)'.[20]

When the Manchu dynasty collapsed, Xinjiang became virtually independent until 1949. Chinese governors had little control over the rebellious local population, relying on Russian help to maintain nominal presence. Initially, Han Chinese strongman Yang Tseng-hsin asserted his authority, but his assassination in 1928 sparked riots between the local Turkic people and the Chinese Muslims under his successor, Chin Shu-jen. In 1933, Turkic rebels captured Urumchi, with Kulja left as the only place under Chinese control. The Chinese took shelter in an enclave they had built in Kashgar. The governor implored Britain to send troops from India to rescue them, but Britain declined, instead supplying some arms.[21] Russia became increasingly alarmed by the rebellion spreading to its part of Turkestan and by Japan's encroachment in the region through Manchuria and Mongolia. It believed that Japan sought to establish a Greater Mongolia and consequently engineered a coup by a Chinese general, Sheng Shih-tsai, who assumed control of its administration. Britain was concerned yet unable to intervene. India's Foreign Secretary H. A. F. Metcalfe noted that Russia was in full control of Xinjiang:

> The general conclusion arrived at is therefore that Russian influence and indeed pre-dominance in Sinkiang is firmly established in the spheres of both commerce and general administration. It does not appear that the Government of India can do anything effective to check or counteract this

natural process, which must continue unless the Chinese Government are able to re-establish their authority over the Provincial Government.[22]

British influence waned, and trade with India halted. The communist revolution in Russia reignited Britain's apprehensions regarding its designs in Central Asia, while Hitler's rise in Germany posed a new threat in Europe. The Soviet Union, the reorganized Russian empire after the revolution, briefly allied with Hitler on the brink of the Second World War. However, Hitler's subsequent invasion compelled the Soviet Union to pull back its forces from Xinjiang to defend its core cities. Although China welcomed Sheng Shih-tsai's shift in allegiance to Chiang Kai-shek's government, Russia's complete withdrawal left China exposed, triggering violence targeting both Chinese and Russians.

The Russian retreat gave Britain the opportunity to encourage China to revive its control over Xinjiang. In 1943, Ashley Clarke of the British Foreign Office wrote to R. Peel of the India Office, asserting that China had historically ruled Xinjiang 'from time immemorial'. He acknowledged that the region's Muslim population had revolted frequently but concluded saying, 'our advantage lies in strengthening the Chinese connexion. The Province is not strong enough to maintain an absolutely independent existence, and under Chinese rule it will be less of a military danger and we shall have more chance of reviving the Indian trade routes than if the territory came under the Soviet or Japanese domination.'[23]

Peel concurred, writing, 'it would doubtless ... be preferable for Sinkiang to be controlled by China as being the weaker military power than Russia'.[24]

Emergence of the Chinese Communist Party

After the overthrow of the Romanov dynasty in 1917 and the creation of the Soviet Union, Russia rekindled its interest in China, now with a revolutionary fervour. With its support, the Chinese Communist Party was set up in Shanghai in 1921. The party made steady progress among labour and agrarian organizations and soon gathered influence. But the Soviets doubted the feasibility of communism in a primarily agricultural country and advised cooperation with Sun Yat-sen.

Within two years in 1923, Sun Yat-sen proclaimed himself president of the Kuomintang or Nationalist government in Canton, appointing Chiang Kai-shek as the military commander. The Soviet Union aided both the Nationalists and the Communists. Nonetheless, after Sun Yat-sen's death in 1925, Western powers drew Chiang Kai-shek away from the Communists. Accusing the Communists of attempting to take over the government after Sun's death, Chiang severed ties with them. Despite Soviet advice against resistance, the Communists staged revolts in several provinces in the south and established a base in Jiangxi (Kiangsi). However, they were also riven with infighting, compounded by Moscow's interference. Chiang responded with a brutal massacre of their activists in Shanghai. One of the Communist Party leaders, Mao Zedong, fled west with his followers into the mountains in Yunnan, thus starting what came to be called the Long March. From Yunnan, Mao moved north to Sichuan on the Tibetan border.

After driving the Communists out of Shanghai, Chiang sent his army to recover Beijing from the local warlord. He then claimed that he had united the country and, in October 1928, declared the Nationalist Government of China with its capital at Nanjing. To strengthen his credentials in the party, Chiang married Soong Mei-ling, the sister of Sun's widow. Both sisters, belonging to the wealthy Soong family, were Christians, and like Sun, Chiang also converted. Western powers, including Britain, recognized his government. This is widely regarded as the end of the Warlord Era and the beginning of the Nationalist government. In reality, the break with the Communists had sparked a new civil war in China – between the Nationalists and the Communists.

During the Long March, Mao had an unpleasant encounter with Tibetans in Sichuan. The 90,000-strong communist forces had occupied the edge of the Tibetan plateau, where there was barely enough resources to sustain the local population. The Tibetans fled to the forest and launched guerrilla attacks. Mao recorded that many stragglers were killed by the Tibetan 'barbarians'.[25]

From Sichuan, Mao proceeded north and reached Yenan in the Shaanxi (Shensi) province. This region, on the edge of Inner Mongolia, was safely out of the reach of Chiang's army and conveniently close to the Soviet Union. In December 1936, Mao set up the headquarters of the Chinese Communist Party in Yenan and began to rebuild his army with Russian support.

In December 1936, a significant incident unfolded when Chiang Kai-shek ordered his army to attack the communist base in Yenan. When he flew to Xian to oversee the operation's success, the local warlord imprisoned him, demanding a greater role in his government. Alarmed by the situation and keen for China to put up a united front against Japan and relieve pressure in Manchuria, the Soviets intervened. They dispatched a Communist Party leader, Zhou Enlai, from Yenan to mediate the dispute and secure Chiang's release.

Japan's Invasion of China

After the First World War, Britain rewarded Japan for joining the anti-German war coalition by giving it all German concessions in China on the assurance that it would protect China from Russia. Japan took this as a licence to acquire more Chinese territory. In 1931, it conquered Manchuria and parts of Inner Mongolia from China. The following year, it formed the state of Manchukuo (Manchuguo) in Manchuria with the deposed Manchu emperor Pu Yi as its ruler. At twenty-three years old, Pu Yi made an ironic return to the homeland of his ancestors. Manchukuo lasted until Japan's defeat in the Second World War.

In 1937, Japan attacked mainland China, and the Soviet Union emerged as the only country willing to help China for the next two years. It supplied 1,000 planes, 2,000 pilots and 500 military advisers, along with three loans totalling US $250 million.[26] However, when the Second World War started, Soviet attention turned to Europe, and assistance slackened. Support finally ceased in

June 1941, following Germany's invasion. Subsequently, the Soviet Union signed a neutrality pact with Japan to concentrate on the German invasion, under which it recognized Japan's control over Manchuria, reciprocated by Japan recognizing Soviet control over Outer Mongolia.

China found itself abandoned – a situation that changed when Japan attacked the United States.

China's Role in the Second World War

In December 1941, Japan's attack on the US naval base at Pearl Harbor in Hawaii prompted the US to join the war alongside the Allies, comprising Britain, Russia and others. With China, where half of Japan's army was tied up, once again acquiring strategic importance, the US opened its coffers. By 1946, the United States had granted US $1.54 billion in loans to China – and also ensured its participation in key Allied meetings and declarations.[27] China's ambassador to the US, T. V. Soong (brother of Chiang's wife, Soong Mei-ling), participated in a meeting of the big three allies – the US, Soviet Union and Britain – marking the formation of the United Nations as a military alliance on 1 January 1942.

This catapulted China into the league of the US, the Soviet Union and Britain – even though both Britain and the Soviet Union had reservations about its inclusion. The Soviets, supporting the Communists, questioned the inclusion of Nationalist China in the declarations relating to the war in Europe since it had no stake there. But the US needed China against Japan and made it a party to the Four-Nation Moscow Declaration in October 1943.[28] In December 1943, President Roosevelt of the US, Prime Minister Churchill of Britain and Chiang Kai-shek met in Cairo, Egypt, where the Cairo Declaration was issued, assuring the complete restoration of Chinese territories occupied by Japan. In 1943, the US and Britain relinquished all treaty rights acquired on its soil by force to persuade China to intensify its war against Japan.

Within China, however, the Nationalists and the Communists were busier fighting each other than the Japanese. The US tried to mediate but with no success. Keen on enlisting the Soviet Union's help in the war against Japan, US President Roosevelt flew to Yalta for a meeting with the Soviet leader Joseph Stalin and Churchill. The resulting Yalta agreement of February 1945 allowed the big three to share the spoils of war after their anticipated victory. In Asia, Stalin persuaded Roosevelt to accept the return of the territories lost by Russia to Japan in the 1904 war. Concurrently, they agreed to recognize China's sovereignty over Manchuria – as long as the Soviets maintained control of its railway line and could use some ports. Chiang sent T. V. Soong and his foreign minister, Wang Shih-chieh, to Moscow to negotiate a treaty before attacking Japan, essentially reconfirming the Yalta deal. The Soviet Union agreed to recognize Chinese sovereignty over Manchuria and Xinjiang, while China agreed to give up its claim to Outer Mongolia.

When Germany surrendered in May 1945, the Soviet Union redirected its attention eastwards, attempting to capture as much of Manchuria as possible from Japan before its inevitable defeat. But the US pulverized Hiroshima and Nagasaki by unleashing its atom bombs upon them in August, prompting Japan's immediate surrender. On the very day of the bombing in Hiroshima, Soviet troops attacked Manchuria and continued their campaign for two weeks after Japan's capitulation. But the US and Britain were in no mood to see Manchuria under Soviet control. They compelled it to withdraw and return the region to China.

Chiang Kai-shek responded quickly by dispatching a large force to take control of the province. This prompted Stalin to go all-out to assist the Communist Party, which annihilated Chiang's troops. Manchuria became the graveyard of the Nationalist forces.

Nationalists vs Communists

The US attempted once again to mediate between the two parties. Yet both factions remained confident of military victory, intensifying the civil war. Frustrated by its failure at mediation, the US, with Japan defeated, reassessed China's strategic importance and decided against committing the kind of military force required to be effective in such a large country. It also did not believe China to be a threat to its regional interests, even if it fell to the Soviets. In early 1947, it abandoned efforts to bring the two parties together and withdrew its special ambassador, the celebrated general George C. Marshall. With the Americans gone, the communist forces marched rapidly southwards, capturing Beijing in January 1949 and Nanjing three months later. Chiang Kai-shek and his forces retreated to Canton before ultimately escaping to Taiwan in December of that year.

Mao declared the establishment of the People's Republic of China on 1 October 1949 – twenty-eight years since the formation of the Chinese Communist Party. The Soviet Union recognized it the following day, with other communist countries doing so in quick succession. India became the first non-communist country and Britain the first major western country to establish diplomatic relations, both in early 1950.

Soon after his victory in China, Mao spent two months in Moscow, returning only after securing the Treaty of Friendship, Alliance and Mutual Assistance in February 1950. Under the treaty, the Soviet Union promised to defend it against Japan and its allies. He also received clearance to invade Tibet with an assurance of support.

But what became of Tibet when the Manchu empire fell?

Tibet in a map of north India, 1916. It shows the border of north-east Kashmir passing through Aktagh, about 20 kilometres north of Karakoram Pass. Aksai Chin is depicted as a territory of Kashmir and Tibet as a part of the Chinese empire. The McMahon Line had not yet been made public.

TURKESTAN
KOKO-NOR
KAN-SU
CHINESE EMPIRE
EASTERN OR GREAT TIBET
D'YUL OR TIBET
SI-CHUEN
Pass of
Pom
BHOTAN
YUN-NAN
LUSHAY HILLS
UPPER BURMA
Shan States
Nau Country
INDO-CHINA
LOWER BURMA
BAY OF BENGAL
MOUTHS

9

An Independent Tibet

When Younghusband invaded Lhasa in 1904, Thubten Gyatso, the Thirteenth Dalai Lama, fled north to Urga (now Ulaanbaatar) in Mongolia. Arriving in November, he stayed as a guest of the highest lama of Mongolia, the Jetsun Dampa, where he was visited by Beijing-based diplomats from the US, Japan and Germany. However, suspicious that he was colluding with Russia, Britain advised its minister in Beijing, Ernest Satow, not to let him return to Lhasa.[1]

Once again, the Dalai Lama sent Dorjiev to St Petersburg to seek help. The tsar was non-committal, but the move irritated Britain, which delivered a sharp rebuke to the Dalai Lama through Beijing. India's governor-general, Minto, also summoned the Panchen Lama and warned him against joining Russia's conspiracies. Rumours that the Dalai Lama intended to return with an armed escort of Buryat Mongols, to which Dorjiev belonged, infuriated Britain even more. China threatened to depose him if he colluded with Russia.

With no solace from Russia and his hospitality in Urga running cold, the Dalai Lama relocated to the Kumbum monastery in Amdo in 1906. He stayed there for nearly two years, hoping for the situation to improve in Tibet. It was while he was there that Tibet's fate was sealed – in the Convention of 1907. Satow's successor, John Jordan, met the Dalai Lama's envoy, telling him that Britain–Tibet relations had improved since Younghusband's expedition, and that the Dalai Lama should return to Tibet.

But when the Dalai Lama travelled to Beijing in 1908, he only found ailing Manchu rulers and a government run by the British mission. He was told to return to Lhasa and present his case to the ambans. From his deathbed, the Guangxu emperor gave him a new seal, designating him 'Sincerely Obedient'. Two centuries earlier, the seal granted to the Fifth Dalai Lama had included more exalted and purely religious titles: 'Universal Ruler of the Buddhist Faith' and 'Holder of the Sceptre'.[2] An imperial order was also issued, commanding the Dalai Lama to obey the laws of the 'Sovereign State of China' and exhorting Tibetans to do the same.[3]

This denigrating treatment cannot be attributed to any newfound strength of the emperor. Both he and Empress Dowager Cixi were gravely ill, dying within a day of each other during the Dalai Lama's stay. Nor were the Manchus irreverent to him. On Cixi's request, he performed a ritual for her long life. He left Beijing in December 1908, after spending only two months there, and reached Lhasa the following year.

Tibet's condition had deteriorated during the Dalai Lama's five-year exile. China had exploited his absence to aggressively enforce its authority, appointing warlord Zhao Erfeng (Chao Erh-feng) as warden of the Marches – the mountainous terrain between Sichuan and Tibet – and as an additional amban to Tibet. He was nicknamed 'Zhao the Butcher' for his merciless persecution of the Khampas in Sichuan and the neighbouring Kham region of Tibet. Despite this, the British mission in Beijing reported that he enjoyed an excellent reputation. The Sichuan province saw a new governor – the warden's brother, Zhao Ersun (Chao Erh-sun). China asked for, and received, permission from the British to establish telegraph links between Beijing and Lhasa through Hong Kong and Kolkata, which became the established route for messages between the two capitals and soon of travel by Chinese officials.

Meanwhile, Zhao 'the Butcher' continued his predations against Tibet. In February 1910, his troops invaded Lhasa. The Dalai Lama appealed in vain to Russia for help before fleeing once again – this time to India. The Dalai Lama's flight further whetted China's appetite; there were even fanciful plans to invade India via Tibet. A British official, H. C. Wilton, wrote that there were some – a small minority – in China who hoped that this would be possible: 'The present Chinese policy in Thibet includes, therefore, the building up of an effective fighting force of 40,000 Tibetans, stiffened by a small number of Chinese soldiers, and a coalition of China, Nepal, Thibet, Bhutan, and Sikkim against India.'[4] Zhao Erfeng created a new province in eastern Tibet, Xikang, that had traditionally served as the frontier between the two countries.

Britain gave shelter to the Dalai Lama in India and appointed Charles Bell, a diplomatic officer who had learnt Tibetan during his stay in Bhutan, as his interlocutor. But it refused to change its stand on Tibet's status. As a precautionary measure, it conveyed a 'friendly representation' to China to avoid any complications for neighbouring countries, especially one inconsistent with the Convention of 1906.[5] While sheltering the Dalai Lama, Britain informed both Russia and Japan of its actions, claiming that it had not been made aware of China's invasion and that the Dalai Lama would be provided shelter in accordance with his high rank. It also said that it had conveyed to China the necessity of maintaining an effective government in Tibet that Britain could engage with, in accordance with the agreement of 1906. Moreover, it told the Dalai Lama that Britain would not intervene in Tibet.

Britain's conciliatory policy encouraged the tottering regime in Beijing to depose the Dalai Lama, stripping him of his status as an incarnation, issuing an edict depriving him of all his titles and withdrawing imperial support to his Yellow Sect.[6] Britain's mild reaction elicited a fierce outburst from China, which launched into a litany of complaints against the Dalai Lama. China said that in the fifty days in Lhasa after his return, the Dalai Lama had not met the amban and cut off his (the amban's) transport and communication links with China. It denied that Zhao Erfeng had demolished monasteries, claiming that he had only destroyed one in retaliation against the killing of a Chinese official by its lamas. China also sent letters to the kings of Nepal and Bhutan, reminding them they were under its sovereignty and should not take instructions from 'bad people'.[7]

China's aggression, combined with the outbreak of violence in Tibet, impelled Britain to adopt a firmer stance. Cautioning China that the situation had escalated beyond control and indicating readiness to intervene if any British life or property were damaged, Britain stationed a small force on the border at Gnatong. This chastened China somewhat and, unable to find a substitute for the Dalai Lama, it appealed to Britain to let him return. Britain replied that it would not compel him to do so but continued to cooperate with China.

When the Manchu dynasty fell, Chinese soldiers in Tibet revolted against their commanders – not only killing some of them but also looting the locals. This sparked resistance across the country. Zhao Erfeng was assassinated in Chengdu, while the Chinese garrison at Batang in eastern Tibet faced a massacre. Two associates of the amban were killed, and all four members of the kashag, who had collaborated with the Chinese, were executed.

The collapse of the Manchus brought little change to China's imperial policy towards Tibet. Both the Nanjing and Beijing governments vied with each other to assert their claim. The provisional constitution framed by the Nanjing government in March 1912 listed Tibet as a province of China. In Beijing, Yuan Shikai issued a presidential order the following month, declaring the Mongolian, Tibetan, Manchu and Hui people to be national minorities who were all part of the territory of the new Republic of China. He set up a bureau in charge of Mongolian and Tibetan affairs and offered to send an envoy to the Dalai Lama for discussions. However, the Chinese position in Tibet had become untenable, leading Yuan Shikai to withdraw its troops. Rather than risk a land journey through the rebellious Kham province, he ordered their return through India – with Britain's help. China's official statement on this event is illustrative of the way China writes its history. The Chinese general in Lhasa communicated that peace had been restored in Tibet and his troops were returning via India – after fulfilling their mission and 'depositing' their weapons.[8]

Beijing also reached out to Nepal, inviting it to join the new republic of five nationalities formed by Yuan Shikai. Nepal declined, citing its status as a Hindu kingdom.[9] The amban also wrote to the king of Bhutan to acknowledge Chinese suzerainty.

The revolt in Tibet and expulsion of the Chinese forces reignited Britain's security concerns. It became evident that China was unable to control Tibet and its presence was fuelling unrest. But instead of advocating for Tibet's independence from China, it merely warned against the oppressive behaviour of Chinese officials, advising China not to interfere in the internal administration of the country. It also called for a written agreement on the number of troops China could station in Tibet. Until such an agreement was reached, all communications between China and Tibet via India would be suspended, except for the expelled Chinese troops allowed to return through India. China would be permitted to maintain a representative with a small armed escort in Lhasa.[10]

Amidst the chaos, China did not respond. An internal memo prepared by the India Office in London for the British cabinet described the dilemma of sustaining a benign Chinese control over Tibet:

> [T]he Tibetans have ejected the present Amban, stated that they do not require one, and apparently formally declared their independence. How then are the Chinese to assert the rights which we have recognised? ... The only answer is apparently to offer the Chinese our good offices to induce the Dalai Lama to accept the Amban with an escort of say, 300 men, in return for Chinese acceptance of the Memorandum.[11]

The memo expressed hope that the Dalai Lama would accept the proposal as a good bargain.

Yuan Shikai decided to make amends with the Dalai Lama. In October 1912, he sent him a message restoring his temporal and ecclesiastical title of 'Loyal and Submissive Vice-Regent, Great Good, and Self-Existent Buddha', urging him to take over the affairs of the country as one of the 'five races united into one family'. The Dalai Lama replied that he had not asked for his former rank, stating his intention to exercise both temporal and ecclesiastical powers in Tibet.[12]

The period from 1904 to 1912, during which China tried to assert its control over Tibet, was one of strife within Tibet and disturbance along India's north-east frontier. Once the Chinese were thrown out in 1912, Tibet became relatively quiet, while China sank into chaos.

The Dalai Lama's Return

Upon his return to Lhasa in January 1913, the Dalai Lama soon set about reorganizing the government, declaring that he and his predecessors had only maintained a patron–lama relationship with the Manchu emperors. He decreed that 'documents and decrees which the Han brought to Tibet must not be observed'.[13]

A declaration was issued invoking Lord Buddha to assert the legitimacy of his government: 'Lord Buddha, from the glorious country of India, prophesied that the reincarnations of Avalokiteśvara, through successive rulers from the early religious kings to the present day, would look after the welfare of Tibet.' It characterized the historical relationship between the Buddhist rulers of China, Mongolia and Manchuria and the lamas of Tibet as purely ecclesiastical: 'During the time of Genghis Khan and Altan Khan of the Mongols, the Ming dynasty of the Chinese, and the Qing dynasty of the Manchus, Tibet and China cooperated on the basis of benefactor and priest relationship.' As for China's invasion of Sichuan and Yunnan, the declaration said it represented a failed attempt to colonize Tibet: 'The Chinese intention of colonizing Tibet under the patron-priest relationship has faded like a rainbow in the sky'.[14]

While Tibet views these decrees as a declaration of independence, China dismisses them as rebellion against the feudal Qing dynasty, not secession from the motherland. It attributes the Dalai Lama's actions to British instigation.

But how could the Dalai Lama defend his weak country from a powerful opponent like China? He understood he needed international support. In 1913, Tibet signed a treaty with Mongolia in Urga declaring that they had freed themselves from Manchu rule, separated from China and become independent states. They proclaimed and recognized each other's sovereignty and asserted mutual friendship based on the Buddhist faith, agreeing not to permit other countries to interfere in their internal affairs and to assist each other against dangers from both within and beyond.[15] Contemporary China deems the treaty illegal and maintains its 1924 agreement with the Soviet Union, which declared Outer Mongolia a part of China.

The Dalai Lama also approached Britain and Russia for help. He wrote to King George V: 'We pray that, if it be possible, Your Majesty and the Emperor of Russia will consult together, and that you and he will each depute a representative to Lhasa, for the benefit of Tibet, and that the Power, both Temporal and Spiritual, may remain with the Tibetans themselves.'[16] Britain, however, refused to budge from its old line on Tibet. In his reply, the king reiterated that Tibet was under Chinese 'suzerainty':

> Your Holiness is already aware that my government is adopting means to effect a settlement between your country and China and to establish good relations between the British Empire, China and Tibet. I trust that the meeting between representatives which is to take place at Simla will be fruitful and good results will bring peace to the people of Tibet.[17]

The meeting to which King George referred was proposed by Britain to ensure Tibet did not secede from China during the upheaval of the Manchu dynasty's fall. Britain was well aware that neither China nor Tibet was party to the Anglo-Russian Convention of 1907. It decided to address this lacuna through a meeting at which both would be present. China accepted the invitation because, as

Chinese historians admit, 'At that time, the government of the Republic of China had not been widely recognised internationally. Various political forces in China were not unified. Politically, the government of the Republic of China needed recognition and support from powers in the world.'[18]

Defining Tibet's Status and Limits

The Dalai Lama's assertiveness in Lhasa had become a concern for Britain. With his diplomatic outreach, he had been solidifying Tibet's international standing and asserting its authority along the Sichuan province border. The Viceroy of India reported ongoing conflict after the Tibetans had expelled the Chinese from Lhasa, highlighting security implications and proposing a conference with China and Tibet on 'the future status and limits of Tibet'.[19] Secretary of State for India Lord Crewe wrote to Foreign Secretary Edward Grey, advising a new agreement with China in view of the change in government there. Britain feared that an independent Dalai Lama would once again turn to Russia and decided to persuade Tibet to accept Chinese suzerainty – in return for some guarantees from China.

The tripartite conference was held in Simla from 1913 to 1914. Lt. Col. Henry McMahon, who was serving as foreign secretary of British India, represented Britain. Lonchen Shatra Paljor Dorje attended from Lhasa. China's representation posed a challenge as both Yuan Shikai in Beijing and Sun Yat-sen in Canton had set up parallel governments, and other countries had recognized one or the other. Just a week before the start of the meeting, in October 1913, Britain accorded recognition to Yuan Shikai's regime and requested Chen I-Fan (called Ivan Chen by the British), a diplomat who had worked earlier at the Chinese embassy in London to be present at the meeting.

The Tibetan delegation came to secure recognition of its independence, along with the delineation of the Tibet–China border in the east, revision of trade agreements of 1893 and 1908 and the rescission of the Britain–China agreement of 1906. It also demanded that the Dalai Lama be allowed to appoint monks for monasteries in China and Mongolia that accepted his leadership and provide alms to Tibetan monasteries.

Chen I-Fan sought to reaffirm Tibet as part of China, with authority to station officials and troops and control over its foreign, military and government affairs.

Negotiations progressed slowly. By February 1914, the delegates agreed to divide Tibet into two parts: Outer Tibet, covering central and western Tibet, including Lhasa, Shigatse and Chamdo; and Inner Tibet, comprising Amdo and parts of Kham. China agreed to recognize Outer Tibet as autonomous, provided it could station some officials and troops in Lhasa. Chen initialled the agreement on 27 April 1914, while the other two parties signed it. However, China later rejected the agreement, refusing to accept the border between Inner Tibet and China as defined by it.

Britain and Tibet held separate negotiations regarding India–Tibet border issues and agreed to what came to be known as the McMahon Line along the Himalayan watershed, establishing the border between Assam province in India and Tibet. This agreement was signed on 3 July 1914, without Chinese participation. India recognizes this agreement as the basis of its boundary with Tibet, while China rejects both the agreement and the border defined by it, maintaining that the treaty violated the 'thousand'-year-old traditional boundary between India and China along the southern foothills of the Himalaya. Today, China alleges that the McMahon Line gave India 90,000 square kilometres of Chinese territory.

Thus, the Simla meeting produced two agreements: the first, the tripartite agreement signed by Tibet and Britain and initialled by China regarding the autonomy of Outer Tibet, and the second between Britain and Tibet on the India–Tibet border in Arunachal Pradesh. China later rejected both.

The reality was that China was in the midst of a civil war and Yuan Shikai's authority was confined to Beijing and its precincts. Still, he took advantage of Britain's rivalry with Russia to hold out on ratifying the tripartite agreement. Britain's primary concern was gaining Russia's consent to the agreements. Edward Grey wrote, 'I do not at all like the idea of signing with Tibet alone without China. It is too flagrant a violation of the Anglo-Russian Agreement.'[20] Viceroy Hardinge responded by saying that China was holding out on signing the agreement because it was banking on Russia rejecting it.

Britain kept Moscow informed of the progress and ensured that the conference's outcome was within the framework of the Convention of 1907. McMahon wanted a British representative to be stationed in Lhasa to maintain peace between Tibet and China. But this was not permitted under the 1907 convention. Efforts to persuade Russia by citing its deal with Mongolia, where it had extracted concessions from China, failed. Russia rejected the argument, linking it with Tibet and Britain did not press the matter. The outbreak of the First World War in 1914 delayed Britain's pursuit of the border settlement with China, while Tibet turned its attention to the Chinese occupation of Kham province.

In 1917, a Tibetan force invaded Chamdo, Kham's capital, and advanced towards the Yunnan province. China, struggling with internal chaos, panicked and appealed to Britain for help. Eric Teichman, the British vice-consul in Beijing, was sent to Tibet to mediate on the basis of a frontier line that 'corresponded very closely to the old historical frontier between China and Tibet'. But China refused to ratify this local agreement, even though it accepted the frontier as the de facto boundary.[21] After the First World War, Britain resumed efforts to settle the unfinished China–Tibet border, though talks broke down in 1921.

Meanwhile, the newly independent Tibetan lamas became increasingly assertive, demanding the expulsion of the British from Tibet. The Dalai Lama struggled to balance relations with Britain and China in order to keep both at bay. But his own problems were equally grave, including a dispute with the Panchen Lama, who fled to China in 1923.

Chiang Kai-shek's Nationalist government in Nanjing declared both Tibet and Mongolia as parts of China and set up an office, the Commission for Mongolian and Tibetan Affairs. Chiang also persuaded the Panchen Lama to establish an office in Nanjing. The Dalai Lama countered by claiming that Tibet owned several monasteries in China where it sent lamas to teach Buddhism. Since the collapse of the Manchu dynasty, however, the new government had not permitted this. He consequently wrote to the British seeking intervention.

Tibet and China at War

In 1930, another military conflict erupted between Tibet and China in Sichuan. The Chinese warlord, Liu Wen-hui, became involved in a dispute between monasteries affiliated with the Dalai Lama and the Panchen Lama. While the Tibetan forces initially saw some success, they were soon overwhelmed by the vastly superior Chinese. The Dalai Lama asked Britain to send a representative to Lhasa to discuss the Chinese threat and relations with Britain, as well to procure some weapons.

Britain sent its political officer in Sikkim, Colonel Weir. Secretary of State for India William Benn expressed scepticism regarding Tibet's capacity to pay for weapons. So, he insisted on maintaining the territorial status quo on the Sino-Tibetan frontier until a formal settlement was reached, emphasizing that Britain had incurred certain obligations towards Tibet while asserting, 'The general basis on which we have proceeded has been that Tibet should be recognised as an autonomous state under Chinese suzerainty.'[22] But China could not pursue its gains, since it was confronted with a much more serious threat in the north – from Japan. Chiang Kai-shek was keen to maintain peace with Tibet. Liu Wen-hui, who was effectively an independent ruler, was also faced with a revolt by his nephew. In 1932, he signed a treaty with Tibet under which the Yangtse River was accepted as the border between Sichuan and Tibet.[23]

Another incident on the Indian border highlighted Tibet's assertive stance of independence during this period. In 1930, when a dispute erupted on the Almora border as Tibet claimed Niland

and Jadhang, a compromise was reached thanks to the political officer in Sikkim who advised accepting the claim in exchange for Tibet recognizing Gomukh and Gangotri as part of India. Tibet accepted the proposal, and the matter was resolved. Since there was no Chinese presence in Lhasa at that time, China was not brought into the proceedings – even by Britain.[24]

Death of the Dalai Lama and the Interregnum

In 1933, the Thirteenth Dalai Lama passed away, plunging Tibet into political uncertainty, as it navigated the intrigues of the long interregnum of selecting a new Dalai Lama. The Tsongdu, Tibet's national assembly, appointed Reting Rimpoche as the regent, though he was only nineteen, seemingly chosen by drawing lots among the three leading lamas.

Following the Dalai Lama's death, Chiang Kai-shek decided to review Chinese policy towards Tibet. Orders were issued to stop hostilities while the government tried to work out a peaceful settlement of the border. Additionally, he instructed that the property of the Tibetans in the Tachin Monastery be restored.[25] The Peking newspaper *Shih Chieh Jin Pao* advocated for steps to improve relations with Tibet, and remove misunderstandings, advising against sending troops and instead training Tibetan troops and selecting the amban from among honest people. It also called for improvement in transport and communication links and that the demarcation of the India–Tibet border be taken up with Britain.[26]

Chiang Kai-shek sent an envoy, Huang Musong, to Lhasa in 1934 to convey condolences on the Dalai Lama's death. Huang journeyed through East Tibet, while his advance party, bearing a substantial sum of money and many gifts, travelled via India. Huang stayed in Lhasa for about six months, during which time he presented a draft agreement asserting Tibetans as one of China's five races. The proposal included the stationing of a Chinese amban in Lhasa, with an armed escort, and stipulated that all senior appointments be approved by China. The kashag sought British involvement, but Huang found this unacceptable, causing the agreement to fall through. Huang also offered a new seal and title for the departed Dalai Lama, which the kashag turned down.

On his return to China, Huang claimed to have successfully re-instated China's authority in Lhasa. He reported that – contrary to some beliefs – Britain wielded no special influence in Tibet, confined by the limits of established agreements. He refuted reports of Tibet severing relations with China and declaring independence, though he acknowledged that the Indian rupee was the standard currency in Tibet, alongside Tibetan notes and the Sichuan 'half-dollar'. Japanese goods dominated the market, followed by British and Nepalese products, with Buddhist articles, Mandarin dresses and official robe ornaments being the only Chinese ones. He also noted that hardly anyone could read or understand Chinese.[27]

To this day, China asserts that Huang had 'supervised' the setting up of the transitional government, reaffirming China's 'harmonious sovereignty' under the Nationalist government. He had demanded renewal of Tibet's tributary status as it was under Manchu rule, including the return of the ambans and the transfer of defence and foreign affairs to the Mongolian and Tibetan Affairs Commission in Beijing. Chinese records claim that Tibet agreed to these terms on the condition of non-annexation as a province of China, which Tibet denies, maintaining that it had demanded the return of its territories east of the Drichu (Yangtse) River and border demarcation. For this, it agreed to resume negotiations and host a Chinese envoy in Lhasa – but refused to allow Chinese troops to be stationed in Tibet.

Huang returned to China via India, leaving two of his men behind in Lhasa, much to Tibetan displeasure. One of them died soon after, and the other's refusal to leave prompted Tibet to request a British liaison office in Lhasa. Consequently, Basil Gould, the political officer in Sikkim, visited Lhasa and opened a mission in 1936. The second Chinese official left in 1938.

Meanwhile, the Tibetan government kept trying to find the reincarnation of the Thirteenth Dalai Lama. The regent and monks settled on a boy in the Qinghai province, but the region was under the control of the warlord Ma Bufang, who had to be bribed so that the young boy could travel to Tibet – a sum China claims to have paid.

In 1940, Chiang Kai-shek sent Wu Zhongxin (Wu Chung-tsin), the director of Tibetan Affairs in the Mongolian and Tibetan Affairs Commission, to attend the enthronement ceremony of the new Dalai Lama. Discrepancies exist between Tibetan and Chinese accounts regarding Wu's role at the ceremony. Tibetan sources assert that the Chinese man participated like other foreign dignitaries, but China claims that Wu presided over the ceremony and approved the new incarnation after due scrutiny. For the beleaguered Chiang Kai-shek, stationing a representative in Lhasa was a proud nationalist achievement, as he could proclaim that Chinese sovereignty over Tibet had been reasserted.

China accuses Britain of obstructing its envoy's mission and blames it for Tibet's resistance. Wang and Gyaincain write that Basil Gould 'rushed' to Lhasa under the pretence of attending the ceremony but actually aimed 'to monitor Wu Zhongxin and undermine the prestige of the Chinese Government in Tibet'.[28] This allegation seems churlish considering Wu and his eighteen-member delegation had travelled to Lhasa from Nanjing via Hong Kong and Kolkata, territories under British rule – they avoided the Chinese overland route because it was arduous and unsafe. The ceremonial Chinese presence in Tibet in this period was sustained by the British, which also bolstered the Chiang Kai-shek government in China.

The Panchen Lama was living in exile in Nanjing when the Dalai Lama died. Both Britain and Chiang Kai-shek were keen to have him return to Lhasa, but the regent, Reting Rimpoche, and others resisted. Even though Britain managed to persuade the Tibetans, the Panchen Lama insisted on returning only with a Chinese military escort, a request declined by Tibet. He subsequently died in China in 1937. Tibet wanted the Panchen Lama's successor to be selected in Lhasa; however, his entourage made the selection in China, endorsed by Chiang Kai-shek in the absence of the Golden Urn.

Britain's Delicate Diplomacy

In February 1941, with Britain facing difficulties in sending supplies to China by sea due to the war, Chiang Kai-shek proposed constructing a road from India through Arunachal Pradesh and the Szechuan province. Britain hesitated on the feasibility or utility of such a road, and Tibet objected to the use of its territory for transit to China. When the United States entered the war in December, Britain started to take the proposal seriously, but Tibet blocked the survey, insistent on remaining neutral in the war. It set up a foreign affairs bureau to deal with the British and Chinese representatives in Lhasa rather than directly with the kashag.

Britain and China exerted pressure on Tibet to accede to the road proposal. Chiang Kai-shek asked the warlords of Qinghai, Sichuan and Yunnan to initiate military action against Tibet and provided assistance for this purpose, leading to another round of border skirmishes. Nevertheless, British and American intervention prevented further escalation. China denied any intent to invade Tibet, with T. V. Soong assuring Churchill in Washington that though Tibet was part of China, it had no plans to invade the region.[29] Tibet eased its trade embargo on China but continued to refuse military equipment transit.

British Foreign Minister Anthony Eden tried to reconcile Tibet's rejection of Chinese overlordship with his country's policy of propping up China as an ally in the Second World War. He outlined his government's policy toward Tibet–China relations for the benefit of both China and the US, as also his own officials. Britain wanted to maintain the 'practical autonomy' of Tibet because it was important to 'the security of India and to the tranquillity of India's north-east frontier'. Eden wrote that Chinese suzerainty over Tibet had been recognized on the condition that Tibet would be regarded as autonomous, adding, 'Any unconditional admission of Chinese suzerainty should be avoided.'[30]

Once the Second World War had ended, Britain made another attempt to settle the Tibet–China border issue. Chiang Kai-shek, who had proved a useful ally in the war, sought rewards. He was also eager to prove that he had brought Tibet back into China's fold. Shen Tsung-lien was swiftly dispatched to Lhasa to hold talks on formalizing an arrangement on an agreed frontier between China and Tibet 'with a large measure of autonomy for Tibet'.[31] Hugh Richardson, the head of the British mission in Lhasa from 1946 to 1950, dismissed the Chinese proposal as a desire to extend its empire, while Olaf Caroe, the head of India's foreign office, suggested that Britain should not allow Tibet to become a source of friction with China.

Despite its own civil war between the Communists and the Nationalists, China kept up its hysteria over Tibet. The Chinese newspaper in Nanjing, *Ch'ien Hsien Jih Pao*, expressed China's concern over losing its influence in Tibet with customary outrage:

> Because of Tibet's proximity to India very frightening things are going on behind the political scene. Britain still has political agents in Lhassa. They have given a Diesel engined electric generator for the use of some members of the Tibetan nobility, with a view to winning friendship. They have set up schools and businesses to carry on economic aggression. There are Lamas who do not know Chinese but who are fluent in English. From the railhead in India, it only takes just over 20 days to get to Lhassa, whereas the journey from China takes 2 or 3 months. These facts have all encouraged the growth of a centrifugal tendency in Tibet and have helped to make Tibet lean towards Britain. Britain has not yet given up her right to station troops in Gyantse. When we look at the outrage that happened at Kowloon, we feel extreme alarm about the future of Tibet. Co-operation between the Chinese Government and the Tibetan people is necessary if we are to remove this alarming threat.[32]

The Asian Relations Conference

In March and April of 1947, the Asian Relations Conference was organized in New Delhi under the leadership of Jawaharlal Nehru, who had become the interim prime minister in September 1946 while the country was still under British rule. A four-member delegation from Tibet participated, along with twenty-six other countries. The backdrop for the conference featuring a map of Asia showed Tibet as an independent country. Mingling with delegates from Asia and Africa and observers from the US, UK, Australia and the UN brought great pride to the Tibetan delegates. Objections were raised by the representatives of the Chinese Kuomintang government to the presence of the Tibetan delegation and the depiction of Tibet on the map.

Nehru's response to China's complaint was ambivalent. As a scholar of world history, he was familiar with Tibet's past. In his 1934 book *Glimpses of World History*, Nehru had written that Tibet had been occupied by China under the Manchu ruler Chien Lung (Qianlong) and incorporated into the Manchu empire.[33] This refrain continued in *The Discovery of India*, which was written a decade later. He referred to his travels to the 'frontiers of Tibet', Buddhism's spread to 'Tibet, China and Mongolia' from India, cooperation between 'Indian, Chinese and Tibetan scholars' of Buddhism and the ancient Nalanda University, which drew students from 'China, Japan, and Tibet'. In all these references, Nehru placed Tibet on the same footing as other countries of the region, treating it as distinct from China.

At the conference, however, he struck a compromise. He let the Tibetan delegation stay but replaced the map with one depicting Tibet as part of China. At the time, he commented:

Unable to understand Chinese attitude to Asian Conference when conference organizers have fully explained the position, which is in no way injurious to Chinese interests. Non-official cultural conference cannot be expected to consider political niceties. We are unable to say whom Tibetans represent till they come.[34]

In his inaugural address, while welcoming delegates to the conference, he named China first, referring to it as 'that great country to which Asia owes so much and from which so much is expected'. He then greeted India's neighbouring countries, 'Afghanistan, Tibet, Nepal, Bhutan, Burma, and Ceylon to whom we look especially for co-operation and close and friendly intercourse'.[35]

Independent India: An Opportunity for Tibet?

The Fourteenth Dalai Lama, Tenzin Gyatso, was still in his teens when the world underwent tectonic changes after the Second World War. He had not completed his religious ordainment, which required him to pass a series of rigorous theological tests before becoming the head of the government. The caretaker government – run by the regent, the kashag and the national assembly – was alert to the changes sweeping through its two giant neighbours, India and China. If anything, Tibet was impetuous; suspicious of both, it saw an opportunity for national resurgence.

During the Dalai Lama's minority, other leaders kept up a merry struggle for power. The regent, Reting Rimpoche, was replaced by the more elderly Taktra Rimpoche, and in April 1947 Lhasa was rattled by a revolt at the Sera monastery led by Reting Rimpoche with suspected Chinese support. An attempt on the regent's life was swiftly put down by Tibetan forces – though the violence left the public horrified. Reting Rimpoche was arrested and brought to Lhasa, where he died in custody amidst rumours of foul play. The British embassy in Nanjing stated that while China's support for the insurrection could not be confirmed, Chinese press reports showed a clear bias in favour of Reting and the rebelling monks.

On the eve of India's independence, Britain sent a message to Tibet informing that the new Indian government would inherit all its treaty rights as the successor state, but that it would continue to 'take a friendly interest in the prosperity of the Tibetan people and the maintenance of Tibetan autonomy'. Tibet now reposed its faith in Britain for protection, expecting it to help against both India and China, and requested its aid in securing the return of the 'Tibetan territories' from India. A missive was delivered through the Indian Mission in Lhasa and the office in Gangtok. Contrary to the accepted Tibetan practice, it was written in English and did not bear a signature or seal. As it was not in the official format, the political officer in Sikkim wanted to return it. Regardless, both offices transmitted it.[36] The message read:

> We would like to express our gratitude for your message which states that His Majesty's Government will continue to consider any further maintenance of Tibet's Independence and common welfare of her people as they have done so hitherto … Regarding our request to return of excluded Tibetan territories gradually included into India and regarding trade relations affecting general economic welfare of Tibet we have discussed the matter with Government of India when India was under British administration. And it becomes [necessary that] Government of Tibet must continue the negotiations with new Government of India in near future. Hence, we hope that His Majesty's Government will also support in achieving our desire.[37]

The British High Commission did not respond to Tibet's message, informing the Indian government that it had no desire to get involved in controversial issues between India and Tibet.

Tibet appeared to perceive independent India as potentially weak and divided, presenting the perfect opportunity to recover certain territories. Leslie Fry of the British High Commission speculated that Tibet could try to play China and India against each other and recommended that Britain remain neutral. Correspondingly, Tibet seems to have sent a similar letter to China, seeking the return of its traditional lands.[38]

B. N. Mullick, the head of India's intelligence agency, noted that Tibet's claim adversely affected India's sympathy towards Tibet: '[T]his unfounded and ill-advised claim made by the Tibetan government resulted in the temporary loss of a certain amount of Indian sympathy for Tibet'.[39] Tibet's demand for hard currency from India for its exports, primarily wool, further strained relations. Eighty per cent Tibet's wool exports went to India and the remainder to China. Tibetan traders sold it in India for rupees, which was then exported by Indian traders to the United States, resulting in Tibet earning no hard currency. It now insisted on receiving hard currency from India to buy gold from the United States.

At the same time, Tibet sought to buy arms from India, particularly rifles and ammunition. The latter supplied some but refused to sell mortars and anti-aircraft weapons.

India retained the British representative for political affairs in Lhasa, Hugh Richardson, as the head of the Indian Mission. Its first communication to Tibet requested recognition as the successor state of British India and ratification of the 1914 Simla convention.

Tibet Asserts (1947–1949)

In November 1947, Tibet sent a trade delegation led by Tsipon Shakabpa to India, Britain, the United States and China. It travelled on Tibetan passports – a first for the country. China protested immediately, but India clarified that Tibetans did not need passports for entry. However, the Indian government refused to entertain the commercial requests of the delegation until it was recognized by the latter as the successor state of British India. With no mandate on this issue, the delegation deferred it to Lhasa. India made no reference to Tibet's earlier territorial demands. The delegation also demanded US $2 million as outstanding payment for exports,[40] which India rejected, asserting that Tibet's exports primarily went to India, where the wool was repacked before being re-exported.

The delegation left for China in January 1948, entering on Chinese passports issued in Kolkata. The Chiang Kai-shek government insisted that the delegation sign its new constitution declaring Tibet as a province of China. Upon refusal, it was detained until the new constitution had been adopted. Later, China asked Tibet to send a representative to the new Chinese national assembly, which the latter refused.

China insisted on the delegation travelling to the United States and Britain on Chinese passports; yet, after declaring their intention to return to India, once they reached Hong Kong, the delegation obtained British and American visas and travelled on Tibetan passports. The US embassy claimed that its visa had been issued on plain paper.

China kept close track of the Tibetan delegation. In Washington, its ambassador sought to attend the meetings between the Tibetan delegation and US officials. But the delegation refused. To avoid acrimony with China, the US government arranged an 'informal' meeting at the State Department, without granting the Tibetans a call on President Truman.

In London, the British Foreign Office initially objected to the visit, with the Commonwealth Relations Office arguing that Britain's relations with Tibet were governed by the Simla Convention. It was the intervention of Sir Basil Gould, the retired political officer in Sikkim, which facilitated its reception as a trade delegation and thereby a meeting with the lord chamberlain on behalf of the king. A request by the Chinese ambassador to accompany it was ignored but Britain kept him informed in 'very general terms'.[41] As for the effectiveness of the meetings, though, the American historian Melvyn C. Goldstein reveals: 'The Tibetans were treated courteously, but neither of the two Western countries offered them any new political support. They both acknowledged by their treatment that Tibet possessed some degree of international identity independent of China, but they refused to treat Tibet as a fully independent polity.'[42]

The delegation returned to India in January 1949. By then, the sensitive successor-state issue had been resolved, and Tibet received some assistance from India. This included purchasing machinery and conducting a preliminary survey of mineral resources. Tibet also wanted to import gold through India, which was hesitant for fear of it being smuggled back, but eventually yielded to relentless requests and released US $250,000 for the purchase of American gold bullion. This was carried to India and sent on mules to Tibet.

China's Looming Invasion

As the civil war in China intensified, the Tibetan government became concerned about its fallout. In July 1949, the kashag expelled the Chinese representative, Chen Xizhang, and asked Chinese personnel working in schools and hospitals to leave. These moves were denounced by the Chinese Communist Party. Then in November, a month after the communist takeover, Tibet conveyed a strong message, warning against any border crossings and expressing a desire to open negotiations for the return of the territories taken by China 'some years back'.

Such provocation could not have come at a more inopportune moment. The Communist Party was fired up by an urge to recover China's imperial glory, threatening to attack neighbouring countries on the pretext of liberating them from capitalism and imperialism. In addition to Tibet and Xinjiang, the Communist Party's map of China included parts of Korea, Vietnam, Mongolia, Myanmar, Malaysia, India, Nepal, Sikkim and Bhutan. The *Hsin Hwa Pao* newspaper ran an editorial stating:

> The affair of expelling the Han Chinese and Kuomintang officials at Lhasa was a plot undertaken by the local Tibetan authorities through the instigation of the British imperialists and their lackey the Nehru administration of India. The purpose of this anti-Chinese affair is to prevent the people in Tibet from being liberated by the Chinese People's Liberation Army.[43]

The Tibetan government was not unaware of these renewed threats, recognizing the ominous portents these dramatic Chinese victories held for its independence. Many Tibetans realized that their forces were in no position to confront those of the Chinese; some hoped that China would invade Taiwan before Tibet. India's political officer in Sikkim, Harishwar Dayal, visited Lhasa twice in 1949 to discuss Tibet's request for military assistance. While India supplied some arms and military training, they were woefully short of the Tibetan government's perceived needs, as the latter wanted to increase its army from 13,000 to 100,000 men.

In December 1949, Tibet appealed to Britain and the United States for support in securing membership in the United Nations.

Drawing attention to the 'impending threat of Communist invasion', the kashag implored them to help preserve Tibet's 'independence and freedom' and secure its place as a member of the United Nations. There is no indication if this request was made to India as well. The British high commissioner sought the views of Foreign Secretary K. P. S. Menon, who told him that Tibet had not approached India.[44]

Soon after seizing power, Mao set three targets for his forces: Hainan, Taiwan and Tibet. In September 1949, the commander in chief of the People's Liberation Army (PLA), Zhu De, announced at a party meeting the decision to 'liberate' the whole of China's territory, including Tibet. This was incorporated into the Party's Common Programme and approved unanimously by the National People's Conference.[45] The new Chinese government called upon Tibet to send a delegation to Beijing to negotiate the peaceful liberation of Tibet. Soon, the Chinese forces invaded the Gansu, Qinghai and Xinjiang provinces. The young Panchen Lama and his entourage bolstered the communists, refusing to flee to Taiwan with Chiang Kai-shek and instead pledged their loyalty to the new regime in China.

Reports speculating China's invasion of Tibet also started to appear in the media shortly after the communist win. The *Manchester Guardian* stated in November 1949 that it was likely to occur in the summer of 1950.[46]

Tibet decided to send diplomatic missions to Nepal, India, the US and the UK to seek their support, especially for its UN membership bid. Britain turned down the request, indicating that admission into the UN would be subject to the approval of the Security Council – which was sure to be vetoed. It advised Tibet, therefore, to reach out to India and the US. After the US also refused to receive the delegation, these plans were abandoned. It then agreed to hold talks with China, asking for them to be organized in Hong Kong. Once again Shakabpa was appointed to lead the delegation. Tibet also launched its own broadcasting station, Radio Lhasa, to counter Communist China's propaganda.

Shakabpa's mandate was to secure an assurance from China that it would respect Tibet's territorial integrity and independence and avoid meddling in the Dalai Lama's rule. China assented to send a representative to Hong Kong – though only to escort the delegation to China, where the talks would take place. The Tibetan delegation arrived in India in March 1950 but could not travel to Hong Kong because Britain rescinded the visas initially granted on their Tibetan passports and advised them against the journey.

Britain also asked the US to consult the Government of India prior to any action. The US accordingly informed Tibet that it 'should first ask GOI for additional aid and if refused then ask GOI [for] friendly cooperation by permitting the passage of aid it wanted to secure from abroad'.[47]

With its delegation unable to travel to China, the Tibetan government requested that the talks be held in India, which was rejected by China.

Early India–China Exchanges about Tibet

India was confronted with the Tibet problem soon after gaining independence, still grappling with the aftermath of the country's partition and war with Pakistan. The Chinese Communist Party did not take kindly to Jawaharlal Nehru championing freedom movements across Asia. Its party-controlled mouthpieces accused him of being a hireling of Anglo-American imperialism, leading the anti-communist movement in Asia, and claimed that the Indian 'bourgeoisie' harboured designs on Tibet, Sikkim and Bhutan.

Nehru had appointed Kavalam Madhava Panikkar, an erudite minister who had served the princely states of Bikaner and Patiala, as the ambassador to China. Panikkar travelled first to Nanjing, the capital of the Nationalist government. When the Communist Party seized power, he advised Nehru to recognize their regime. Nehru did not need any prodding; his disappointing visit to the US in 1949, where he observed strong anti-communist sentiment and a willingness to back colonial and authoritarian countries in opposition to it, had made him eager for allies who shared his principles. Nehru stood for the freedom of all subjugated countries of Asia and Africa, determined for India not to be identified with colonialism and keen to develop close relations with China and Russia, as they claimed to share this ideal.

Panikkar, on the other hand, soon became infatuated with Mao's party. The party's hospitality towards him, coupled with its military claims, had left him enthralled, and he took it upon himself to promote the regime. He advised Nehru to visit China and bought into the peace and friendship proclamations with India, accepting its territorial claims unquestioningly, overlooking – even condoning – the brutalities of the government against its own people. He pleaded that the communists were 'overwhelmed by the immensity of the problems facing them' and displayed childlike excitement for the revolution: 'The spirit here is something magnificent and it will be of the greatest benefit to us, if some of our younger men could come and see what is happening in China.'[48] The Communist Party could not have asked for a better ambassador.

All critical Chinese statements went unreported, and hints of hostility overlooked. Repeated references to Nehru as the running dog of imperialism were glossed over. Panikkar also chose not to question China's claim to Tibet or its stated goal of exporting communism abroad, readily accepting its argument that such interference in the affairs of other countries was necessary to counter America. Even so, his attitude to the Chinese communists was not without contradictions. He proclaimed that China's government was not truly communist, rather an 'effective coalition'. At the same time, he had nothing but admiration for communism, going on to describe one of its leaders who befriended him as a 'Communist par excellence'. The violent expulsion of the Kuomintang leadership from the mainland raised no doubts or alarms in Panikkar's mind about the Communist Party's intentions.

In June 1950, Panikkar informed Delhi of China's eagerness to bring Taiwan and Tibet into its fold. An attack on Taiwan was imminent, but military action against Tibet would likely only occur if it did not respond to the offered autonomy. A month later, he said that the Chinese were keen on peaceful negotiations with Tibet and cautioned India against getting unsolicited advice. He accused the Tibetans of stalling negotiations and suggested that India should only counsel China if Tibet put up serious opposition that led to a prolonged conflict.[49]

Tibet approached Hugh Richardson, the sole foreign representative in Lhasa, asking him to request Indian intervention and use its friendly relations with China to stop the impending invasion. It also hoped to secure India's help in arranging a meeting between Shakabpa and the Chinese ambassador in Delhi. India's external affairs ministry asked Panikkar to tell the Chinese that the Tibetan delegation was waiting in India for a visa from the British to travel to Hong Kong. It asked him to reassure China that India held no interest in Tibet; in fact, it was among the first countries to recognize the Communist Party regime. India merely wanted China to settle its dispute with Tibet by peaceful means in accordance with the UN Charter. To China's allegations of foreign influence on Tibet, India clarified that no British or US missions were present in Lhasa, and the British officer heading the Indian mission was on transfer orders.

In the larger interest of world peace, the ministry implored Panikkar to approach Zhou Enlai, China's prime minister, even at the risk of being denied: 'We should like you to make representations urgently, on lines indicated, to Chou-En-Lai. We have taken into account the possibility of a rebuff but are satisfied that risk must be taken in larger interests of world peace.'[50]

Panikkar met Zhou Enlai on 22 August, who told him about China's sensitivity regarding Tibet, considering it an internal matter. It did not accept Tibet's semi-autonomous status or any limitation of Chinese sovereignty over it. Despite this blunt, categorical message, Panikkar informed Nehru that he believed China would not attack Tibet 'unless all efforts at peaceful negotiations have been exhausted'. China had ruled out talks in New Delhi and declared Tibetans a national minority. Its delegation would have to come to Beijing for talks. Panikkar himself was supportive of China's policy on Tibet, likening it to India's handling of Hyderabad, suggesting that China would use military force only if the Tibetans 'prove themselves too OBDURATE [*emphasis in the original*]'.[51]

A significant portion of his meeting with Zhou Enlai was dedicated to discussing Taiwan. Panikkar expressed concern about the global ramifications of a potential Chinese invasion and urged Nehru to join Britain in preventing the US from using Taiwan as an excuse to attack China. He also wanted India to persuade America to soften its opposition to Communist China's membership in the UN.

China welcomed India's conciliatory policy on Tibet, especially its statement indicating it did not have 'any political or territorial ambition in Tibet'. Then China enlarged the ambit of the peaceful impact of this policy: 'Not only China [but] other countries neighbouring China and India, such as Pakistan, Nepal etc., may also live peacefully together.'[52]

The Tibetan delegation, led by Shakabpa, met Prime Minister Nehru on 8 September, informing him that Tibetans wished to continue their religious way of life. Like every race, they had a right to their independence and looked to India for help. Shakabpa said that his delegation wanted to hold talks with the Chinese in Delhi – or at least in Hong Kong – since they would not have the freedom to fully negotiate in Beijing. He pointed out that China had come to India for the Simla Conference of 1914. Nehru replied that India could only give diplomatic support to Tibet. He said that if China invaded, neither India nor any other country could provide military assistance, as at the time of the Simla Conference China was weak – which was not the case now. He advised the delegation to accept China's proposal for talks in Beijing and not to demand full independence as 'talks could proceed only on the basis of Tibetan autonomy under the suzerainty tof China'.[53]

The following day, Shakabpa met K. P. S. Menon for a detailed discussion. He asked what India meant by 'autonomy' to which Menon replied ambiguously, stating that it was difficult to define exactly but it certainly would not include setting up diplomatic missions abroad. Shakabpa mentioned existing trade treaties and privileges that India enjoyed in Tibet, which Menon emphasized were based on treaties recognized by the Chinese government and India intended to maintain them. The former told Menon that the Chinese charge d'affaires in New Delhi had said that China intended to station troops in Tibet. Menon responded that China was precluded from doing so in 'Outer Tibet' under the Convention of 1914, but some arrangement might be feasible.[54]

Nehru shared Panikkar's concern about the outbreak of a world war if China attacked Taiwan and the US came to its rescue. This would bring the Soviet Union in support of China. Nehru directed Panikkar to notify the Chinese that India supported their claim to Taiwan but an invasion of the island would lead to a major war 'and possibly even a world war'. On Tibet, he conceded that China's invasion 'might well upset the present unsuitable equilibrium and let loose dangerous forces. Some of our border States will be affected ... But I am more concerned with the larger issues which this involves.' He expressed the hope that if China were to follow a path of wisdom it would result in a 'much more enduring settlement with goodwill and will redound to China's credit'.[55]

India was now confronted with the question of a Chinese attack on Tibet. In December 1949, at a meeting with the British high commissioner, India's secretary general of the external affairs ministry, Girija Shankar Bajpai,* ruled out military intervention and said that by accepting the Communist Party regime, India would be able to protect its interests in Tibet. But, according to the high commissioner, Bajpai also expressed his personal opinion that doing so would be unpleasant and was unlikely to make China friendlier to India or less dependent on the Soviet Union. Rather presciently, he said that a split between China and the USSR was possible – but not for several years. China was showing itself to be very hostile and wanted to stir up trouble in India and Southeast Asia in the hope of dominating the region, and any retreat on Tibet would also affect

---

* The external affairs ministry had a secretary general above the foreign secretary till 1963.

Nepal. Bajpai said that his advice to his prime minister would be along similar lines, though he expected strong opposition.[56]

At the United Nations, India supported Communist China's case to replace Nationalist China. India's ambassador to the United States, Nehru's sister Vijayalakshmi Pandit, told Panikkar to persuade the Chinese to tone down their rhetoric against the United States and refrain from openly threatening Tibet and its Southeast Asian neighbours until the question of its admission was resolved. But while China itself seemed unconcerned about such niceties, Nehru pleaded on its behalf in an interview with *U.S. News & World Report*:

> The Government of China is a national coalition with the Communist Party as a dominant partner. The coalition is composed of all sections of the nation, including some members of the Kuomintang who pledged to work for a common program for democratic advance. Mao Tse-tung [head of the Chinese Communist Government] has openly declared that China at this stage is a new democratic state preparing itself for socialism. It has a mixed economy as its immediate objective and a coalition Government as its present machinery.[57]

Nehru also wrote to British Foreign Minister Ernest Bevin, urging him not to allow US-led forces in South Korea to cross the 38th Parallel since it would prompt China to retaliate. Panikkar was advocating for China to exercise moderation, but he did not think that external pressure would help exert influence as it was already being isolated internationally. Bevin dismissed China's threat of intervening in Korea as a bluff, while Nehru cautioned that the threat of war should not be ignored.

Nehru's enthusiasm for working with China was not shared by the Chinese Communist Party. Durga Das, the editor of a prominent Indian newspaper, wrote about his interaction with Nehru regarding threats to Tibet in 1949:

> In September, the Communist radio asserted that Tibet was a part of China and that 'the British and American imperialists

and their running dog Nehru are now plotting a coup in Lhasa for the annexation of Tibet'. I asked Nehru for his comments and he told me this was the Communist Chinese reaction to his permitting a Kuomintang mission to pass through India. He said he would not quarrel with China over Tibet. He would not take Curzon's role and establish Indian influence in Lhasa.[58]

China's leadership did not take kindly to condescending sermons from India. Mao had Stalin's full support and, with atomic bombs in the Soviet arsenal, he was raring for war and wanted to swiftly reconquer Tibet before moving on to Korea. In June, Chinese forces had already occupied the Demar area, south of the Yangtse River, which was treated as a demilitarized area where Tibet maintained two wireless operators.

Shakabpa used his stay in New Delhi to engage with US embassy officials. On an earlier visit, US Ambassador Loy Henderson had told him that the United States planned to bolster its relations with Tibet. He had even recommended that the US government send a mission to Lhasa, especially after the victory of the Soviet-backed communists, which had alarmed the US about the spread of communism in Asia.

But it wasn't until the Korean War that the US re-engaged in Asia, responding to the communist invasion of South Korea in June 1950 with the Security Council's authorization of a multinational force under its command. Soon, the US started recruiting allies in Asia and began to view Tibet through the prism of the Cold War. While Britain continued to advise caution about Tibet's remoteness and inaccessibility, and to consult with India, the US informed New Delhi it would send arms to Tibet through India.[59]

In Lhasa, preparations were underway for the investiture ceremony of the young Dalai Lama, who had turned fifteen in July. The 17th of November was chosen as the auspicious day for the ceremony.

On 7 October 1950, China attacked Tibet.

10

China Reconquers Tibet

After defeating the Nationalist Party, the Chinese Communist Party laid claim to all territories of the disintegrated Manchu empire and threatened to reassert influence over former tributary states like Myanmar, Korea and Vietnam. It spawned communist parties in these countries and supported their efforts to seize power by force.

PLA's Invasion of Tibet

In Tibet, China's action was swift and deadly. Its army, euphemistically called the People's 'Liberation' Army, launched an attack on 7 October 1950, commanded by Deng Xiaoping and Liu Bocheng, capturing the town of Chamdo and the entire Kham province within weeks. Ngapo Ngawang Jigme, the Tibetan governor of Kham, offered resistance but received no support from Lhasa. The kashag was overwhelmed by the enormity of the situation. Several monasteries refused to oppose China's invasion because of internal rivalries and the hope that, like the Mongols and Manchus, the Chinese communists would not interfere in their religious affairs. Ngapo surrendered, but the Chinese army did not advance on Lhasa. It halted in Chamdo to open surrender negotiations with Ngapo acting as the interlocutor. During this period, Robert Ford, a British wireless operator hired by Tibet earlier in the year to start a radio station, was taken prisoner.[1]

Reports of the invasion soon started trickling into India, though they were denied by both the Indian government and Shakabpa's delegation in New Delhi. China announced its invasion through an official handout in Beijing on 25 October to Xinhua (New China News Agency) stating 'People's army units have been ordered to advance into Tibet to free three million Tibetans'.

Panikkar did not bother to report this development to New Delhi. When newspapers carried the news the following day, the Ministry of External Affairs pulled him up. Unsure of his messages to the Chinese, he was sent a note to hand over to the foreign minister. This missive expressed India's 'deep regret that in spite of the friendly and disinterested advice repeatedly tendered by them, the Chinese Government should have decided to seek a solution of the problems of their relations with Tibet by force instead of by the slower and more enduring method of a peaceful approach'.[2] China responded three weeks later:

> On August 31, 1950, the Chinese Ministry of Foreign Affairs informed the Indian Government through Ambassador Panikkar that the Chinese People's Liberation Army was going to take action soon in west Sikang according to set plans, and expressed the hope that the Indian Government would assist the delegation of the local authorities of Tibet so that it might arrive in Peking in mid-September to begin peace negotiations.[3]

It said that India, in its *aide-mémoire* of 26 August 1950, had acknowledged China's sovereign rights over Tibet. But when China began exercising this right and driving out foreign forces and influences to facilitate regional autonomy and religious freedom for the Tibetan people, the Indian government was obstructing it. China reiterated that Tibet was an internal matter, categorically rejecting foreign interference, declaring that its troops were there to liberate the Tibetan people from Anglo-American influences and assuring that Tibet's way of life and autonomy would not be disturbed. China accused Tibet of intentionally delaying the departure of its delegation to Beijing at the behest of countries hostile to China and requested India's help in sending it to Beijing.

In Lhasa, Taktra Rimpoche resigned as regent and requested the fifteen-year-old Dalai Lama to take charge, which he did on the day of his investiture. Shortly after the investiture ceremony in December, the entire top leadership of Tibet – including the Dalai Lama and the kashag – fled to Yatung on the border of Sikkim. China initially held talks with Ngapo Ngawang Jigme in Chamdo, but subsequently took him to Beijing, insisting on conducting negotiations there. The Tibetan government appealed to Britain, the US, India and the UN for help, specifically requesting India's intervention to halt the attack and pleaded that it could not engage in talks under duress. India counselled China to negotiate with the Tibetan government, citing its own restrained approach in the cases of French and Portuguese territories in India. But China maintained that Tibet was an internal matter in which India had no right to interfere.

Panikkar came up with an ingenious explanation for China's invasion of Tibet, informing Delhi that it feared Anglo-American machinations in Tibet via Nepal. Additionally, with plans for a military operation in Manchuria, China did not want to leave its southern flank exposed. He wrote: 'Recent attack by Moscow Radio on Nepal as an Anglo-American satellite and fear that Chou En Lai expressed of Nepal intervention add weight to these considerations.'4 He added that the Chinese were wary of an incipient world war, perceiving Tibet as a potential threat.

India's Dilemma

India found itself on the horns of a dilemma. If Tibet was a part of China, as acknowledging its suzerainty implied, then could the Chinese military entering Tibet be deemed an invasion? The Tibetans certainly didn't see it that way, and there was sympathy for them in India. The invasion somewhat hardened the government's stance, advising Tibet against sending its delegation to Beijing for talks. It even offered asylum to the Dalai Lama in India if he wished. The Indian government instructed Richardson to stay at his post in the Indian mission in Lhasa since the withdrawal of the mission would be 'a great blow to the Tibetans'. But it refused to sponsor Tibet's appeal to the United Nations, citing its recognition of China's suzerainty over Tibet.[5]

US Ambassador to India Loy W. Henderson approached Nehru soon after the Chinese invasion, asking if the US could help in any way. Nehru turned this down emphatically, stating that such help would be impractical and 'would immediately provide the fullest justification to China for what she had done'. Henderson persisted, arguing that China might extend its reach to the Indo-Tibetan frontier. Nehru dismissed such concerns, highlighting 'the hard and uninhabitable Table-land of Tibet' on the other side. He conceded, though, that the presence of Communist China on the border would require 'normal precautions to keep the border safe from intrusion or infiltration'. But Nehru did not see why China would be concerned about the border with India. In contrast, there was greater risk with the Sino-Burmese frontier since it was undefined in many places.[6]

For Nehru, Tibet was an irritant in his larger endeavour of bridging the Cold War divide by building relations with Communist China. When Tibet appealed to the United Nations, he wrote to India's permanent representative in New York: 'I have a strong feeling that the future of Asia is rather tied up with the relations between India and China. I see both the U.S.A. and the U.K. on the one hand and the U.S.S.R. on the other, for entirely different reasons, are not anxious that India and China should be friendly towards each other.'[7]

Meanwhile, Panikkar continued to advocate for China, characterizing Tibet's appeal to the UN as an American conspiracy to intervene in China's internal affairs. The discussion in the UN would only intensify the bitterness in China against the rest of the world. He claimed that talks were underway with Tibet, hinting at the possibility of a small contingent of the Chinese army being allowed to enter Lhasa peacefully. Both claims were later refuted by the kashag, which stated that there had been no official talks with China in Chamdo and accused the Chinese of deceit and breaking their promises repeatedly, such as giving elaborate assurance to the Khampas before clamping down on them at the first opportunity.

India's stand on Tibet's status also became embroiled in a semantic debate over 'suzerainty' and 'sovereignty'. In an aide-mémoire telegraphed to Panikkar on 24 August 1950, India had defined Tibet's status as 'harmonious adjustment of legitimate Tibetan claims to autonomy within the framework of Chinese Sovereignty'.[8] This was handed over to the Chinese government two days later and was cited by China in its response to India's concern about the invasion. The use of the term 'sovereignty' was not a typographical error. Two months later, New Delhi once again told its embassy in Beijing that India supported Tibetan autonomy within the framework of Chinese 'sovereignty'. Later, on 2 November, it used the term 'suzerainty' to describe the relationship. Panikkar protested against being asked to convey a changed stance, noting China's suspicion that India had made the change under foreign influence. He asserted that the Chinese had felt aggrieved that India viewed its action to safeguard its security in Tibet as increasing international tension. Panikkar questioned whether it was worthwhile to strain relations with China by further pursuing the issue.[9]

Nehru dismissed the switch in terminology as 'academical', writing to Panikkar:

> We have always laid stress on the autonomy of Tibet. Autonomy plus sovereignty leads to suzerainty. Words are NOT important [and summarised his Tibet-China policy as] Our present policy is primarily based on avoidance of world war; and secondly on maintenance of honourable and peaceful relations with China ... If a peaceful settlement is arrived at there and Tibet's autonomy recognised, this should meet Chinese demands and satisfy, more or less, both Tibet and India.[10]

Panikkar reassured Nehru of China's continuing goodwill towards India and attributed the controversy to a 'misunderstanding'. He advised New Delhi on handling the thorny issue of the disputed border, which was being repeatedly raised by the Indian representatives in Lhasa and Gangtok:

> Our one and dominant interest in Tibetan position is the MACMOHAN [i.e., McMahon: *sic*]. My submission is that on the basis of their present note on respect for each other's boundaries and territorial integrity we must take our stand and be prepared to enforce it. Chinese understand that point very well, but it is equally important to take steps on the border to drive the point home. I feel sure that the present misunderstanding can be cleared up if handled with moderation and understanding.[11]

With the Indian ambassador in Beijing painting a rosy picture of the communist government, it fell to the Indian officials in Lhasa and Gangtok to alert New Delhi to the lurking dangers. India's political officer in Sikkim, Harishwar Dayal, and the trade agent in charge of the Indian mission in Lhasa, Hugh Richardson, advised New Delhi to assist the frail Tibetan government in its negotiations with Beijing to safeguard its autonomy and India's treaty rights in Tibet. Dayal cautioned against giving unconditional recognition to the Communist Party regime. He pointed out that in January 1950, New Delhi had pledged diplomatic help to Tibet when China would raise the Tibetan question. Dayal recommended persuading China to conduct talks with Tibet in New Delhi, since a Tibetan delegation would 'virtually be prisoners in Beijing'.

> The Government of India, for their part, have already given ample proof of their anxiety to respect Chinese sentiment; but they should not sacrifice their own interests in Tibet, or fail in their obligation to the Tibetan Government, through fear that their interest in the Tibetan question might be distasteful to the new Government of China.[12]

He further advised:

> It seems desirable at this time … to avoid making concessions
> to Chinese claims in advance and giving the impression that
> India is NOT concerned in what happens in Tibet. That would
> only stiffen the Chinese attitude and might make for greater
> difficulties between India and China later on.[13]

Dayal challenged China's contention that its invasion of Tibet was
aimed at eliminating the 'Kuomintang reactionary clique', reminding
that the KMT had never controlled Tibetan affairs and that its
Lhasa mission had been expelled the previous year. He warned,
prophetically, that after annexing Tibet, China might raise its old
claims to 'Ladakh, Darjeeling, Sikkim, Bhutan and tribal tracts of
Assam as well as their own claim to suzerainty over Nepal'.[14]

Richardson also expressed Tibet's anguish:

> Tibetans justifiably feel disconcerted every time Government of
> India refer to Chinese SUZERAINTY over Tibet and accept
> it as GOSPEL truth, even when there have NOT been any
> traces of that SUZERAINTY in Tibet for 30 years. Does
> SUZERAINTY never die, and if it does how long does it
> take?[15] [*emphasis in the original*]

Dayal and Richardson were not the only officials raising concerns
with New Delhi. Even within the government, questions were being
asked. Secretary-General Bajpai in the external affairs ministry
wrote to Nehru in October, as soon as news of China's invasion
of Tibet became public. He stated that China's action sharply
contradicted India's efforts to establish friendly relations with it:

> At the risk of misunderstanding, unpopularity and odium,
> we have been pressing China's legitimate claims as regards
> entry into the United Nations, Formosa[16] and a voice in the
> Korean settlement. We have had little appreciation of this …
> If China's response to our endeavour for friendship with her
> is to [take] unilateral action against our neighbours, then, I
> submit, China's friendship can be of little value to us.[17]

Both Bajpai and Foreign Secretary Menon were unhappy with Panikkar's unwillingness to convey India's concerns to China. Bajpai lambasted Panikkar for having been 'lamentably weak' and persisting in his erroneous acceptance of Chinese claims and maps, questioning Panikkar's excuses for China's invasion.[18] Neither the US nor Britain had access to Tibet and China's fear of an invasion through the country could only be due to its distrust of India. He recommended sending a stern message to China.[19] Bajpai even compared Panikkar to Britain's ambassador to Germany under Hitler, Neville Henderson:[20] 'It gives me no pleasure to write in this manner about the head of an important mission, but there is no gainsaying the fact that, in this matter of Tibet, we have been served badly. I only hope that our protest will not be delayed or orally "watered down".'[21]

Menon criticized Panikkar for being 'half-hearted' in making India's representations and failing to appreciate that not merely India's honour but also its interests were involved in Tibet and the McMahon Line. India's trade missions in Gyantse and Yatung and its representation in Lhasa would all be jeopardized by China's invasion.

Bajpai advised Panikkar to convey India's 'grave concern' on China's invasion of Tibet, reminding him that China had been misrepresenting India's stand on the Korean War in its propaganda. However, keeping in mind Nehru's reluctance to embarrass either his ambassador or China, he suggested that this could be conveyed informally 'if facts warrant'.[22]

These complaints persuaded Nehru to instruct Panikkar to 'informally' convey India's 'grave concern' about the development, prefacing it with an expression of 'friendly feelings towards China and our continued efforts as regards her entry into the United Nations, future of Formosa and association in the final solution of Korean problem'. He also told Panikkar to remind Zhou Enlai that India was not doing this for any political or economic advantage but 'out of genuine friendship for a great neighbour whose cooperation in the cause of world peace and enhancement of Asia's weight and dignity in international councils, we value and consider necessary'.[23]

Nehru showed an intemperate outburst against Dayal and Richardson for outspokenness in a note to the secretary-general and foreign secretary. He wrote that he was 'a little tired' of their despatches 'full of advice to us as to what we should do and criticism of us for we may have done'. To him, their messages indicated 'a lack of confidence in the Government of India and an apprehension that we might do the wrong thing unless they stop us from doing it … They live in remote parts, cut off from the rest of the world, and judge all world events from their own immediate environments. They appear to have hardly any conception of broad policies in terms of what is happening in the world.'[24]

On Nehru's instruction, Foreign Secretary Menon sent a telegram to the Indian mission in Lhasa and the political officer in Sikkim, telling them that certain communications from them were 'dogmatic, disputatious and admonitory' and advising them to accept government decisions gracefully and follow them faithfully.[25]

Tibet Surrenders: The Seventeen-Article Agreement

On 23 May 1951, Ngapo signed a seventeen-article agreement in Beijing accepting China's annexation of Tibet. China took over its defence and foreign affairs and promised to maintain Tibet's autonomy. It agreed not to change 'Tibet's internal system and the inherent power of Dalai Lama', nor its Buddhist culture and institutions. Tibet, in turn, agreed to drive out imperialist forces from its soil and welcome the Chinese PLA, whose expenses would be borne by China.[26]

Two months later, the high lamas in Yatung met to discuss the agreement. Those who opposed China had already fled the country, and there was little opposition. The lamas present advised the young Dalai Lama to accept the agreement, which he did in a telegram to Mao.

Once the agreement was approved by the Dalai Lama, General Zhang Jingwu (Chang Ching-wu) travelled to Lhasa through India, arriving in Kolkata from China, before going by air to Bagdogra and then by road through Sikkim to Yatung. The Chinese general had his first meeting with the Dalai Lama at Yatung, then travelled ahead of him to Lhasa. The welcome given to him there must have been decidedly cold because when the Dalai Lama arrived a few days later, the general complained bitterly about his reception and accommodation. Three days later, on 9 September, the Chinese army marched into Lhasa from Chamdo – a year after the invasion. There were not many Chinese in Lhasa at the time, but 10,000 Chinese soldiers flooded into the city in less than a year.[27] As the number of Chinese swelled, a food shortage developed. China requested permission from India to import 10,000 tons of food, which India acceded to, and 3,000 tons of rice were allowed to transit into Tibet.[28]

The Indian embassy in Beijing made a favourable assessment of the seventeen-article agreement, writing that the position of the Dalai Lama and Tibet's autonomy would be respected: 'On the whole, [the] agreement would appear to be a reasonable one reconciling China's claim to sovereignty with Tibet's right to autonomy and desire for non-interference with existing political and social structure.' It pointed out that China would not accept India's direct links with Lhasa but might allow the existing arrangement to continue, cautioning that the agreement gave sufficient powers to China to change the system whenever it desired.[29]

This assessment was at variance with that of Sumul Sinha, who had been in charge of the Indian mission in Lhasa since Hugh Richardson's retirement in December 1950. Sinha reported that the Tibetan prime minister, Lukhangwa, had told him he found the agreement repugnant and would be willing to lead a resistance movement if the Dalai Lama so desired and that 'further resistance would have been possible had NOT His Holiness desired peace through negotiation'. Sinha wrote that among the people of Tibet there was bewilderment and anxiety.[30] In April 1952, the Chinese asked the Dalai Lama to dismiss Lukhangwa and threatened the Potala Palace with gunfire if he did not. Lukhangwa resigned.

Russia's Support for the Invasion

China's invasion of Tibet had not only been approved but encouraged and supported by Stalin. When Mao went to Moscow after seizing power, he told Stalin he was planning to attack Tibet, to which Stalin responded: 'It's good that you are preparing to attack. The Tibetans need to be subdued.'[31] When China attacked, Moscow supported it and alleged that the US and Britain were conspiring to make Tibet part of the anti-communist bloc. A *Pravda* despatch from Beijing on 26 October 1950 stated that Tibet was the 'last region of the continental part of the Republic which is still under the oppression of foreign imperialism'.

This is confirmed by the Russian diplomat, Lukin, who writes that, once Mao had seized power, Stalin advised him to establish firm control in Xinjiang and Tibet:

> Stalin also recommended that Mao Tse-tung seize and keep under firm military control Sinkiang (a former Russian and Soviet sphere of influence) and Tibet, eliminating British and other foreign influence there. To please the Chinese Communists, he abandoned his support for the pro-Soviet Eastern Turkestan Republic.[32]

The Soviets actively supported China in strengthening its hold on Tibet. Ever since flights started between Hong Kong and Kolkata, this had become the most convenient way to get to Lhasa, as the eastern and northern routes were both long and arduous. The Soviet Union began helping China build a road from Xinjiang, through Aksai Chin, that bypassed the traditional route connecting to Ladakh. In 1952, the British newspaper the *Times* reported that the USSR was linking Xinjiang to Tibet by road, and the British embassy in Moscow had confirmed that it was likely that Soviet engineers were assisting the Chinese army. A map showed the alignment of the road running east of Akai Chin. British experts expressed surprise as it did not go through the typical passes in the mountains.[33] Later, it was revealed that the road passed through Aksai Chin, which both the Soviet Union and Britain regarded as part of India. This was possibly why the Russian map did not show the route passing through Aksai Chin. China used this road to occupy Aksai Chin and lay claim to it.

Although China called its invasion a 'peaceful liberation', Wang and Gyaincain acknowledge that 114 PLA soldiers and 180 Tibetan troops were killed or wounded in the battle of Chamdo, which the Chinese army captured in the first wave of its invasion.[34]

By the time Tibet signed the agreement with China, the US had realized it needed to support the Dalai Lama, who felt abandoned by the international community. But Britain's stated policy was that it had handed the baton to India regarding initiatives on Tibet and it continued to dissuade the US from taking the initiative, even speaking on behalf of India. Its embassy in Washington informed the US that the Indian government would not be pleased to see American involvement in Tibet and would not support Tibet's appeal to the UN, stating that one of the principles motivating India was that its relations with China should not worsen due to developments in Tibet – and that Tibetan resistance was futile.[35] While this accurately summarized the Indian government's position, there was no justification for Britain to speak on India's behalf, especially considering Britain's anti-communist stand in the Cold War. Even though it was against the communist bloc, Britain continued to advocate differing policies towards the Soviet Union and China.

India's Internal Debate on its Tibet Policy

In political circles, India's Tibet policy was controversial and criticized by opposition leaders like Jai Prakash Narayan and Dr Ram Manohar Lohia. Within the ruling Congress Party, voices of dissent arose from Home Minister Vallabhbhai Patel and J. P. Kripalani, a senior leader.

The Ministry of External Affairs had a practice of circulating telegrams from its missions abroad to key ministers. Telegrams sent by officials in Lhasa and Sikkim had not impressed the prime minister but they alarmed Patel. On 7 November 1950, he wrote to Nehru describing the Chinese action as 'little short of perfidy', lamenting that India had let Tibet down and would not be able to rescue the Dalai Lama. Patel expressed surprise that Ambassador Panikkar had been 'at great pains to find an explanation or justification for Chinese policy and actions', observing that the tone of China's letters to India was that of a 'potential enemy' and made a perceptive comment, stating 'even though we regard ourselves as the friends of China, the Chinese do not regard us as their friends'.

Patel pointed out that the 1914 convention, on which India's stance was based, had not actually been signed by China. In any event, China's interpretation of its 'suzerainty' over Tibet was different from India's. He cautioned that the communists were just as good or bad imperialists as any other political force and that India's communists were in touch with their comrades abroad, adding that there was an urgent need to take measures to secure India's border and seek an early meeting to discuss security issues.[36]

Nehru was rattled by Patel's letter. He recorded two notes, one the day after and the other ten days later. These were neither a reply to Patel nor an instruction to his office to take action on his letter but merely expounded his thoughts on China and Tibet.

In the notes, Nehru dismissed the notion of a military threat from China and the necessity for India to take specific defensive actions. However, he shared Patel's distrust of Panikkar: 'I think that our Ambassador at Peking has not always represented our point of view with sufficient force to the Chinese Government'. Nevertheless, he doubted 'that a more forcible expression of it would have made a great difference'. He repeated Panikkar's explanation of China's invasion of Tibet as an act to secure its territory before the impending world war triggered by the Korean crisis: 'This may be due to the general fear of a world conflict and, therefore, to solve the Tibetan problem, according to their lights, before this world conflict begins.' He also exonerated China of the widely held belief that it had deceived India, noting that China had consistently maintained its position of incorporating Tibet into its territory.

On the security implications of China's invasion, Nehru ruled out any danger of military operations on any scale on the border. He envisioned potential threats only in the case of a world war or if India became belligerent with China. He emphasized the need to guard against 'infiltration and intrusion of small groups', stressing that the frontier posts needed to be strengthened 'from the point of view of watch and ward as well as intelligence'. He also advised improved communications in Assam and adjoining areas, suggesting the possibility of erecting airfields. While he proposed a closer association with Burma, Nehru ruled out a military alliance, citing India's inability to bear the burden of defending it.[37]

In a debate in the Indian Parliament in December 1950, Nehru tried to assuage members by telling them that India was committed to finding a peaceful solution and while it recognized China's suzerainty over Tibet, it was 'anxious that Tibet should maintain the autonomy it has had for at least the last forty years'. Some members objected to his acceptance of China's suzerainty, demanding that the people of Tibet should have the final say in deciding its future. Nehru conceded:

> [S]ince Tibet is not the same as China, it should ultimately be the wishes of the people of Tibet that should prevail and not legal or constitutional arguments ... But it is a right and proper thing to say and I see no difficulty in saying to the Chinese Government that whether they have suzerainty over Tibet or sovereignty over Tibet, surely, according to any principles, the principles they proclaim and the principles I uphold, the last voice in regard to Tibet should be the voice of the people of Tibet and of nobody else.[38]

Patel, however, did not have time to pursue the matter. He died on 15 December 1950. But he was not the only prominent Indian leader to be concerned about China's annexation of Tibet; President Rajendra Prasad shared similar concerns. Being a constitutional figure, he did not express his views in public, but towards the end of his term confided in Durga Das, who later wrote:

Prasad felt very strongly that India's diplomatic approach to China was riddled with weaknesses and a proneness to wishful thinking. The 'Hindi-Chini bhai bhai (Indians and Chinese are brothers) honeymoon', he told me, did not blind him to Beijing's ultimate aims and real feelings towards India. He was greatly upset at the Indian Government's impassivity when Tibet was occupied by the Chinese Reds. His words of caution to Nehru, he said, had fallen on deaf ears. The Prime Minister had been misled by his Ambassador in Beijing, Panikkar. With his eyes moistened, Prasad observed: 'I hope I am not seeing ghosts and phantoms, but I see the murder of Tibet recoiling on India.'[39]

Nehru did not let China's invasion of Tibet hinder his pursuit of a partnership with China to promote Asia's resurgence. In 1952, he sent a government delegation headed by Vijayalakshmi Pandit, who was deeply impressed with Mao, pondering whether he reminded her more of Gandhi or Stalin. She admired Zhou Enlai as a distinguished statesman with an infectious sense of humour, and found life in Beijing much more relaxing and joyful than in Moscow, where she had earlier served as the ambassador.[40]

The same year, Nehru accepted Zhou Enlai's proposal to convert the Indian mission in Lhasa into a consulate. This confirmed India's acknowledgement that Tibet was a part of China and reversed the practice of the office reporting to New Delhi, as it had since its inception in 1936. As a consulate-general, it would now report to the Indian embassy in Beijing.

Nehru then made his first visit to Beijing in 1954. Two years later, Zhou Enlai attended celebrations in Delhi marking the 2,500th anniversary of the Buddha.

The Dalai Lama also visited India in 1956 to attend the festivities. He informed Nehru about the clashes between the Tibetans and Chinese since 1955. In response, Nehru advised that they accept Chinese suzerainty with maximum internal autonomy and carry out internal reforms to prevent Tibet from being isolated from the rest of the world. The Dalai Lama disagreed, asserting that Tibet could not have internal autonomy under China, as it was a different country – culturally, economically and politically. He argued that there was no previous record of Tibet being under Chinese suzerainty, except for limited periods, and Tibet had enjoyed complete freedom from 1910 to 1950, until it was coerced into accepting a treaty that promised it internal autonomy, which China had failed to honour.[41]

During his stay, the Dalai Lama met with Tibetan refugees and learnt the depth of their resentment towards the Chinese occupation. Despite being impressed with India's democracy and free political environment, in sharp contrast to Communist Party rule in China, he returned to Tibet to complete his religious education.

The Dalai Lama's Flight to India

After the Khampa Rebellion, a series of events unfolded rapidly. Mao Zedong launched his ambitious programme, the Great Leap Forward, to catapult China to the front ranks of the global powers. However, it led to disastrous consequences and provoked a popular uprising that was brutally repressed, subsequently killing millions of people. The impact of this crackdown was particularly devastating for Tibet, where rumours circulated that the Chinese intended to imprison their spiritual leader. In response, the Dalai Lama fled to India in March 1959. In the wake of his departure, about 80,000 Tibetans escaped to India, Bhutan and Nepal.

The next month, the Dalai Lama met Nehru in New Delhi, recounting the events of the Khampa Rebellion and the bitter fighting that ensued, with both sides suffering heavy losses. He detailed China's repression and anti-religious propaganda, expressing his apprehension about being imprisoned. When Nehru asked about his desired relations with China, the Dalai Lama said, 'Tibetans expect the achieving of independence in the long run'. Nehru dismissed this as impractical, saying that 'the whole world cannot bring freedom to Tibet unless the whole fabric of the Chinese state is destroyed'.[42]

He urged the Dalai Lama to refashion his policy based on reality, pointing out that even with support of the US, the UK and other countries, Tibet could not be freed. India, he said, could not give direct advice to the Chinese because they suspected India of trying to grab Tibet. Nehru urged the Dalai Lama to keep the door open for a negotiated settlement. India could help but, as he put it: 'At the moment our relations with China are bad. We have to recover the lost ground. By threats to China or condemnation of China, we do not recover such ground.'[43]

Nehru also ruled out the idea of India recognizing the Tibetan government in exile, citing international law. India would have to close its consulate in Lhasa, resulting in loss of contact with Tibet. The Dalai Lama argued that the consulate had served the old Tibetan government that had been dissolved, but Nehru rejected this, saying that it would be an act of war against China. The Dalai Lama assured him of his intention not to embarrass India or spoil its relations with other countries.[44]

Nehru's Tibet Policy Unravels

After the arrival of the Dalai Lama, Nehru's Tibet policy started to unravel, coming under attack from both pro-China and pro-Tibet factions in India. China questioned India's claim that the Dalai Lama was merely an honoured guest in his capacity as a religious leader who would not be permitted to indulge in political activity. It accused India of inciting insurgency in Tibet.

Throughout the 1950s, Chinese leaders had played along with Nehru, refraining from questioning his stand on the border. In March 1959, Nehru wrote to Zhou Enlai that the India–Tibet border followed the geographical principle of the watershed on the crest of the High Himalayan Range. He also cited the following international agreements between India and the Central Government of China for most parts of the border:

- The Anglo-Chinese Convention of 1890
- The treaty of 1842 between Jammu–Kashmir and Tibet
- The McMahon line in the north-east[45]

Zhou replied in September, refusing to discuss the Sikkim border because China did not recognize it as part of India and dismissing the other two because they were not authorized by the Central Government of China. He declared that even though the early British and Indian maps had been similar to Chinese maps 'British and Indian maps [had] later unilaterally altered the way the Sino-Indian boundary was drawn'.[46]

Sometime in 1958, China had released an undated map of Tibet showing Arunachal Pradesh and Aksai Chin in Tibet, which was reported by the British embassy. The legend on the map, in Chinese stated: 'The map has been based on the pre-Resistance War [i.e., pre-1937] Shen-pao Atlas. Internal Administration Areas have been revised according to new material.'[47]

Nehru told the Parliament that he was 'greatly distressed at the tone of the comments and the charges made against India by responsible people in China'. He countered Chinese allegations of 'Indian expansionism' in Tibet, explaining that it was the British who pursued such a policy, not India. He outlined his policy on Tibet, citing the three factors that governed it: '(1) the preservation of the security and integrity of India; (2) our desire to maintain friendly relations with China; and (3) our deep sympathy for the people of Tibet.'[48] He acknowledged that the second and third objectives 'slightly contradict each other ... and that is the difficulty of the situation ... It would be a tragedy not only for India and, and possibly for China, but for Asia and the world if we develop some kind of permanent hostility.'[49]

The uprising in Tibet also brought Nehru face to face with the immensity of disaffection among Tibetans and the brutality of Chinese repression. He realized that Tibet had signed its agreements with China under duress and there was strong resentment against it, even in India. Nehru accepted that these feelings were probably shared by other Asian Buddhist countries. His earlier counsel to the Dalai Lama to reach an amicable settlement with China was shattered by how the PLA had unleased repression.

Still, Nehru refused to accept that Tibet was fighting for its independence against an imperial power. In a debate in parliament on taking the Tibet issue to the UN, he cited the policies of Britain and Russia on its international status:

> Internationally Tibet has not been regarded as an independent country. It has been considered an autonomous country but under the suzerainty or sovereignty of China. That was the attitude, before India became independent, of the United Kingdom and Russia (the Soviet Union as well as Czarist Russia). The rest of the world did not pay the slightest attention to Tibet.[50]

He rejected demands to support Tibet in the UN, arguing that India's action 'should be constitutional and justifiable in law and we should hope for results which will help us to achieve the objective aimed at'. The matter could be taken up in the UN on two counts – violation of human rights and aggression – and he dismissed both as inadmissible. Human rights, he declared, applied only to those who had accepted the UN Charter, which China had not. And aggression could only be by one sovereign country over another.

Rejecting Tibet's plea for human rights and defence against aggression, Nehru dismissed the two main organs of the United Nations – the General Assembly and the Security Council – as ineffective debating forums, citing the example of Hungary, where European nations had not been able to do anything. He concluded that taking the matter to the UN would 'probably produce reactions on the Chinese Government which will be more adverse to Tibet and the Tibetan people than even now'.[51]

But he also conceded now that Tibet's seventeen-article agreement with China was forced and held China responsible for building an empire through military conquest: 'From fairly early in history they have had a sensation of greatness. They called themselves the Middle Kingdom, and it seemed natural to them that other countries should pay tribute to them.'[52] History, he said, had shown the world that a strong China was an expansionist China. When asked by opposition members why he had not raised the border question with China when it invaded Tibet in 1950,

Nehru defended India's decision: 'From the very first day this problem about our frontier was before us. The question was whether we should raise it in an acute form at that stage. We decided not to – whether it was right or wrong you can judge now – and still we do not see how we could have decided otherwise.'

Some members enquired as to why India had recognized China's annexation of Tibet without securing acknowledgement of the McMahon Line. Nehru responded that India's objections would not have made any difference: 'It is rather infantile to think that they would have been frightened by our saying it.'[53] Tibet stood abandoned and helpless.

11

Tibet in the United Nations

When China invaded, Tibet decided to appeal to the UN, but it needed a member state to sponsor its case. After failing to sway Britain, it sought India's sponsorship. India firmly declined, citing two primary reasons: 'New China', a term euphemizing the Communist regime, lacked representation in the UN, and Tibet lacked international recognition. Additionally, India deemed Tibet's proposal for a plebiscite 'unfeasible'.[1]

Bajpai conveyed to the British High Commissioner in New Delhi, H. C. Roberts, that Tibet had consulted India regarding raising the issue of China's invasion at the UN. While declining sponsorship, India pledged to support the appeal on the broader principle that China's use of force was unjust, subsequently instructing the Indian mission in New York accordingly.

Ultimately, Tibet transmitted its appeal via telegram. The joint plea by the kashag and the Tibetan national assembly contested China's assertion of popular support in Tibet for the invasion, culminating in a passionate appeal:

> The problem is simple, the Chinese claim Tibet as a part of China; the Tibetans feel that racially, culturally and geographically, they are far apart from the Chinese. If the Chinese find the reactions of the Government of Tibet to their unnatural claim NOT acceptable, there are other civilised

methods by which they could ascertain the views of the people of Tibet, or should the issue be purely judicial they are open to seeking redress in an International Court of Law. The conquest of Tibet by China will only enlarge the area of conflict and increase the threat to the Independence and stability of other Asian countries.

We, Ministers, with the approval of His Holiness Dalai Lama entrust the problems of Tibet in this emergency to the ultimate decision of the United Nations, hoping that the conscience of the world would NOT allow the disruption of our State by methods reminiscent of the jungle.[2] [*emphasis in the original*].

The appeal was relayed to the Indian Mission in Lhasa, then forwarded to the political officer in Sikkim before it finally reached New Delhi – the only means available to Tibet to communicate with the outside world.

El Salvador stepped forward to sponsor Tibet's plea in the General Assembly. However, the Security Council, tasked with maintaining international peace and security, did not address the issue.

The UK's Ambassador to the UN, Gladwyn Jebb, leaned towards supporting Tibet's appeal and advocating for its independence. He corresponded with his government, suggesting that the UK could present a robust resolution in the Security Council. If vetoed (as was expected), the matter could then be raised in the General Assembly under a 'Uniting for Peace' resolution, akin to the approach taken with Korea previously. Jebb acknowledged India's stance against absolute independence for Tibet but expressed personal support for it.[3] The British government instructed Jebb, however, not to make any comment on China's suzerainty, maintaining that Tibet had a right to appeal as a non-member state under Article 35(2). This ambivalence put the onus on India and opened a small window of opportunity for it to build international opinion in favour of Tibet's independence. But the question remained: would India rise to the challenge?

India's Stance

India's main priority in the UN during this period was to secure China's seat for the new Communist regime, displacing the Nationalists who had taken refuge in Taiwan. Nehru informed India's Permanent Representative to the UN, Benegal Narsing Rau, that the invasion of Tibet did not affect India's position on China's claim to UN seat. Rau in fact claimed that India's support for Communist China's case was aimed at deterring any potential invasion of Tibet. In an interview with the Columbia Broadcasting System, he contended that had Communist China been made a UN member, it would not have invaded Tibet: 'The very fact that it might have been called upon to account for its actions before a world tribunal might have deterred any invasion.'[4]

India's reaction to Tibet's appeal underwent change as it further crystallized. On 16 November, the external affairs ministry communicated to its New York mission a preference for the matter to be considered by the Security Council rather than the General Assembly. It asked the mission to approach Britain and the US – and if they agreed, to impress upon El Salvador the need for postponing the matter.[5] The ministry then directed the mission to endorse the proposal for consideration but avoid using recrimination or strong rhetoric that could impede a peaceful settlement.

India ultimately decided not to support Tibet's appeal and limited itself to urging China to respect Tibet's autonomy – not independence – and peacefully resolve the issue without resorting to arms.[6] Foreign Secretary Menon rationalized this about-turn in an internal note, stating that 'in the first flush of our indignation against the Chinese invasion of Tibet, we said that we would support this appeal, though we would not sponsor it'. But the idea for such a debate was dropped because it was deemed to be not helpful.[7] This rationale was further elaborated in a telegram to the political officer in Sikkim explaining India's policy: '[I]t must be realised that neither we nor U.N. can give active help to Tibet and a heroic policy of condemnation can do Tibet little good.'[8]

El Salvador's resolution, invoking Article 1 of the UN Charter, stated that 'the peaceful nation of Tibet has been invaded without any provocation on its part by foreign forces proceeding from the territory controlled by the Government established at Peiping'. Condemning the 'unprovoked aggression', it called for the formation of a General Assembly committee to recommend measures.[9] Tibet had also demanded that the Chinese forces withdraw to the east of the Yangtse River, which marked the traditional boundary between China and Tibet.

On 24 November, El Salvador proposed that the General Committee include the Tibetan question on the agenda of the General Assembly. Britain requested a postponement, which was supported by India's representative, Jam Saheb of Nawanagar, advocating for peaceful talks. The Soviet Union wanted the item to be deleted, viewing it as China's internal affair. The American delegation agreed to the adjournment, following the Indian lead. Nationalist China, occupying the China seat, did not oppose the postponement as the use of force was against Chinese interests and had been prompted by the Soviet Union. The motion for postponement was adopted unanimously, and no date was fixed for further consideration. The issue never came up for discussion again.[10]

According to the UN Charter, the Security Council bears the responsibility for maintaining international peace and security, encompassing a broad mandate to counter any threat, regardless of its origin. In fact, the UN's primary focus was the threat from World War II enemy states Germany and Japan, who were not members. Despite no international recognition, Tibet's right to self-determination, promised to all 'peoples' under the UN Charter, remained valid – a principle recently acknowledged by India in Jammu and Kashmir. And in 1950, the UN had authorized its first military action against North Korea for invading South Korea, carried out by a coalition of nations led by the United States. North Korea was supported by the Soviet Union and China, and neither faction in Korea was a member of the UN.

India's stand on Tibet was out of sync with its own emerging foreign policy, as were its arguments against raising the matter in the UN. It regarded adopting a resolution in the UN as a heroic but futile policy of condemnation. This stance was at variance with India's regular sponsorship of resolutions against apartheid, disdainfully ignored by South Africa. The argument that Tibet could not receive military assistance because of its remoteness did not fly, as Lhasa was more accessible from India than any part of China.

There was internal disagreement over India's policy. Bajpai was unhappy with Nehru's decision believing it was not in accordance with India's earlier decision to support Tibet. He thought the matter should have been discussed in the General Assembly, since it was the world's forum, and even contemplated resigning. When he spoke to Menon, the latter reported it to Nehru, who wondered if such a situation could be averted by getting Tibet to withdraw its appeal.[11]

The Empires Stay Aloof

According to a report of the British High Commissioner to India, the United States had considered recognizing Tibet's independence during the civil war between the Communists and the Nationalists. But the idea was abandoned as such recognition would seem 'indecent' to the Nationalists and 'provocative' to the Communists.[12]

The first official statement by the US on the status of Tibet, in 1943, had been favourable to China:

> [T]he Chinese Government has long claimed suzerainty over Tibet and the Chinese constitution lists Tibet among areas constituting the territory of the Republic of China. This Government has at no time raised the question regarding either of the claims.[13]

However, when the Communist Party seized power in 1949, the US position somewhat changed, stating: 'The United States Government believes that Tibet should not be compelled by duress to accept violation of its autonomy and that the Tibetan people should enjoy the rights of self-determination.'[14]

The Soviet Union's policy on Tibet, like Britain's, was based on the Convention of 1907 recognizing Chinese suzerainty over the country. This was the foundation for Stalin's advice to Mao Zedong in 1950 to annex Tibet. Records from the declassified archives at Wilson Center in Washington DC reveal that during their meeting on 22 January 1950, Mao thanked Stalin for sending an air regiment to China, enabling the PLA to transport provisions for the invasion of Tibet.[15]

Russia also supported China's claim to Bhutan, citing its declared sovereignty over Tibet. In 1951, the official newspaper *Pravda* reported that Britain had unlawfully taken the province of Bhutan and the neighbouring Sikkim princedom from Tibet in 1890. The paper praised China for its peaceful liberation of Tibet and had, earlier, also listed Ladakh among the Tibetan territories conquered by the British.[16]

Later UN Resolutions

The Tibetan question would not come up again in the UN General Assembly until the Dalai Lama's exile and the 1959 uprising. In October that year, Malaysia and Ireland sponsored a resolution referring to the 'distinctive cultural and religious heritage of the people of Tibet' and to the 'autonomy which they have traditionally enjoyed' in its preamble. The resolution demanded 'respect for the fundamental human rights of the Tibetan people and for their distinctive cultural and religious life'. It did not mention their demand for independence or China's occupation. In fact, it did not mention the People's Republic of China at all. The resolution was adopted forty-five votes in favour, nine against and twenty-six abstentions.[17] India abstained.

Two years later, Malaysia and Ireland were joined by El Salvador and Thailand in sponsoring another resolution that also did not mention China but, in addition to calling for the protection of the fundamental human rights and freedoms of the people of Tibet, called for 'their right to self-determination'. This resolution received fifty-six votes in favour and ten against. India was one of twenty-nine abstentions.[18]

The third and last resolution came in 1965 with the same four sponsors, along with Nicaragua and the Philippines. It deplored the continuing violation of the fundamental rights and freedoms of the people of Tibet but without any reference to self-determination. It received forty-three votes in favour and twenty-six against, with twenty-two abstentions.[19] India voted in favour, with its representative accusing China of genocide and violating the seventeen-article agreement of 1951. This change became possible because China had invaded India three years earlier, and there was new leadership in India: Jawaharlal Nehru had died the previous year and Lal Bahadur Shastri had succeeded him.

After Communist China replaced Nationalist China in the UN in 1971, prospects for another resolution on Tibet faded. The only one to be adopted within the UN system was in 1991, in the UN Sub-Commission on Prevention of Discrimination and Protection of Minorities – a subordinate body of the UN Commission on Human Rights. The resolution criticized China's policy in Tibet and urged it to respect the human rights and fundamental freedoms of the Tibetan people.

Some countries have continued to voice concern over China's human rights violations in Tibet. In the debate on China's Universal Periodic Review in 2024 in the UN Human Rights Council, twenty-four countries mentioned Tibet.

Divergent Fates of Mongolia and East Turkestan

Tibet's fate is in sharp contrast to Mongolia's, which despite similar historical circumstances, regained independence because of a quirk of destiny.

When the Manchu dynasty collapsed, Mongolia declared independence, as did Tibet. In December 1911, its highest-ranking cleric assumed the title of Bogd Khan (Holy Ruler) and launched a military campaign to recover Inner Mongolia. Based on its understanding with Britain, Russia refrained from recognizing Mongolia's independence, but oscillated between supporting China and taking the region under its wings. The following year, it signed a protocol with Mongolia promising military assistance. The year after that, it issued a joint declaration with China recognizing its suzerainty to prevent Japan from claiming the region.

Mongolia, meanwhile, continued efforts to assert independence. In 1913, it signed a treaty of friendship and alliance with Tibet – its sister Buddhist country fighting similar imperial powers – but the arrangement was rejected by both Russia and China.

However, by this time, the outbreak of the First World War had diverted Russia's attention to Europe. Within two years, in 1915, Yuan Shi-kai, who had consolidated his position in north China, invaded Mongolia and compelled it to sign a treaty accepting Chinese suzerainty. After the war, the Russians drove out the Chinese and, following Bogd Khan's death in 1924, set up the Mongolian People's Republic.

At the Yalta conference in February 1945, Stalin insisted on keeping Mongolia within his sphere of influence, promising not to annex it. In return, he agreed to surrender the concessions obtained from China in Manchuria. Chiang Kai-shek accepted this arrangement in the hope that Stalin would stop colluding with the Chinese Communist Party.

Falling in the Soviet Union's sphere of influence proved fortuitous for Mongolia, as it emerged an independent country when the former disintegrated. Inner Mongolia remained under Chinese rule and continues to be so today.

East Turkestan, on the other hand, suffered the same fate as Tibet because both Britain and the Soviet Union upheld their arrangement to leave it with China, where it is known by its Chinese name – Xinjiang. Among the five non-Han countries annexed by China during the Mongol and Manchu periods, only Outer Mongolia has been able to break free, although China remains unreconciled to its loss.

12

Tibet under Chinese Occupation

After occupying Lhasa, China swiftly moved to consolidate its hold over the country. In March 1952, the Communist Party rewarded the young Panchen Lama by escorting him back to the Tashilhunpo monastery accompanied by 2,000 Chinese soldiers. Two years later, he and the Dalai Lama attended the National People's Congress (NPC) and the Chinese People's Political Consultative Conference (CPPCC) in Beijing. The Dalai Lama was elected vice-chairman of the NPC and the Panchen Lama vice-chairman of the CPCC, the 'highest leading positions ever held by the Tibetan leaders in China'.[1] This is telling of the actual position of Tibet, challenging China claims that Tibet became a part of it in 1271 CE. It took seven centuries for a Tibetan leader to attain such a position in their supposed 'motherland'.

However, the Tibetan people remained restive under Chinese rule. In 1955, an armed rebellion – instigated by some monks who had accompanied the Dalai Lama to Beijing – broke out in Sichuan, east of the Yangtse River. It soon spread to neighbouring Garze before being suppressed by the Chinese army with many rebels killed and others fleeing to India. The resistance expanded into a widespread revolt that came to be called the Khampa Rebellion, with several Tibetan army commanders joining in. China accused the US of supporting the rebels and air-dropping weapons.

Amidst the backdrop of a burgeoning global anti-communist movement led by the US, in 1957 it launched a Central Intelligence

Agency (CIA) operation in Tibet from Pakistan. A member of two western military alliances, the Central Treaty Organization (CENTO) and the Southeast Asia Treaty Organization (SEATO), Pakistan facilitated the airdropping of Tibetan resistance fighters and weapons into Tibet from the Dhaka airbase in East Pakistan (now Bangladesh). In July 1958, China protested to India regarding this operation – but not to Pakistan.[2]

Tibet without the Dalai Lama

The Dalai Lama's flight led to another uprising in Lhasa that China violently crushed, with the Communist Party's red flag being hoisted on the Potala Palace. Hundreds of Tibetans committed suicide when they were unable to escape. Senior officials and monks were imprisoned and tortured, including army commander Tsarong, who died in prison in May 1959. Ngapo and the Panchen Lama were elevated to top positions, but the real power continued to be vested in the People's Liberation Army.

The rebellion spread across Tibet and lasted three years. According to Chinese sources, about 90,000 people participated, of which 23,000 were treated as chief culprits. Wang and Gyaincain state that the PLA suffered 1,551 casualties and 1,987 wounded.[3] So devastating was the impact of the repression that even the Panchen Lama had difficulty accepting it. In 1962, he wrote to Zhou Enlai that between 1959 and 1962, 97 per cent of Tibet's 2,500 monasteries had been destroyed or closed. Mao was infuriated with the Panchen Lama and had him thrown in prison, where he remained for ten years. He was rehabilitated in 1978, after Mao's death.

In 1965, China created the Tibet Autonomous Region and appointed Ngapo its first governor.

The Cultural Revolution in China brought the second round of cultural destruction in Tibet in 1966. General Zhang Guohua destroyed most centres of cultural and historical importance in Lhasa, including ancient statues at the Jokhang temple. China maintains that it respects Tibetan religion and culture even though, according to its own white paper, there had been excesses during the Cultural Revolution: 'During the period of the "cultural revolution" (1966–1976), however, in Tibet as in other parts of China, the policy on freedom of religious belief was disrupted, and sites and facilities for religious activities were seriously damaged.' It claims that these were restored later.[4]

After Mao's death in 1976, the Panchen Lama mustered the courage to write what he had dared not in his earlier letter – revealing that 15 to 20 per cent of all Tibetans, perhaps half of all the adult population, had been arrested during the period and subjected to inhuman atrocities.[5] The repression outlived Mao, as did the liberation struggle. There were riots in Lhasa in 1987 and 1989 and again in 2008–2009, which found an echo elsewhere in the world too. There have also been repeated cases of self-immolation by the Tibetans.

By this time, the Tibetan diaspora had become active, and the Dalai Lama was no longer the sole leader of the movement overseas. Younger leaders were more assertive and less ambivalent in their call for independence. The Tibetan Youth Congress professed loyalty to the Dalai Lama while questioning his policies, and it became a significant force in framing Tibetan opinion.

These young leaders also re-energized the Dalai Lama, who visited Europe for the first time in 1973 and the US in 1987, where he was more forthcoming – with his characteristic geniality. His prestige grew in the world, as did awareness of the Tibetan cause. In his 1989 Nobel Peace Prize acceptance speech, he referred to China's 'forty years of occupation' and outlined the basis on which Tibet–China relations need to be defined, as enshrined in the agreement made during the Tang period:

> Any relationship between Tibet and China will have to be based on the principles of equality, respect, trust and mutual benefit. It will also have to be based on the principle that the wise rulers of Tibet and China laid down in a treaty as early as 823 AD, carved on the pillar which still stands today in front of the Jokhang, Tibet's holiest shrine in Lhasa, that 'Tibetans

will live happily in the great land of Tibet and the Chinese will live happily in the great land of China'.[6]

An estimated 1.2 million Tibetans have died as a result of China's invasion and occupation. After plundering Tibetan monasteries during the Cultural Revolution, China is now eliminating Tibetan culture through regimented education. Roughly three out of four students in Tibet are forced to study in residential schools and younger children are taken to boarding kindergartens. Mandarin has replaced Tibetan in educational institutions.

China's Claim over Tibet

The claim of China over Tibet warrants an analysis. When did Tibet become a part of China, according to the latter? What is the basis of its claim? Chinese historians have divergent views on both questions, ranging from religious bonds to imperial conquest, with the dates of annexation varying from antiquity to the eighteenth century.

Elliot Sperling, in *The Tibet–China Conflict*, recently observed that China has been rewriting its version of its historical relations with Tibet:

> The idea that Tibet became a part of China in the thirteenth century is a very recent construction. In the early part of the twentieth century, Chinese writers generally dated the annexation of Tibet to the eighteenth century. They described Tibet's status under the Qing with a term that designates a 'feudal dependency', not an integral part of a country.[7]

The Manchu administration, which ended in the early twentieth century, did not include Tibet among the eighteen provinces of China.

Chinese historian Huang Fensheng, in 1953, wrote that Tibet became part of China at the end of the eighteenth century:

> In the 57th year of the Qianlong period (1792), following the despatch of troops to put down the Gurkha incursion

into Tibet and the subsequent military victory, the so-called 'Regulations for Resolving Tibetan (Matters)' were promulgated. They established the equal rank of the *amban* with the Dalai and Panchen, and his direct authority to control political, military, religious, financial, communications, and transportation matters. Tibet at that point became wholly a part of China's territory.[8]

In a Communist Party-endorsed history of China, Bai Shouyi declares Tibet to have been a part of China since ancient times, citing Tibet's desire for good relations and exchange of gifts as proof of its acceptance of China's sovereignty.[9]

Proprietorship of the Dalai Lama

In an effort to legitimize its rule, China claims ownership over the institution of the Dalai Lama, the most revered body in Tibetan culture, and regards the Dalai Lama as its appointee and dependent on its patronage. This is despite the fact that, during the 267 years of Manchu rule in China, only two Dalai Lamas visited Beijing – one in the early years of the dynasty and the other in its dying days. The Fifth Dalai Lama visited the city in 1652–1653 at the invitation of the Kangxi emperor, and the Thirteenth in 1908 while in exile.

An entourage of 3,000 accompanied the Fifth Dalai Lama. He stayed at the Huangsi (Yellow Temple) specially built in his honour and exchanged titles with the emperor. He also went to Mukden in Manchuria, the ancestral home of the Manchus, and performed prayer ceremonies at their ancestors' graves. The visit was treated with the reverence of an honoured priest rather than a vassal.

After spending two months in 1908 in Beijing, hoping for support against the British, the Thirteenth Dalai Lama realized that the Manchu dynasty itself was surviving on British support. The emperor and the empress dowager, Cixi, died during his stay, forcing him to return to Lhasa and deal with Britain on his own. The current Dalai Lama – the Fourteenth – was the third and last to visit Beijing, in 1954.

The first time the Manchu emperor appointed or authenticated a selection was of the Eighth Dalai Lama, when Chinese troops were occupying Lhasa. The Tibetans saw his predecessor as a puppet of China. He'd had a stormy life, including a period of exile from Lhasa. On his death in 1757, the Qianlong emperor sent a Tibetan lama in his court, Rolpe Dorje, to supervise the discovery of the next Dalai Lama's incarnation. Later, Qianlong sent an urn – the Golden Urn – and instructed that it be used to draw lots for selecting the Dalai Lama.

Tibetan Buddhism reached its pinnacle under the patronage of Manchu rulers, spreading from the Himalaya to Siberia. While China now maintains that this establishes its claim over Tibet, the opposite conclusion – that Tibetan Buddhism prevailed in China during Manchu rule – is more appropriate.

In the early years of its occupation, China had prohibited the system of reincarnation, but after 1990, under the guise of restoring Tibetan traditions, it has permitted the practice and asserted the exclusive right of approval. Since then, the number of officially registered lamas has increased significantly.

Official Statements on Claim to Tibet

Shortly after the Dalai Lama's flight, in May 1959, the Chinese Communist Party published its first official claim to Tibet in a book entitled *Concerning the Question of Tibet*. It referenced historical relations during the Tang period, citing a treaty proclaiming unity between the two regions thus: 'The chaos in Tibet was brought to an end, and unity was achieved when Mongko, Emperor Hsien Tsung of the Yuan dynasty, sent an armed force to Tibet in 1253. Tibet was then incorporated into the Yuan Empire, and it has been a part of the territory of China ever since.'[10]

The book blames the British and Nehru for conspiring to split Tibet from China in the twentieth century, declaring that when the Manchu dynasty collapsed, 'the British imperialists lost no time in inciting their protégés, the reactionaries of the upper strata in Tibet, to stage a revolt' and undermining the 'normal' relations between the Chinese central government and the local government of Tibet. Subsequently, in the late 1940s, the British and the Americans tried to thwart the 'peaceful liberation' of the 'Tibet region of China'. The Chinese premier, Zhou Enlai, claimed that at the Simla meeting, Britain had tried to detach Tibet from China by referring to its sovereignty over it as 'China's so-called suzerainty'.

Furthermore, Zhou Enlai argued that Britain had illegally surveyed Aksai Chin and attempted to invade Xinjiang, only to be rebuffed by China for trying to alter the 'traditional customary line in the western sector of the Sino-Indian border'. China claims Aksai Chin as part of Xinjiang and Ladakh of Tibet, based on this 'line'.

White Paper on Tibet

In September 1992, China released a white paper, *Tibet: Its Ownership and Human Rights Situation*. The first of this two-part paper now represents China's official stand on Tibet, available on the website of the Permanent Mission of China to the UN. The first part offers evidence to establish its 'ownership' of Tibet and the second lists the benefits of Chinese rule to the Tibetan people since 1950.

The ownership claim begins with the conquest of Tibet by the Mongols in the thirteenth century, with Chinggis Khan establishing a khanate in north China and, in 1247, a religious leader of Tibet's Sakya sect pledging allegiance to his successor. In 1271, Tibet was placed under the rule of Kublai Khan, under the Yuan name, and the troops stationed there. Chinggis Khan is regarded as a Chinese ruler who reunited the country and restored its rightful external territories, including Mongolia, Turkestan and Tibet. Kublai Khan reaffirmed his Chinese identity by adopting a Chinese name for his dynasty.

The paper states that Tibet revolted in 1290, when troops were sent to put it down. In 1368, the Mings replaced the Yuans in China and 'inherited' the right to rule Tibet. They chose to continue the Yuan practice of receiving tributes from religious leaders in Tibet and bestowing honorifics on them. In 1587, the Ming emperor conferred the title of Dalai Lama on the head of the recently founded Gelug sect. The Qing (the Manchu dynasty) maintained the Ming practice. When the Zunghar Mongols took control of Tibet, a Qing army had to be sent in 1719 to throw them out and the Qing emperor reorganized Tibet's government, appointing high commissioners (the ambans) in 1727. By 1793, the administration was reorganized once again through the Authorized Regulations for the Better Governing of Tibet, which was necessitated by Nepal's invasion of Lhasa, and a regular Chinese army of 3,000 was stationed in Tibet.

The white paper also covers ancient links between the Tibetan race and the Han people who lived in the central plains of China. During the Tang period (618–907 CE), marriage ties existed between the Tibetan royal families and Hans, and a treaty signed in 641 CE. It cites an inscription from the period: 'The two sovereigns, uncle and nephew, having come to the agreement that their territories be united as one, have signed this alliance of great peace to last for eternity! May God and humanity bear witness thereto so that it may be praised from generation to generation.'[11]

Maintaining that both Britain and India recognize Tibet as part of China, the paper even asserts, 'There was no such word as "independence" in the Tibetan vocabulary at the beginning of the twentieth century.'[12] On the Dalai Lama's flight, it states that a rebellion instigated by anti-China forces broke out among Tibetans in Xikang province who raised the banner of independence, but it failed and ended with the rebels and the Dalai Lama fleeing to India in 1959. Riots erupted again in Lhasa in 1987 and lasted for several years. These disturbances are attributed to the Dalai Lama clique and foreign forces.

The second part of the white paper portrays Tibet as a poor and backward country steeped in feudal serfdom, claiming that the rule of the Chinese Communist Party liberated the serfs that constituted 90 per cent of the population. It is argued that they welcomed the Chinese because they had no human rights and lived in abject poverty, while the serfs' owners 'enjoyed a life more luxurious than the wealthiest in many countries in the world'. China claims that it implemented democratic reforms in agriculture as Tibet's serfs were 'no longer able to bear the exploitation and oppression [and] had spontaneously risen to oppose Tibetan government officials and serf owners many times'.[13]

The paper also claims that though both Chinese and Tibetan languages are spoken in Tibet, Tibetan enjoys first place. It does admit that during the Cultural Revolution (1966–1976), freedom of religion was disrupted in China and religious places suffered serious damage, but claims that this was later rectified.

EPILOGUE
No Endgame in Sight

Tibet's current plight is the result of a combination of miscalculation and misfortune. Its misfortune was that Britain and Russia left it in the Chinese empire, refusing to support its bid for independence even after the collapse of the Manchu dynasty. Had either of them annexed it at that time, or earlier, Tibet would be a free country today. Instead, neither supported Tibet's appeal to the UN, leaving it to India and the US. The absence of international support left Tibet at China's mercy.

Many Tibetans were taken in by the Chinese Communist Party's assurances of respect for their autonomy and religion. They remembered how the Manchu emperors had revered their lamas and were willing to trust China's new rulers. Tibet was rudderless and divided during the long interregnum of the minority of the Fourteenth Dalai Lama. Tibet's strongest defence against China was its special relationship with India. But some of its officials got carried away by their misplaced belief that Britain's withdrawal would leave India weak and that now was a good time to assert itself. After the withdrawal of the British, Tibet hoped to get back territories it had ceded to India.

Many in independent India inadvertently played into China's hands by joining its slogan of liberation for the downtrodden. A section of Indians found Tibet's theocracy obscurantist and were seduced by the revolutionary ideas of the Chinese Communist Party. They were taken in by its claims of championing anti-colonialism and solidarity with the people of Asia.

Both Tibet and India read the changes in the imperial game after World War II incorrectly. India expected China to partner it against Western imperialism. But Britain was no longer the dominant player in Asia, and they little realized that the formidable Mao–Stalin alliance represented the new imperial threat for the continent. Stalin was the dominant partner in this, and he divided the spoils of Central Asia with China. This, as we all know, proved providential for Mongolia and fatal for Tibet.

China's Rise as a World Power

China has now successfully rebuilt its empire, while the more powerful British empire has practically faded into history and the Russian Federation is evermore engulfed in the continued repercussions of the Soviet Union's breakup. China clung tenaciously to its territorial claims through years of military defeat, foreign occupation and civil war. Its diplomats refused to surrender territory at the negotiating table and, when they did, their government denounced the treaties as 'unequal'.

This persistence has paid off handsomely. Few countries question China's territorial claims or look upon it as a colonial power. For over a century, Britain held on to its ambivalent characterization of China's rule over Tibet as 'suzerainty' until 2008, when, faced with a severe economic crisis, it succumbed to China's pressure and recognized it as enjoying 'sovereignty' over Tibet. This was followed by a statement in the British parliament, where Foreign Secretary David Miliband declared the concept of suzerainty to be outdated, removing any lingering doubts about Britain's stance on Tibet: 'We have made it clear to the Chinese Government, and publicly, that we do not support Tibet's independence.'[1]

China's transformation from a lumpen country to an economic and military powerhouse has worsened the prospects of independence for Tibet. China's Communist Party – underpinned by the philosophies of Confucius, Sun Tzu and Mao Zedong – has created a political narrative and a deeply held conviction that its 'century of humiliation' was caused by disunity and military weakness. A highly centralized government and strong military are supremely important to it to prevent a recurrence of such ignominy.

Thus, even though China claims to be a multinational state, its government is so centralized that it has only one time zone for a country spanning 5,000 kilometres, east to west. It maintains that the non-Han nationalities are ethnic minorities who voluntarily became part of China and hold the status of 'autonomous regions'. In its version of history, the PLA 'liberated' the delinquent territories and brought them back to the motherland – though rarely is a non-Han chosen as a member of the apex political body, the Politburo. No Tibetan has ever been appointed to it.

China is the only one among the world's top ten economies that is not a multiparty democracy. It has not ratified the International Convention of Civil and Political Rights. Its citizens suffer capital punishment at a higher rate than any other country, and it has developed sophisticated technologies to spy on its people. The autocratic rule of the Communist Party is by no means unquestioned in China. There have been numerous popular movements against it – all brutally repressed. The non-Han people have borne the brunt of the brutalities, but even within the party there have been violent power struggles.

In 1957, Mao admitted that since the Communist Party came to power, 700,000 people had been killed and 2.5 million arrested. Odd Arne Westad estimates those killed between 1949 and 1955 at 4 to 5 million, excluding the casualties of the 1946–1949 civil war between the Communists and Nationalists.[2] These killings pale into insignificance when compared to Mao's Great Leap Forward in 1958, which killed 45 million people, mainly farmers, from hunger and disease. Later, Mao launched the Cultural Revolution (1966–1976) to purge his opponents from the party.

In Mao's last years, as he lay incapacitated, four of his close associates – the Gang of Four – seized power. After his death in 1976, the gang disbanded and Deng Xiaoping, who took over, gave some economic freedom to the people; but political repression continued. In 1989, the party used tanks to crush peaceful protesters in Beijing's Tiananmen Square. A decade later, a spiritual movement, the Falun Gong or 'Wheel of Law', was equally violently suppressed. This was followed by the persecution of other religious groups, particularly Christians, who were viewed with suspicion.

Despite its dismal human rights record, China has successfully established itself as a world leader, becoming the second-largest economy, as well as the largest manufacturer and exporter – while still claiming the privileges of a developing country. It has not joined the G-77, the association of developing countries, but participates in all its activities as 'G-77 plus China'. It is the world's largest emitter of greenhouse gases but refuses to make mitigation commitments in climate change negotiations like other industrialized countries.

In 1951, the UN General Assembly adopted a resolution declaring that China had engaged in aggression in Korea. Twenty years later, it voted to displace Taiwan in the UN, turning China overnight from an international pariah to a veto-wielding permanent member of the Security Council.[3] China has used this position to consolidate its hold over other UN bodies. Between 2019 and 2021, Chinese nationals headed an unprecedented four UN specialized agencies. It has also refused to allow Taiwan to become a member of the UN, arguing that there is only one China and only one government can represent it. The rest of the world has accepted this, even though Korea is represented by two governments – as was Germany during the Cold War. In violation of the UN Charter, China periodically threatens to invade Taiwan. So complete is Taiwan's isolation that few countries have diplomatic relations with it, for fear of offending China, and it can only participate in international sports events as Chinese Taipei.

China remains unreconciled to the loss of any territory ruled from or conquered by its former rulers – be it Mongolia, Taiwan or the islands of the East China and South China seas – and considers their reconquest a historical duty.

It is also rankled by the refusal of its traditional 'tributary' states in East and Southeast Asia to recognize its overlordship. In its early years, it became the self-declared leader of revolutionary movements in Asia and Africa, funding and arming their communist parties. In November 1949, President Liu Shaoqi told the Conference of Asian and Australasian Trade Unions that '[t]he path of the Chinese people's victory ... is the path which should be taken by the people of many colonial and semi-colonial nations who struggle for national independence and people's democracy'.[4] China promoted armed insurgencies in India, Myanmar, Malaysia, Indonesia, Vietnam, Cambodia and the Philippines.

Until 1952, China's foreign policy mainly consisted of exporting the communist armed struggle. Then there was a moderate phase when it professed friendship with fellow developing countries in Asia and Africa; it participated in the Panchsheel Declaration with India in 1954 and the Bandung Conference of Afro-Asian Countries in April 1955. But the Great Leap Forward brought this conciliatory phase to an end. China then targeted countries like Vietnam, Indonesia and Algeria, though it had little success winning friends or exporting revolution. In 1965, Indonesia experienced severe backlash against the communists and a subsequent right-wing military coup. But China continued to supply arms to the Burmese Communist Party and the Khmer Rouge in Cambodia, and it has stubbornly refused to publicly renounce its policy of promoting 'People's Wars' in other countries.

Fearing China-supported communist parties, five countries in Southeast Asia – Indonesia, the Philippines, Malaysia, Singapore and Thailand – formed the Association of Southeast Asian Nations (ASEAN) in 1967. China condemned it as an American creation.

Despite vociferous criticism of Communist China, the US, then under President Richard Nixon, reached out in 1971 as part of the American effort to encircle the Soviet Union. After World War II, China had relied on its communist brother, the Soviet Union, to build its military strength but relations weakened after Stalin and finally ruptured around 1960 when the Soviet Union terminated its nuclear assistance. When the Soviet Union signed the Partial Test Ban Treaty with the United States in 1963, China launched a vicious campaign of calumny against Soviet Premier Nikita Khrushchev, accusing him of betraying communism, and tested the nuclear bomb the following year. In 1969, China and the Soviet Union clashed violently across their borders. Nixon took advantage of this split to isolate the Soviet Union and weaken China's support for North Vietnam. China quickly used this rapprochement to promote its economic development and international standing.

China's irredentism has led to armed conflicts with Korea, India, Russia and Vietnam, as well as confrontation with all its neighbours. In 1974, it seized the Paracel Islands (called Xisha by China) in the South China Sea from South Vietnam, which appealed to the US for help. But the US had started its withdrawal from Vietnam after the Paris Peace Accords the previous year and was unwilling to let anything undermine its efforts to improve relations with China. In 1978, Vietnam signed a treaty of friendship and cooperation with the Soviet Union, which incensed China. It invaded Vietnam, claiming the act was a 'self-defensive counter-attack'. China also used terms like 'punishment' and 'teaching a lesson' for its action – a throwback to the days when its emperor would chastise vassal states for impudence.

In 1992, China passed a law claiming sovereignty over nearly all of the South China Sea, including the Spratly Islands (called Nansha in Chinese). The Paracel Islands are now entirely under its control, while parts of the Spratly Islands are occupied by Vietnam, Malaysia, the Philippines and Taiwan. Both island groups are disputed, but China refuses to accept international mediation or the application of the UN Convention on the Law of the Seas (UNCLOS) to resolve the issues peacefully under international law.

With the turn of the twenty-first century, China's military strength was augmented by its economic power, multiplying its power base manifold. In 2013, it launched an economic programme to transform China into a transport hub and promote foreign trade with the construction of large infrastructure projects abroad through Chinese companies. Initially known as the Silk Road Economic Belt, before being renamed the One Belt One Road scheme and finally the Belt and Road Initiative, the projects have done little to boost the economic development of the recipient countries, with many of them falling into debt traps. China has instituted the usurious practice of seizing their assets to recover its loans. In 2017, it took the port of Humbantota from Sri Lanka on a ninety-nine-year lease for non-payment of dues. Ironically, Britain's lease on Hong Kong in 1898 was for the same term.

Silent Suffering

Tibet has little chance of getting help from the United Nations against its powerful occupier. The passive resistance of its people has earned universal sympathy and admiration but their claim to be a sovereign state under foreign occupation has been clouded by their leaders' muddled arguments and drowned out by China's vociferous bullying.

The Tibetan people have defied China's military by clinging to their faith and endured their misfortune with stoic resilience. China's repression of its own Han Chinese people leaves no scope for minorities like the Tibetans to enjoy any political or human rights. Beijing has also targeted Tibet's religious institutions in an attempt to break the spirit and solidarity of its people. According to Chinese President Xi Jinping, even Tibetan Buddhism 'should be guided in adapting to the socialist order and should be developed in the Chinese context'.[5]

For Tibetans, fleeing the country is the only recourse. There are about 150,000 Tibetans living in exile, mostly in India, where the Dalai Lama also lives. The Tibetans in exile have established the Central Tibetan Administration, which is based in Dharamsala, Himachal Pradesh, to manage their affairs and relations with other countries. It is headed by a president directly elected by the Tibetans in exile, a parliament and an executive council (kashag), although no country recognizes it as a government-in-exile.

China has supplanted the former Soviet Union as the main threat to western supremacy – one much more profound than Russia ever was. While there is talk of the return of the Cold War of the 1950s – in which the West was pitted against the communist alliance of the Soviet Union and China – China continues to successfully play both sides, maintaining close economic and military ties with Russia while providing enough inducements to keep the West enticed.

China is the current winner of the imperial game, and there is no end in sight to its occupation of Tibet. Even though the Dalai Lama has divested himself of all temporal powers, handing them to the Central Tibetan Administration, the de facto government-in-exile, there will inevitably be a void after him. The long interregnum of the rebirth, selection and growing up of the new Dalai Lama is bound to be embroiled in controversy. While the lamas in exile will select the child according to the directions left behind by the Dalai Lama, China is unlikely to recognize him and will certainly appoint its own. There is little prospect of a smooth reincarnation, given the continuing wrangles over other senior lamas like the Panchen Lama and the Karmapa Lama.

The role of the government-in-exile will become critical, as will the attitude of other countries, particularly India and the US. The Tibetan political leadership will have to become more assertive, and India and the US less ambivalent about their support towards it. That is the only ray of hope for the Tibetan people in their long struggle for statehood and sovereignty.

ANNEXURE 1

Principal Ruling Dynasties in China

Shang	16th–11th c. BCE
Zhou	1045–256 BCE
Qin	221–206 BCE
Han	202–220 CE
Sui	581–618
Tang	618–907
Song	960–1279
Yuan (Mongol)	1271–1368
Ming	1368–1644
Qing (Manchu)	1644–1911

Qing (Ch'ing) Dynasty 1644–1912

Founded by Hong Taiji (1636–1643)

Pinyin	Wade–Giles	
Shunzhi	Shun-chih	1644–1661
Kangxi	K'ang-hsi	1662–1722
Yongzheng	Yung-cheng	1723–1735
Qianlong	Ch'ien-lung	1736–1795
Jiaqing	Chia-ch'ing	1796–1820
Daoguang	Tao-kuang	1821–1850
Xianfeng	Hsien-feng	1851–1861
Tongzhi	T'ung-chih	1862–1875
Guangxu	Kuang-hsü	1875–1908
Xuantong (Pu Yi)	Hsuan-t'ung	1909–1912

ANNEXURE 2

Chinese Names in the Latin Script

Pin Yin	Wade–Giles
Anqing	Anking
Anxi	An-hsi
Beijing	Peking
Jin Shuren	Chin Shu-jen
Chunghow	Ch'ung-hou
Cixi	T'zu-hsi
Duan Qirui	Tuan Ch'i-jui
Fuzhou	Foochow
Gansu	Kansu
Gaozu	Kai-tsu
Gong	Kung
Guangdong	Kuang-tung
Guangxi	Kuang-hsi
Guangxu	Kuang-hsü
Guangzhou	Kuang-chou
Guomindang	Kuomintang
Hangzhou	Hangchou
Hankou	Han-k'ou
Heilongjiang	Hei-lung-chiang/Hei-lung-kiang
Hong Xiuquan	Hung Hsiu-ch'üan
Huang He	Huang Ho
Hubei	Hupeh
Jiangsu	Kiangsu/Chiangsu
Jiaqing	Chia-ch'ing
Jilin	Kirin
Jin Cheng	Tsin Cheng/Chin Cheng

Kangxi	K'ang-hsi
Kung Fuzi (Confucius)	K'ung-fu-tzu
Lanzhou	Len-Chu
Li Hongzhang	Li Hung-chang
Li Yuanhong	Li Yüan-hung
Liaodong	Liaotung
Liaoning	Liao-ning
Liu Bocheng	Liu Po-ch'eng
Mao Zedong	Mao Tse-tung
Nanjing	Nanking
Nian	Nien
Ningbo	Ningpo
Qi Gong	Ch'i Kung
Qianlong	Chien Lung
Qing	Ch'ing
Qinghai	Ch'ing-hai
Shanxi	Shan-hsi
Shi Huang Di	Shih Huang-ti
Shunzhi	Shun-chih
Xikang	Sikang/Hsikang
Suzhou	Soochow
Taizong	T'ai-tsung
Tang	T'ang
Tianjin	Tientsin
Tongzhi	T'ung-chih
Zongli Yamen	Tsungli Yamen
Wu Zhongxin	Wu Chung-tsin
Xiamen	Hsia-men (Amoy)
Xian	Hsi-an
Xianfeng	Hsien-feng
Xinjiang	Sinkiang/Hsin-chiang
Xuantong	Hsuan-tung
Xuanzang	Hiuen Tsang
Yongzheng	Yung-cheng
Yu Gang	Yu Kang
Yu Zan	Yu Tsan
Yuan Shikai	Yüan Shih-kai
Zeng Guofan	Tseng Kuo-fan
Zeng Jize	Tseng Chi-tse

Zhang Jingwu	Chang Ching-wu
Zhao Erfeng	Chao Erh-feng
Zhao Ersun	Chao Erh-sun
Zhejiang	Che-chiang
Zhengtong	Cheng-t'ung
Zhong Zong	Chung-tsung
Zhou Enlai	Chao En-lai
Zhu De	Chu Teh
Zhu Yuanzhang	Chu Yüan-chang
Zhujiang	Chu-kiang (Pearl River)
Zuo Qiuming	Tso Ch'iu-ming
Zuo Zongtang	Tso Tsung-T'ang

Notes

Abbreviations

NAI: National Archives of India
UKNA: UK National Archives
PMML: Prime Ministers' Museum and Library; formerly Nehru Memorial
Museum and Library; and Teen Murti House Museum and Library

Introduction: The Game

1   This century, according to China, starts from the First Opium War
    (1839–1842) and ends with the Communist Party takeover in 1949.
2   There was a skirmish on the northern border of Afghanistan in 1885,
    known as the Panjdeh Incident, in which only Afghan forces were involved.
3   Charles Bell, *Tibet: Past and Present*, quoted in Peter John Brobst, *The
    Future of the Great Game* (Akron, Ohio: University of Akron Press, 2005),
    71.
4   O. Edmund Clubb, *20th Century China* (New York: Columbia University
    Press, 1964), 378.
5   Ian Brownlie, *Principles of Public International Law* (Oxford: Clarendon
    Press, 1973), 280.
6   This peace settlement, comprising the treaties of Münster (between the
    Holy Roman Empire and France and its allies) and Osnabrück (between the
    Holy Roman Empire and Sweden and its allies), brought the devastating
    religious war in Europe, the Thirty Years War, to a close. It is regarded by
    many scholars as marking the beginning of modern international relations
    based on the principles of equality of sovereign states and non-interference
    in their internal affairs.
7   This convention of seventeen American countries defined the criteria of
    statehood and the rights and duties of states. It declared that the political
    existence of a state is based on self-declaration and is independent of
    recognition by other states. This 'declaratory' theory of statehood is more
    widely accepted than the 'constitutive' theory which lays greater emphasis
    on recognition by other states.
8   Yuval Noah Harari, *Sapiens: A Brief History of Humankind* (London:
    Vintage Books, 2015), 225.

1. Tibet: Monastic Heights

1   S. W. Bushell, 'The Early History of Tibet from Chinese Sources', *Journal of the Royal Asiatic Society*, vol. 12, no. 4, 1880, 435–541. A legation is a diplomatic mission lower than an embassy. Britain set up its legation, headed by a minister, in Beijing in 1861. It was upgraded to an embassy, with an ambassador, in 1935.

2   Bradford Chamber of Commerce, 'Letter dated 21 November 1895 to the India Office', *Papers Relating to Tibet* (London: Darling & Son, 1904), 51.

3   Rinchen Dolma Taring, *Daughter of Tibet* (New Delhi: Allied Publishers, 1970), 237.

4   Bai Shouyi, *An Outline History of China* (Beijing: Foreign Languages Press, 2010), 14.

5   David Crystal, *The Encyclopedia of Language* (New York: Cambridge University Press, 1987), 310.

6   Taring, 63.

7   Charles Bell, a British civil servant who wrote extensively on Tibet, regarded the Tibetan language as belonging to the same linguistic family as Burmese. He regarded Tibetans and Mongols as a kindred race belonging to the same religion.

8   Dawa Norbu, 'Indo-Tibetan Cultural Relations Through the Ages', *Himalayan and Central Asian Studies Journal*, vol. 13, no. 1, 2009, 34.

9   B. N. Puri, *Buddhism in Central Asia* (Delhi: Motilal Banarsidass, 1987), 15.

10   *Tsenpo* was the title used by kings in Tibet.

11   John K. Fairbank, Edwin O. Reischauer and Albert M. Craig, *East Asia: Tradition and Transformation* (Boston: Houghton Mifflin Company, 1973), 111.

12   Sarat Chandra Das, *A Journey to Lhasa and Central Tibet* (London: John Murray, 1902), 151.

13   Wang Jiawei and Nyima Gyaincain, *The Historical Status of China's Tibet* (Beijing: China Intercontinental Press, 1997), 8.

14   Bai, *An Outline History of China*, 194.

15   *Rimpoche* is an honorific in Tibetan, meaning the 'precious one'. It is also spelt Rinpoche.

16   Sam van Shaik, *Tibet: A History* (New Delhi, Amaryllis, 2012), 52.

17   All these texts were translated from Sanskrit and Pali into Tibetan. During the Mongol rule of China, thousands of Buddhist texts were translated from Tibetan into Mongolian.

18   Wang and Nyima, *The Historical Status of China's Tibet* (Beijing: China Intercontinental Press, 1997), 13.

19   Ye Lang, Fei Zhengang and Wang Tianyou (eds.), *China: Five Thousand Years of History and Civilization* (Hong Kong: City University of Hong Kong Press, 2007), 68.

20   Bai, *An Outline History of China*, 213.

21   Wang and Nyima, *The Historical Status of China's Tibet*, 17.

22 Vicomte D'Ollone, (trans. Bernard Miall), *In Forbidden China: The D'Ollone Mission*, Boston, Small Maynard and Company, p 11–12.
23 D'Ollone, *In Forbidden China*, 180.
24 Tachienlu. Also called Tatsendo and Kangding.
25 D'Ollone, *In Forbidden China*, 195.
26 Ibid., 309.
27 Sonam Joldan, 'Historical Relationship between Tibet and Ladakh', in Siddiq Wahid (ed.), *Tibet's Relations with the Himalaya* (New Delhi: Academic Foundation, 2017), 155.
28 Margaret W. Fisher, Leo E. Rose and Robert A. Huttenback, *Himalayan Battleground: Sino-Indian Rivalry in Ladakh* (New York: Frederick A. Praeger, 1963), 56.
29 Das, *A Journey to Lhasa and Central Tibet*, 52.

2. Mongol Empire: Connecting Eurasia

1 Charles R. Bawden, *Mongolian Traditional Literature* (London, Kegan Paul Ltd, 2003), xvi.
2 *Khan* is a Mongol title for a ruler. It became popular later among the Pashtuns of Afghanistan. The Mongols used *Khagan* for a *Khan of khans*, or emperor.
3 The Jurchen were a people who lived north of China in the region now known as Manchuria. They were ethnically close to the Mongols and the Japanese and spoke sister languages, called the Tungusic or the Altaic family. In China, these people – considered the ancestors of the Manchus – are called Nüzhen.
4 The ocean is a symbol of supreme power in Mongolia. The title was tautological because Gyatso also means ocean in Tibetan, as does Chinggis.
5 Bell, *The People of Tibet*, 16.
6 Peter C. Perdue, *China Marches West: The Qing Conquest of Central Eurasia* (Cambridge, Massachusetts: Harvard University Press, 2005), 66.
7 Panchen Lama was recognized as an incarnation of *Amitābha* (Boundless Energy), the spiritual guide of *Avalokiteśvara*, whose incarnation was the Dalai Lama himself.

3. Chinese Empire: Conquering Barbarians

1 S. Wells Williams, *The Middle Kingdom* (New York: Wiley and Putnam, 1848), 7. The italics are from the original.
2 A league was a measure of distance used in Europe. In England, on land, it was equal to 3 miles, or 4.8 kilometres. The diameter of China would thus be between approximately 2,400 and 2,900 kilometres, a remarkably accurate estimate of the country's size if Tibet and Sinkiang are excluded.
3 Thomas Thornton, *A History of China from the Earliest Times to the Treaty with Great Britain in 1842* (vol. I) (London, Wm. H. Allen and Co., 1844), 5.
4 Thornton, *A History of China*, 8.
5 Ibid., 9.

6   Quoted from China's Historical Archives in Matthew W. Mosca, *From Frontier Policy to Foreign Policy: The Question of India and the Transformation of Geopolitics in Qing China* (Stanford: Stanford University Press, 2013), 262.

7   Martin Stuart-Fox, *A Short History of China and Southeast Asia* (Crows Nest: NSW, Australia, Allen & Unwin, 2003), 24.

8   Thant Myint-U, *Where China Meets India: Burma and the New Crossroads of Asia* (London: Faber and Faber, 2012), 191.

9   Hugh Fraser (British Chargé d'Affaires in Beijing), Letter dated 22 January 1877 (London: Royal Geographical Society, RGS/NE/7i), 4.

10 Quoted from China's Historical Archives in Matthew W. Mosca, *From Frontier Policy to Foreign Policy: The Question of India and the Transformation of Geopolitics in Qing China* (Stanford, CA, Stanford University Press, 2013), 80.

11 Immanuel C. Y. Hsü, *The Rise of Modern China* (6th ed.) (New York, Oxford University Press, 2000), 133.

12 Article III of the Treaty of Peace, Friendship, and Commerce, between Great Britain and China, signed at Tientsin, 26 June 1858, *Hertslet's China Treaties, Vol. I* (New York, Cambridge University Press, 1908), 20.

13 John Keay, *China: A History* (New York, Basic Books, 2009), 476.

14 Peter C. Perdue, *China Marches West: The Qing Conquest of Central Asia* (Cambridge: Harvard University Press, 2005), 512.

15 The Karmapa Lama is the head of the Karma Kagyu, the largest sub-sect of the Kagyu sect of Buddhism in Tibet.

16 Morris Rossabi, 'The Ming and Inner Asia', *The Cambridge History of China* (vol. 8) (Cambridge, Cambridge University Press, 1998), 245.

17 Wang and Nyima, *The Historical Status of China's Tibet*, 33–34.

18 This family of languages is also called the Altaic group.

19 Keay, *China*, 501.

20 Pamela Kyle Crossley, *The Manchus: Peoples of Asia* (Cambridge: Blackwell Publishers, 1997), 113.

21 Das, *A Journey to Lhasa and Central Tibet*, 178–79.

22 C. D. Bruce, 'Chinese Turkestan' [paper read on 24 April 1907 at the Proceedings of the Central Asian Society], 7. This route across the Khunjerab Pass is used by the Karakoram Highway built by China.

23 These Muslim Chinese are called Dungans by the Russians, possibly derived from Tunganis, the name given to them by Turkic people – Gansu was called Tangut by the Mongols.

24 N. Prejevalsky, *The Tangut Country and the Solitudes of Northern Tibet, Vol. II*, trans. E. Delmar Morgan (London: Sampson Low, Marston, Searle and Rivington, 1876), p 10–11.

25 Another book, discovered in Dunhuang in 1900, the *Vajracchedikā Prajñapāramitā Sūtra*, popularly known as the *Diamond Sutra* believed to have been written between the second and fourth centuries CE is considered to be the oldest surviving book in the world.

26 Marc Aurel Stein, *Preliminary Report on a Journey of Archaeological*

and Topographical Exploration in Chinese Turkestan (London: Eyre and Spottiswoode, 1901), 11, 64.

27 Marc Aurel Stein, *Ancient Khotan: Detailed Report of Archaeological Explorations in Chinese Turkestan* (Oxford, Clarendon Press, 1906), viii.

28 Keay, *China*, 523.

29 Sinkiang can also be translated as 'new borderland'. The Manchus had used this name for other borderlands they conquered until they moved further to newer borderlands. In the western region they never went any further, so the name remained.

30 Perdue, *China Marches West*, 211.

31 The Manchus had three levels of nobility: (i) Imperial clansmen, (ii) Titular nobles, like *kung*, considered as the equivalent of a duke by the British, and (iii) Bannermen.

32 Hsü, *The Rise of Modern China*, 50.

33 Ibid., 53.

34 Ibid., 8.

35 Ibid., 8.

36 Wang Ke, *The East Turkestan Independence Movement 1930s–1940s*, trans. Carissa Fletcher (Hong Kong: Chinese University Press, 2018), 13.

37 Jonathan Fenby, *History of Modern China* (London: Penguin Books, 2008), 1.

38 Hsü, *The Rise of Modern China*, 440.

39 Perdue, *China Marches West*, 542.

40 Crossley, *The Manchus*, 11.

41 Quoted in Perdue, *China Marches West*, 510.

42 Quoted in Perdue, *China Marches West*, 511.

43 Bai, *An Outline History of China*, 419.

4. Russian Empire: Quest for Warm Waters

1 Keay, *China*, 520.

2 The three feudatories were lords of fiefdoms in Yunnan, Guangdong and Fujian provinces.

3 There were three other agreements thereafter, namely, the Treaty of Aigun in 1858, which China calls an 'unequal' treaty, on the Amur River; the Treaty of Peking in 1860; and the St Petersburg Treaty in 1881. In 1891, Russia started construction of the Trans-Siberian railway.

4 Archibald R. Colquhoun, *Russia Against India: The Struggle for Asia* (London: Harper and Brothers, 1901), 202.

5 James Stone, 'Bismarck and the Great Game: Germany and Anglo-Russian Rivalry in Central Asia, 1871–1890', *Central European History*, vol. 48, no. 2, 2015, 157.

6 Aleksey Kuropatkin (1848–1925) and L. N. Sobolev were among the prominent Russian generals who conquered Central Asia. Kuropatkin became war minister (1898–1904). Sobolev, who was obsessed with invading India, wrote a book on the invasions of India.

7 Charles Marvin, *Russia's Power of Attacking India* (London, W. H. Allen & Co, 1885), 7.

8   Lawrence James, *Raj: The Making and Unmaking of British India* (London, Softback Preview, 1998), 89.

9   Spencer Walpole, *History of England* (vol. 5, 245), quoted in K. W. B. Middleton, *Britain and Russia: An Historical Essay* (London, Hutchinson & Co. 1945), 55.

10   C. A. Bayly, *Empire and Information: Intelligence Gathering and Social Communicating in India, 1780–1870* (Cambridge: Cambridge University Press, 1996), 140.

11   Henry Rawlinson, *England and Russia in the East* (London: John Murray, 1875), 279.

12   Ibid., 336.

13   Charles E. Drummond Black, *The Rival Powers: Central Asia* (London: Archibald Constable and Company, 1893), 132.

14   Demetrius Charles Boulger, *England and Russia in Central Asia* (London: W. H. Allen & Co., 1879), 309–310.

15   Ellis Ashmead-Bartlett, Statement in the House of Commons on 1 August 1881, *Hansard, Vol. 264, Observations* [website], hansard.parliament.uk/Commons/1882-08-01.

16   Ellis Ashmead-Bartlett, Statement in the House of Commons on 15 February 1882, *Hansard, Vol. 266, The Answer in Question to the Queen's Speech: Report* [website], hansard.parliament.uk/Commons/1882-02-15.

17   Middleton, *Britain and Russia*, 71.

18   Colquhoun, *Russia Against India*, 20.

19   Panjdeh is now in Turkmenistan, close to the tri-junction with Iran and Afghanistan.

20   Middleton, *Britain and Russia*, 75.

5. British Empire in China: Power to Trade

1   The Arabs had derived the name *firangi* from the Franks, who were prominent crusaders in the Middle Ages.

2   George Macartney had been governor of Madras (now Chennai) from 1780 to 1786.

3   Robert Bickers, 'Britain and China, and India, 1830s–1947' in Robert Bickers and Jonathan J. Howlett (eds.), *Britain and China, 1840–1970: Empire, Finance and War*, New York, Routledge, 2016, 58.

4   Hsü, *The Rise of Modern China*, 166.

5   James Bradley, *The China Mirage* (New York: Little, Brown and Company, 2015), 17.

6   Thomas Bowlby, *An Account of the Last Mission*, quoted in Stephen Platt, *Autumn in the Heavenly Kingdom* (London: Atlantic Books, 2013), 103.

7   Stephen Platt, *Autumn in the Heavenly Kingdom*, 173.

8   Ibid., 245.

9   R. S. Gundry, *China and Her Neighbours* (London: Chapman and Hall Ltd., 1893), 295.

10   Middleton, *Britain and Russia*, 78.

11   Clubb, *20th Century China*, 13.

12 Odd Arne Westad, *Restless Empire: China and the World Since 1750* (London: Bodley Head, Random House, 2012), 54.

13 Fairbank, Reischauer and Craig, *East Asia*, 481–82.

14 D. Coates, *The China Consuls: British Consular Officers, 1843–1943* (Hong Kong: Oxford University Press, 1988), 142.

15 Platt, *Autumn in the Heavenly Kingdom* 302.

16 Robert K. Douglas, *China* (Chicago: H. W. Snow and Son, 1907), 220.

17 Robert Hart was a member of Britain's Chinese Consular Service. He was knighted in 1882.

18 John Pratt, *China and Britain* (London: Collins, 1945), 116.

19 Hsü, *The Rise of Modern China*, 273.

20 Benjamin Disraeli, Debate in UK House of Commons on Address to Her Majesty on the Lords Commissioners' Speech on 5 February 1863, [website] https://hansard.parliament.uk/Commons/1863-02-05.

21 Bickers, 74.

22 Rutherford Alcock became minister in the Chinese embassy in Peking from 1865 to 1870.

23 Palmerston, Debate in the UK House of Commons on 31 May 1861, *Hansard*, vol. 163, Affairs of China. Available: https://hansard.parliament.uk/Commons/1861-05-31.

24 Palmerston, Statement in the House of Commons on 20 May 1864, *Hansard*, vol. 175, Affairs of China: Observations. Available: https://hansard.parliament.uk/Commons/1864-05-20.

25 Palmerston, Statement in the House of Commons on 31 May 1864, *Hansard*, vol. 175, Affairs in China: Resolution. Available: https://hansard.parliament.uk/Commons/1864-05-31.

26 Palmerston, Statement in the House of Commons on 20 May 1864, *Hansard*, vol. 175, Affairs of China: Observations. Available: https://hansard.parliament.uk/Commons/1864-05-20.

27 Austen Layard, Statement in the House of Commons on 6 July 1863, *Hansard*, vol. 172, Our Relations with China. Available: https://hansard.parliament.uk/Commons/1863-07-06.

28 Austen Layard, Statement in House of Commons on 22 April 1864, *Hansard*, vol. 174, Civil War in China. Available: https://hansard.parliament.uk/Commons/1864-04-22.

29 Stephen R. Platt, 'British Intervention in the Taiping Rebellion' in Robert Bickers and Jonathan J. Howlett (eds.), *Britain and China, 1840–1970: Empire, Finance and War* (New York: Routledge, 2016), 55.

30 Kashgar, Khotan, Yarkand, Yangihisar, Aksu, Kucha and Korla.

31 The representative, Dr Henry Cayley, was a medical doctor who proved as adept at reporting on the medical state of the Ladakhi people as on the rapid developments in East Turkestan.

32 Wang Ke, *The East Turkestan Independence Movement*, 23.

33 Fairbank, Reischauer and Craig, *East Asia*, 600.

34 Thomas Francis Wade, Letter No. 186 dated 26 July 1871, Foreign Department, Government of India, National Archives of India (hereinafter referred to as NAI).

35 Ironically, General Tso was to become famous in the United States a century later because of the culinary dish 'General Tso's Chicken' that was introduced by a Chinese chef who fled to Taiwan after the Communist takeover and then migrated to the US.

36 David Pong, 'Keeping the Navy Foochow Yard Afloat: Government Finance and China's Early Modern Defence Industry, 1866–75', *Modern Asian Studies*, vol. 21, no. 1, 1987, 131.

37 Reuters Staff, *Factbox China's first public loan*, Report dated 9 December 2010, Reuters website.

38 The Hong Kong and Shanghai Bank had been founded by a Scotsman, Thomas Sutherland. He opened it in Hong Kong in 1865 and, a month later, in Shanghai. It gave its first loan to the Chinese government in 1864 and then issued most of its public loans.

39 Immanuel C. Y. Hsü, 'The Late Ch'ing Reconquest of Sinkiang: A Reappraisal of Tso Tsung-T'ang's Role', *Central Asiatic Journal*, vol. 12, no. 1, 1968, 58.

40 Hsü, 'The Late Ch'ing Reconquest of Sinkiang', 50.

41 Charles Gordon, Letter dated 4 July 1880 to Sir J. Hennessy, governor of Hong Kong, UK National Archives (henceforth referred to as UKNA), FO 881/4521, 167.

42 F. R. Plunkett [British diplomat in Russia], Letter dated 3 November 1880, UKNA, FO 418/10, folio 143.

43 Dr Samuel Halliday Macartney belonged to the same family as George Macartney, who had visited the court of the Qianlong emperor in 1793. He was a medical doctor who married a Chinese and worked for the Chinese government, initially in China and later in the Chinese legation in London.

44 Hsü, *The Rise of Modern China*, 324.

45 Lord Dufferin [Britain's ambassador to Russia], Letter to Earl Granville of 28 January 1881, UKNA, FO 418/10, 10.

46 Immanuel C. Y. Hsü, 'British Mediation of China's War with Yakub Beg, 1877', *Central Asiatic Journal*, vol. 9, no. 2, 1964, 149.

47 Fenby, 31.

48 Thomas Wade, Letter dated 27 January 1880 to Salisbury, UKNA, FO 418/10, 20.

49 Memorial from Tsêng Chi-tsê, Chinese Minister in England. Translated annexure to Consul A.R. Hewlett, Letter dated 28 December 1880, *Correspondence respecting the Russo-Chinese Treaty, 1881*, UKNA, FO 418/11, p.13

50 Demetrius Charles Boulger, *The Life of Yakub Beg: Athalik Ghazi, and Badaulet; Ameer of Kashgar* (London: W. H. Allen & Co., 1878), viii.

51 Boulger, *England and Russia in Central Asia*, 24.

52 Boulger, *The Life of Yakub Beg*, 22.

53 Boulger, *The Life of Yakub Beg*, 40.

54 Hsü, *The Rise of Modern China*, 297.

55 British ministers in China included Sir Rutherford Alcock (1865–1870), Sir Tomas Wade (1871–1882), Sir Harry Parkes (1883–1885), Sir Ernest Satow (1902–1906) and Sir John Jordan (1906–1920).

56 Odd Arne Westad, *Restless Empire: China and the World Since 1750* (London: Bodley Head, Random House, 2012), 195.

57 S. Wells Williams, *Our Relations with The Chinese Empire*, San Francisco, University of California, 1877, 9.

58 Quoted in Alexander Lukin, *The Bear Watches the Dragon* (New York: M. E. Sharpe, 2003), 50.

6. British Empire in India

1 *Moscow Gazette*, 9 (21) February 1892 [translation annexed to letter dated 2 March 1892 from R. Morier, British ambassador to Russia], Foreign Department, Secret-F. Nos. 358–59, NAI.

2 'From Peking to Kashgaria', *Proceedings of the R. G. S.* (February 1890), quoted in R. S. Gundry, *China and Her Neighbours* (London: Chapman and Hall, 1893), 304.

3 Colonel Lumsden, British Library, IOR/L/PS/20/MEMO.23, 145.

4 Nicholas R. O'Conor [Britain's minister in Beijing], Letter to Earl of Rosebery, dated 19 December 1893, UKNA, FO 881/6492, 27.

5 Letter dated 14 July 1890 from the Governor-General in Council of India to Viscount Cross, UKNA, FO 881/6131, 4.

6 Map of Turkestan by the Surveyor General of India, 1879, UKNA, WO 78/659.

7 Ney Elias, Officiating Joint Commissioner of Ladakh, UKNA, FO 17/826, 291.

8 Ney Elias, Annexure to letter dated 26 November 1890 of Captain Younghusband, Foreign Department, Government of India K.W. No. 3, NAI.

9 Francis Younghusband, *Report of a Mission to the Northern Frontier of Kashmir, 1889* (Calcutta: Government Printing, 1890), p 8–13.

10 Report of the interview between Captain Younghusband and Pau Ja-Jeu, the Amban of Yarkand, held on 5 September 1890, UKNA, FO 881/6131, 10.

11 Francis Younghusband, Letter dated 16 September 1890 to the Government of India, UKNA, FO 881/6131.

12 Younghusband, *Report of A Mission to the Northern Frontier of Kashmir in 1889* (Calcutta: Superintendent of Government Printing, 1890), p.101.

13 A. Godley, India Office, Letter to the British Foreign Office, dated 14 August 1890, UKNA, FO 881/6131.

14 H. Ramsay, Memorandum of 5 September 1890 on Younghusband's report, UKNA, FO 881/6131, 15.

15 Memorandum of interviews with the Yamên on the subject of the appointment of a British Agent in Chinese Turkestan, 12 September 1890, UKNA, FO 405/54, 10.

16 J. Walsham [British minister in Beijing], Letter to Lord Salisbury, dated 23 July 1891, UKNA, FO 881/6131, 31.

17 Map of the country between Russian and Chinese Turkestan and British India, 1892, UKNA, FO 925/2022.

18 G. T. Feilding, *Route from the Karakorum Pass to Kashgar* (Simla: Government Central Branch Press, 1908), 1.

19 Chinese Taotai, Translation of letter to Capt. Younghusband [annexed to Francis Younghusband's letter dated 23 November 1890], Foreign Department, Secret-F. Nos. 133–134, NAI, 51.

20 Francis Younghusband, Letter dated 23 November 1890, Foreign Department, No. 133, NAI.

21 Francis Younghusband, Letter dated 3 September 1891, Foreign Department, Secret-F. No. 114, NAI.

22 A. Godley [India Office], Letter dated 3 June 1891, UKNA, FO 881/6131, 28.

23 Marquis of Salisbury, Letter dated 12 May 1892, Foreign Department, Secret-F. No. 201, NAI.

24 In 1895 Japan imposed the Treaty of Shimonoseki on China, under which Taiwan was ceded to Japan and the independence of Korea was recognised. It also permitted Japan to take control of Port Arthur and Liaodong Peninsula, though the combined pressure of Russia, France and Germany compelled it to withdraw. Japan's victory made Britain aware of its potential as an ally against Russia in the Far East.

25 John Jordan [British minister in Beijing], Letter dated 13 November 1906, UKNA, FO 228/2311.

7. Britain and Tibet: Forcing Trade

1 Francis Younghusband, *India and Tibet* (London: John Murray, 1910), 29.

2 Matthew W. Mosca, *From Frontier Policy to Foreign Policy: The Question of India and the Transformation of Geopolitics in Qing China* (Stanford, CA: Stanford University Press, 2013), 184.

3 Wei Yuan, *Haiguo tuzhi*, 1844, quoted in Mosca, 287.

4 Quoted in Mosca, *From Frontier Policy to Foreign Policy*, 364.

5 F. Grenard (trans., A. Teixeira de Mattos), *Tibet: The Country and Its Inhabitant* (London: Hutchinson and Company, 1904), p 353–354.

6 Ibid., 358.

7 F. W. A. Bruce [British plenipotentiary to China], Despatch dated 29 March 1864, NAI, Foreign Department, Political-A, No. 53.

8 R. C. Lawrence, Letter dated 10 September 1870, Foreign Department Political A Branch, No. 400, 14, NAI.

9 British minister in Peking, Letter dated 9 April 1873, Foreign Department, Secret-F. No. 257, NAI.

10 Separate Article of the Agreement between Great Britain and China for the Settlement of the Yunnan Case, signed at Chefoo, 13 September 1876, in *Hertslet's China Treaties, vol. 1*, (New York: Cambridge University Press, 1908), 80. Clubb, *20th Century China*, 378.

11 Article IV of the Convention between Her Britannic Majesty and His Majesty the Emperor of China relative to Burmah and Tibet, signed at Peking, 24 July 1886, in *Hertslet's China Treaties, Vol. I*, (New York: Cambridge University Press, 1908), 89.

12 Maharaja of Nepal, Translation of letter to the four Kazis of Lhasa [annexed to letter dated 25 May 1888 from the British Resident in Nepal, Major E. L. Durand], Foreign Department, Secret-E. Nos. 307–08, NAI.

13 Nepal's representative in Lhasa, Report annexed to a letter dated 15 May 1888 from the Maharaja of Nepal, Foreign Department, Secret E., No. 285–86, NAI.

14 Paragraph 1 of the Convention between Britain and China relating to Sikkim and Tibet, 1890, in *Papers Relating to Tibet* (London: Darling & Son, 1904), 6.

15 Article 1, Convention between Great Britain and China relating to Sikkim and Tibet, signed at Calcutta, 17 March 1890, in *Hertslet's China Treaties*, vol. 1 (New York: Cambridge University Press, 1908), 92.

16 Foreign Department of the Government of India, Letter dated 4 July 1893 to the Secretary of State for India in London, in *Papers Relating to Tibet* (London: Darling & Son, 1904), 10.

17 J. C. White [political officer, Sikkim], Letter dated 9 June 1894 to the Commissioner, Rajshahi Division, in *Papers Relating to Tibet* (London: Darling & Son, 1904), 30.

18 Kwei Hwan [Chinese resident in Tibet], Letter dated 14 May 1895 to J. C. White, Political Officer, Sikkim, in *Papers Relating to Tibet* (London: Darling & Son, 1904), 38.

19 J. C. S. Cotton [chief secretary to the government of Bengal], Letter dated 22 July 1895 to the Government of Bengal to the Secretary to the Government of India, in *Papers Relating to Tibet* (London: Darling & Son, 1904), 45.

20 These were the lamas of the monasteries of Drepung, Sera and Gaden.

21 J. C. White, Letter dated 9 December 1898 to the Commissioner of Rajshahi Division, in *Papers Relating to* Tibet (London: Darling & Son, 1904), 96.

22 Wang and Nyima, *The Historical Status of China's Tibet*, 85.

23 George N. Curzon, *Russia in Central Asia in 1889 and the Anglo-Russian Question* (London: Longmans, Green and Co. 1889), p 13–14.

24 Ibid., 157.

25 Ibid., 409.

26 Ibid., 412.

27 Ibid., 297.

28 Ernest Satow, Letter dated 26 August 1903 to Secretary of State Lansdowne, UKNA, FO 800/120, 150. Many years later, in 1944, when British India's Agent-General in Kashgar K. P. S. Menon travelled through the region, he commented that, while the Indian side of the Karakoram Mountains was rugged and barren, the other side had green meadows. This was why the Mir of Hunza was very unhappy with the British for agreeing to cede it to China.

29 Ashley Clark, 107.

30 George N. Curzon, Letter dated 8 June 1901 to the Dalai Lama, in *Papers Relating to Tibet* (London: Darling & Son, 1904), 122.

31 George N. Curzon, Letter dated 13 February 1902 to George F. Hamilton, in ibid., 127.

32 George F. Hamilton, Letter dated 16 August 1901 to George N. Curzon, in ibid., 122.

33 Herbert Adams Gibbons, *The New Map of Asia* (New York: Century, 1919), 27.

34 Odessika Novosti, 12 (25), June 1901 [translation from Russian in a despatch by the British consulate in Odessa], in *Papers Relating to Tibet*, 114.

35 Ernest Satow, Despatch dated 5 August 1902 to the Marquess of Lansdowne in ibid., 140.

36 Charles S. Scott [British ambassador to Russia], Letter dated 2 October 1902 to the Secretary of State, Lord Lansdowne, in ibid., 145.

37 Foreign Department, Government of India, Letter dated 8 January 1903 to the Secretary of State for India, George F. Hamilton, in ibid., 154.

38 Secretary of State for India, Letter dated 4 February 1903 to the Viceroy in India, in ibid., 179.

39 Henry Petty-Fitzmaurice [Lord Lansdowne, secretary of state for foreign affairs], Letter dated 18 February 1903 to Charles S. Scott, British ambassador to Russia, in *Papers Relating to Tibet*, 181.

40 Lansdowne, despatch dated 8 April 1903 to Charles Scott, British ambassador to Russia, in ibid., 187.

41 Lansdowne, Letter to C. Scott, British ambassador to Russia, dated 18 February 1903, UKNA (hereinafter UKNA), FO 800/140, 145.

42 George N. Curzon, Letter dated 26 October 1903 to George F. Hamilton, in *Papers Relating to Tibet*, 215.

43 Yu Kang, Chinese Resident in Tibet, Memorial published in the *Peking Gazette* of 23 May 1903, in ibid., 194.

44 George Hamilton, Letter dated 20 February 1903 to the Viceroy in ibid., 182.

45 George Hamilton, Letter dated 27 February 1903 to the Viceroy in ibid., 185.

46 George Hamilton, Letter dated 1 October 1903 to the Viceroy in ibid., 213.

47 Younghusband, *India and Tibet*, 82.

48 Ibid., 45.

49 Ibid., 45.

50 *Peking Gazette*, 23 May 1903, in *Papers Relating to Tibet*, 194.

51 Lansdowne, despatch dated 17 November 1903, in ibid., 298.

52 Article in the *Shenpao* of 4 February 1904 [translation enclosed with Ernest Satow's letter of 18 February 1904], UKNA, FO 881/8415.

53 Charles Hardinge [British ambassador to Russia], Letter dated 20 June 1904, UKNA, FO 881/8415.

54 George N. Curzon, *Problems of the Far East*, 1894, quoted in Peter John Brobst, *The Future of the Great Game* (Akron, OH: University of Akron Press, 2005), 60.

55 Alastair Lamb, 'Introduction', in Julie G. Marshall (ed.), *Britain and Tibet 1765–1947* (Abington, UK: Routledge, 2005), x.

56 The King's Speech in the House of Lords, *Hansard*, vol. 140, Debated on 15 August 1904. Available: hansard.parliament.uk/Lords/1904-08-15.

57 William Brodrick, Statement in the House of Commons on 28 March 1904, Hansard, vol. 132, Tibet Mission: Views of Chinese Government. Available: hansard.parliament.uk/Commons/1904-03-28.

58   Hardinge's letter of 18 August 1904 and Lansdowne's reply of 24 August 1904, UKNA, FO 800/140, 245, 255.

59   Correspondence between Secretary of State Lansdowne and Britain's ambassador to Russia, Charles Hardinge, September–October 1904, UKNA, FO 800/141, p 11–16.

60   Lansdowne, Statement in House of Lords, Debate on 'The Mission to Tibet', 26 February 1904, *Hansard, Vol. 130* [website], hansard.parliament. uk/Lords/1904-02-26.

61   William Brodrick, Statement in the House of Commons on 18 July 1904, *Hansard, Vol. 138, The Mission to Tibet: Negotiations with Russia*, [website], hansard.parliament.uk/Commons/1904-07-18.

62   Hardwicke [undersecretary of state for foreign affairs], Statement in House of Lords, Debate on 'The Mission to Tibet', 26 February 1904, *Hansard*, vol. 130, 'The Mission to Tibet'. Available: hansard.parliament. uk/Lords/1904-02-26.

63   Ripon, Statement in House of Lords, Debate on 'The Mission to Tibet', 26 February 1904, *Hansard*, vol. 130. Available: hansard.parliament.uk/ Lords/1904-02-26.

64   Nicholas II, Letter dated 4 July 1901 to the Dalai Lama, Archive of the Foreign Policy of the Russian Federation (AVPRF), f. Kitaiskiistol, d.1448, I. 100, quoted in Alexandre Andreyev, 'The Tsar's Generals and Tibet: Apropos of Some "White Spots" in the History of Russo-Tibetan Relations', in Alex McKay (ed.), *Tibet and Her Neighbours* (London: Edition Hansjörg Mayer, 2003), 168.

65   Ekai Kawaguchi, *Three Years in Tibet* (London: Benaras, 1909), 506, quoted in Alexandre Andreyev, 'The Tsar's Generals and Tibet: Apropos of some "White Spots" in the History of Russo-Tibetan Relations', in Alex McKay (ed.), *Tibet and Her Neighbours* (London: Edition Hansjörg Mayer, 2003), 170.

66   Lamb, 'Introduction', in Marshall (ed.), *Britain and Tibet 1765–1947*, x.

67   Ernest Satow's letter of 6 October 1904 to Secretary of State Lansdowne, UKNA, FO 881/8510, 85.

68   Satow, Letter dated 29 December 1904, UKNA, FO 800/121, 126.

69   UKNA FO 17/1754, 381.

70   Article II of the Convention between Great Britain and China respecting Tibet, signed at Peking on 27 April 1906, in *Hertslet's China Treaties*, vol. 1 (New York: Cambridge University Press, 1908), 203.

71   Sergei Yulevich Witte (trans., Abraham Yarmolinsky), *The Memoirs of Count Witte* (New York: Doubleday, Page and Co., 1921), 83.

72   Convention between Great Britain and Russia Respecting Tibet, signed at St. Petersburg, 31 August 1907, in *Hertslet's China Treaties* (New York: Cambridge University Press), 620–22.

73   John Jordan, Letter dated 16 February 1907 to Edward Grey on his meeting with the Chinese minister, UKNA, FO 371/382, 196.

74   Chinese publication, *Shen Pao*, dated 9 October 1907 [translation by the British Legation in Beijing], UKNA, FO 371/382, p 547–548.

75 King's Speech in the House of Lords, 29 January 1908, *Hansard*, vol. 183.
76 British Foreign Office, Memorandum Respecting the Anglo-Russian Convention, UKNA, FO 881/9130, 2.
77 Edmund Fitzmaurice, Speech in the House of Lords, 6 February 1908, *Hansard*, vol. 183. Available: https://hansard.parliament.uk/Lords.
78 Edward Grey of Fallodon, *Twenty-Five Years* (vol. 1, 1925), 165, quoted in Middleton, *Britain and Russia*, 219.
79 Bai Shouyi, *An Outline History of China*, 440.

8. Fall of the Manchus

1   Fenby, *History of Modern China*, 48.
2   Fenby, *History of Modern China*, 55.
3   James L. Hevia, *English Lessons: The Pedagogy of Imperialism in Nineteenth-Century China* (Hong Kong: Hong Kong University Press, 2003), 155.
4   Quoted in Lukin, *The Bear Watches the Dragon*, 38.
5   Ibid., 38.
6   Hevia, *English Lessons*, 164.
7   France had formed this alliance for protection against Germany, which had attacked it in 1870. The alliance lasted till the Russian Revolution in 1917.
8   Gibbons, *The New Map of Asia*, 404.
9   Japan did not quite share Britain's commitment to maintaining the integrity of the Chinese Empire. In 1895, after defeating China, it imposed very harsh conditions under the Treaty of Shimonoseki. It seized the island of Taiwan and compelled China to recognise the independence of Korea. It also occupied Port Arthur and Liaodong Peninsula, although it had to withdraw from there due to the combined pressure of Russia, France and Germany.
10 Clark, Letter dated 27 January 1943, 108.
11 Quoted in Lukin, *The Bear Watches the Dragon*, 55.
12 Ibid., 56.
13 Ernest Satow to Edward Grey, Letter dated 31 March 1906, UKNA, FO 800/44, 65.
14 Fairbank, Reischauer and Craig, *East Asia*, 643.
15 Stuart-Fox, *A Short History of China and Southeast Asia*, 129.
16 Westad, *Restless Empire*, 85.
17 Quoted in Crossley, *The Manchus*, 192.
18 Wolfgang Franke, *A Century of Chinese Revolution 1851–1949* (Oxford: Basil Blackwell, 1970), 64.
19 Fenby, 125.
20 Fairbank, Reischauer and Craig, *East Asia*, 755.
21 British Consul General in Kashgar, Telegram of 6 March 1933, British Library, IOR/L/PS/12/2331.
22 H. A. F. Metcalfe [Foreign Secretary of India], Letter dated 27 July 1936, British Library, IOR/L/PS/12/2382.
23 Ashley Clarke [Foreign Office], Letter dated 27 January 1943, UKNA, FO 371/35768, p 10–11.

24 R. Peel [India Office], Letter dated 2 March 1943, UKNA, FO 371/35768, 86.

25 Jung Chang and Jon Halliday, *Mao: The Unknown Story* (London: Vintage Books, 2007), 195.

26 Hsü, *The Rise of Modern China*, 600.

27 Ibid., 601.

28 This was the Declaration of Four Nations on General Security of 30 October 1943, signed by the US, Soviet Union, United Kingdom and China.

9. An Independent Tibet

1 Ernest Satow, Letter to the Chinese government dated 28 March 1905, UKNA, FO 17/1754, 250.

2 Shaik, *Tibet*, 224–25.

3 Melvyn C. Goldstein, *A History of Modern Tibet, 1913–1951* (New Delhi: Munshiram Manoharlal, 1993), 49.

4 H. C. Wilton, Note of 9 March 1908, UKNA, FO 881/9468, 91.

5 British Foreign Office, Letter to India Office dated 16 February 1910, UKNA, FO 405-314, 9.

6 Goldstein, *A History of Modern Tibet*, 52–53.

7 Chinese Foreign Office, Letter dated 28 October 1910 to William Max-Müller, British ambassador to China, UKNA, FO 405/314, 151–52.

8 Lt Gen Chung Ling and Lien Yu [Minister], Telegram of 28 August 1912, UKNA, FO 405-314, 152.

9 Chandra Shamsher Jang Bahadur Rana [Prime Minister of Nepal], Letter dated 16 March 1913, UKNA, FO 228/2581.

10 John Jordan, Memorandum dated 17 August 1912 presented to China's *Wai-chiao Pu* and internal memo of 27 January 1913, UKNA, FO 405/439.

11 India Office, Memorandum dated 27 January 1913 to the Cabinet, UKNA, FO 405-439, 5.

12 Goldstein, *A History of Modern Tibet*, 59.

13 Wang and Nyima, *The Historical Status of China's Tibet*, 116.

14 Tsepon Shakabpa, *Tibet: A Political History* (New Haven, CT: Yale University Press, 1967), 246–47.

15 An English translation of the Mongol-Tibetan Treaty, 1913, is available in Rajesh Kadian, *Tibet, China and India: Critical Choices, Uncertain Future* (New Delhi: Vision Books, 1999), 204–05.

16 Shaik, *Tibet*, 234.

17 Quoted in ibid., 236.

18 Wang and Nyima, *The Historical Status of China's Tibet*, 121.

19 Lord Hardinge [viceroy of India], Speech to the Imperial Legislative Assembly, October 1913, UKNA, FO 800/98, Folio 268.

20 Edward Grey [foreign secretary], Letter to Lord Crewe, Secretary of State for India, 18 June 1914, UKNA, FO 800/98/103, Folio 350.

21 Ernest Satow, Letter dated 11 January 1928, UKNA, FO 228/3829.

22 Secretary of State for India, Memorandum, July 1930, UKNA, CAB/24/214/31, 235.

23 Goldstein, *A History of Modern Tibet*, 223.

24 Political officer in Sikkim, Letter dated 14 November 1931, UKNA, FO 676/73.

25 Reuters translation of a Chinese government order, 31 March 1934, British Library, IOR/L/PS/12/4177, 221.

26 Reported by the British embassy, British Library, IOR/L/PS/12/4177, p 291–292.

27 Alexander Cadogan, Letter dated 28 February 1935, British Library, IOR/L/PS/12/4177, p 64–66.

28 Wang and Nyima, *The Historical Status of China's Tibet*, 165.

29 Goldstein, *A History of Modern Tibet*, 390, citing USFR, 893.00/64, memorandum of conversation by J. Ballantine [Foreign Affairs, State Department], 31 May 1943.

30 Anthony Eden, Letter dated 22 July 1943, UKNA, FO 371-76314.

31 Basil J. Gould, Telegram dated 4 July 1944, UKNA, FO371/41586.

32 British embassy in Nanjing, Telegram of 25 February 1948, UKNA, FO 371/70042.

33 Jawaharlal Nehru, *Glimpses of World History* (New Delhi: Jawaharlal Nehru Memorial Fund, 1982), 331. Nehru wrote, 'Chien Lung extended his empire by conquering Turkestan in Central Asia and occupying Tibet.' Elsewhere, he talked of China, Tibet and India preserving Ashoka's tradition of greatness (62). He also recounted that Tibet had become independent after the overthrow of the Manchu dynasty (842).

34 Nehru, *Selected Works of Jawaharlal Nehru* (ser. II, vol. 2), 502.

35 Nehru, Inaugural Address at the Asian Relations Conference, 23 March 1947, in *India's Foreign Policy* (New Delhi: Publications Division, Government of India, 1961), 249.

36 Murray, Note dated 24 November 1948, UKNA, FO 371/63943.

37 Leslie A. C. Fry [UK High Commission in New Delhi], Letter dated 7 November 1947, UKNA, FO 371/70042.

38 Goldstein, *A History of Modern Tibet*, 568.

39 B. N. Mullick, *My Years with Nehru: The Chinese Betrayal* (New Delhi: Allied Publishers, 1971), 54.

40 A. W. Selby [British High Commission, New Delhi], Letter dated 9 January 1948, UKNA, FO 371-63943.

41 Telegram from the Commonwealth Relations Office, London, to the British High Commissioner in New Delhi dated 17 December 1948, UKNA, FO 371/70046, 44–45.

42 Goldstein, *A History of Modern Tibet*, 605.

43 Summary of World Broadcasts (pt. V, 1949, no. 17, 27), cited in Tsering Shakya, *The Dragon in the Snows: A History of Modern Tibet since 1947* (London: Pimlico, 1999), 8.

44 Tibet's message to the British High Commission in India dated 3 December 1949 and the High Commissioner's telegram of 13 December 1949, UKNA, FO 371/76314.

45 British Embassy in Nanjing, Report dated 2 November 1949, UKNA, FO 371/76317.

46 *Manchester Guardian*, 18 November 1949, UKNA, FO 371/76314.

47 Tsering Shakya, *The Dragon in the Snows: A History of Modern Tibet since 1947* (London: Pimlico, 1999), 22 [citing *Foreign Relations of the United States*, 1950, 424].

48 K. M. Panikkar, Despatch to Prime Minister Nehru, 1950, Prime Ministers Museum and Library, New Delhi, JN(SG) File 48(I), 106–110.

49 Panikkar, Telegram dated 18 July 1950, PMML, New Delhi, JN(SG) vol. 48, pt. II.

50 MEA, New Delhi, Telegram dated 5 August 1950, PMML, New Delhi, JN(SG) File no. 50(I), 29.

51 Panikkar, Telegram dated 22 August 1950, PMML, New Delhi, JN(SG) No. 52(II), 220. Hyderabad was a princely state which had refused to accede to India after independence.

52 Indian Embassy, Beijing, Telegram dated 21 August 1950, PMML, New Delhi, JN(SG) file no. 52(II), 216.

53 MEA, New Delhi, Record of conversation between the Prime Minister and the Tibetan Delegation on 8 September 1950 [Savingram dated 2 September 1950], PMML, New Delhi, JN(SG) no. 54(II), 203.

54 K. P. S. Menon, Note dated 10 September 1950, PMML, New Delhi, JN(SG) no. 54(II), 287.

55 Nehru, Telegram dated 18.8.1950, PMML, New Delhi, JN(SG) file 52(I), 80–83.

56 H. C. Roberts [UK High Commissioner to India], Telegram of 2 December 1949, UKNA, FO 371/76317.

57 Nehru, Interview to the *U.S. News & World Report*, 15 September 1950, PMML, New Delhi, JN(SG) file no. 55(II), 333.

58 Durga Das, *India from Curzon to Nehru and After* (London: Collins, 1969), 295.

59 Goldstein, *A History of Modern Tibet*, 671, citing a US embassy telegram dated 14 August 1950 on a conversation of the US ambassador with GS Bajpai, secretary-general in the Indian foreign ministry, USFR 611.93B/8-1450.

10. China Reconquers Tibet

1 Robert Ford was released five years later.

2 Nehru, Telegram dated 26 October 1950, PMML, New Delhi, JN(SG) file no. 61(I), 135.

3 Margaret Carlyle (ed.), *Documents on International Affairs 1949–1950: China; The Important Documents of the First Plenary Session of the Chinese People's Political Consultative Conference* (London, Oxford University Press, 1953), 555.

4 Indian Embassy, Beijing, Telegram dated 23 October 1950, PMML, New Delhi, JN(SG) file no. 61(I), 11.

5 MEA, New Delhi, Telegram dated 29 October 1950, PMML, New Delhi, File No. 61(II), 263.

6 Nehru, Record of meeting dated 3 November, PMML, New Delhi, JN(SG) file no. 62(II), 184–185.

7   Nehru, Letter dated 17 November 1950, PMML, New Delhi, JN(SG) file no. 64(I), 162.

8   G. S. Bajpai, Telegram dated 20 November 1950, PMML, New Delhi, JN(SG) 64(II), 271.

9   Panikkar, Telegram dated 16 November 1950, PMML, New Delhi, JN(SG) file no. 64(I).

10   Nehru, Telegram dated 20 November 1950, PMML, New Delhi, JN(SG) 64(II), p 282–283.

11   Panikkar, Telegram dated 19 October 1950, PMML, New Delhi, JN(SG) file no. 64(II), 275.

12   H. Dayal, Memorandum dated 18 April 1950, PMML, New Delhi, JN(SG) file no. 48(I), 172.

13   Savingram dated 2 September 1950, PMML, New Delhi, JN(SG) no. 54(II), 163.

14   Savingram dated 2 September 1950, PMML, New Delhi, JN(SG) no. 54(II), 163.

15   Indian Mission, Lhasa, Telegram dated 14 November 1950, PMML, New Delhi, JN(SG) 63(II), 211.

16   Formosa was the name given to Taiwan.

17   Bajpai, Note dated 12.10.1950, PMML, New Delhi, JN(SG) file no. 59(I), 144.

18   Bajpai and K. P. S. Menon, Notes dated 27.10.50 and 26.10.50, PMML, New Delhi, JN(SG) file no. 61(I), 115–16.

19   Bajpai, Note dated 24 October 1950, PMML, New Delhi, JN(SG) file no. 61(I), 13.

20   Neville Henderson, Britain's ambassador to Germany (1937–1939), is widely derided for becoming very close to the Nazis and for going over the British Foreign Office to Prime Minister Neville Chamberlain, whose closet instructions he claimed to be following.

21   Bajpai, Note dated 27 October 1950, PMML, New Delhi, JN(SG) file 61(I), 115.

22   MEA, New Delhi, Telegram dated 12 October 1950, PMML, New Delhi, JN(SG) file no. 59(I), 205.

23   MEA, New Delhi, Telegram dated 12 November 1950, PMML, New Delhi, JN(SG) 59(I), 205.

24   Nehru, Note dated 19 November 1950, PMML, New Delhi, JN(SG) 64(II), 223.

25   Menon, Telegram dated 23 November 1950, PMML, New Delhi, JN(SG) file no. 65(I), 61.

26   Wang and Nyima, *The Historical Status of China's Tibet*, 214.

27   Taring, 175.

28   Annual Report for 1952 of the Consulate General of India, Lhasa, PMML, New Delhi, JNSG Papers, Folio 170-Part I, 195.

29   Indian Embassy, Beijing, Telegram to MEA, 30 May 1951, PMML, New Delhi, JNSG Papers, Folio 86-II, p 331–332.

30   Telegram from Indian Mission, Lhasa, dated 2 June 1951, PMML, New Delhi, JNSG Papers, Folio 87-II, 238.

31 Record of Talks between I. V. Stalin and Mao Zedong, 22 January 1950, Wilson Center Digital Library, https://digitalarchive.wilsoncenter.org/document/111245.

32 Lukin, *The Bear Watches the Dragon*, 120.

33 'Soviet Linking Road to Tibet', *Times of London*, 5 September 1952 [British Embassy, Beijing, Letter dated 23 September 1952], UKNA, FO 371/99663.

34 Wang and Nyima, *The Historical Status of China's Tibet*, 209.

35 Goldstein, *A History of Modern Tibet*, 791, citing USFR, 793B.00/6-2551, Memorandum of conversation between R. H. Belcher, first secretary of the British Embassy and D. D. Kennedy, acting director of the Office of South Asian Affairs, dated 25 June 1951.

36 Vallabhbhai Patel, Letter dated 7 November 1950, PMML, New Delhi, JN(SG) file no. 62(II), 257–261.

37 Nehru, Note dated 8 November 1950, PMML, New Delhi, JN(SG) file no. 62(II), 342–44.

38 Nehru, 'Statement in Parliament on 7 December 1950', in *India's Foreign Policy* (New Delhi: Publications Division, Government of India, 1961), 302–03.

39 Durga Das, *India from Curzon to Nehru and After* (London: Collins, 1969), 337.

40 Ramchandra Guha, *India after Gandhi* (New Delhi: Pan Macmillan India, 2008), 303.

41 Prime Minister Nehru's notes on his meeting with the Dalai Lama on 26 November 1956, PMML, New Delhi, Subimal Dutt Papers, sub-file 7, 1–3.

42 Record of Prime Minister's meeting with the Dalai Lama on 24 April 1959, PMML, New Delhi, Subimal Dutt Papers, sub-file 9, 18.

43 Record of Prime Minister's Meeting with the Dalai Lama on 24 April 1959, PMML, New Delhi, Subimal Dutt Papers, sub-file 9, 17–21.

44 The consulate closed within three years – in December 1962, soon after China's invasion of India.

45 J. S. Sandhu (ed.), *1962: A View from the Other Side of the Hill* (New Delhi: Vij Books, 2015), 22, 25.

46 Zhou Enlai, Letter dated 8 September 1959 to Nehru, 8, Wilson Center Digital Archive. Available: http://digitalarchive.wilsoncenter.org/document/175958.

47 Report of British embassy in Beijing, dated 12 January 1959, UKNA, FO 371/141619.

48 Nehru, 'Statement in Parliament on 27 April 1959', in *India's Foreign Policy* (New Delhi: Publications Division, Government of India, 1961), 321–23.

49 Nehru, 'Statement in Parliament on 4 September 1959', in ibid., 344.

50 Nehru, 'Statement in Parliament on 4 September 1959', in ibid., 341.

51 Nehru, 'Statement in Parliament on 4 September 1959', in ibid., 346.

52 Nehru, 'Statement in Parliament on 25 November 1959', in ibid., 362.

53 Nehru, 'Statement in Parliament on 9 December 1959', in ibid., 377.

11. Tibet in the United Nations

1   MEA, New Delhi, Telegram dated 22 October 1950, PMML, New Delhi, JN(SG) file no. 60(II), 318.

2   Political Office, Gangtok, Telegram dated 10 November 1950, PMML, New Delhi, JN(SG) file no. 63(I), 18.

3   G. Jebb, Letter dated 14 November 1950 to the British Foreign Office, UKNA, FO 371-84454.

4   Reuters report of 30 October 1950, UKNA, DO 35-2931, 33.

5   MEA, New Delhi, Telegram dated 16 October 1950, PMML, New Delhi, JN(SG) file no. 64(I), 82.

6   MEA, New Delhi, Telegram dated 19 November 1950, PMML, New Delhi, JN(SG) file no. 64(II), 245.

7   Menon, Note dated 22 November 1950, PMML, New Delhi, JN(SG) file no. 65(I), 15.

8   Menon, Telegram dated 23 November 1950, PMML, New Delhi, JN(SG) file no. 65(I), 61.

9   PMI New York, Telegram dated 18 November 1950, PMML, New Delhi, JN(SG) file no. 64(II), 230.

10 PMI New York, Telegram dated 24 November 1950, PMML, New Delhi, JN(SG) file no. 65(I), 146.

11 Menon, Note dated 22 November 1950, PMML, New Delhi, JN(SG) file no. 65(I), 14.

12 British High Commissioner to India, Letter dated 8 November 1949, UKNA, FO 371/76314.

13 A. Tom Grunfeld, 'A Brief Survey of Tibetan Relations with the United States', in Alex McKay (ed.), *Tibet and Her Neighbours* (London: Edition Hansjörg Mayer, 2003), 197.

14 Ibid., 199.

15 '22 January 1950: Record of Talks between I. V. Stalin and Mao Zedong', Wilson Center Digital Archive. Available: http://www.commonprogram. science/documents/111245.pdf.

16 *Pravda* report of 20 June 1951, British High Commission, New Delhi, Letter dated 20 June 1951, UKNA, FO 371/92871.

17 UN General Assembly Resolution 1353 (XIV), Question of Tibet, 834th Plenary Meeting, 21 October 1959. Available: https://digitallibrary.un.org/record/206855?ln=en.

18 UN General Assembly Resolution 1723 (XVI), Question of Tibet, 1085th Plenary Meeting, 20 December 1961. Available: https://documents-dds-ny.un.org/doc/RESOLUTION/GEN/NR0/167/76/PDF/NR016776.pdf?OpenElement.

19 UN General Assembly Resolution 2079 (XX), Question of Tibet, 1403rd Plenary Meeting, 18 December 1965. Available: https://daccess-ods.un.org/tmp/7271571.15936279.html.

12. Tibet under Chinese Occupation

1   Wang and Nyima, *The Historical Status of China's Tibet*, 233.
2   Bruce Riedel, *JFK's Forgotten Crisis: Tibet, The CIA, and the Sino-Indian War* (Washington DC: Brookings Institution Press, 2015), 34.
3   Wang and Nyima, *The Historical Status of China's Tibet*, 249.
4   Permanent Mission of the People's Republic of China to the UN, *White Paper 1992: Tibet; Its Ownership and Human Rights Situation*, 13. Available: https://un.china-mission.gov.cn/eng/gyzg/bp/199209/t19920930_8410933.htm.
5   Chang and Halliday, *Mao*, 556.
6   Dalai Lama, 'Acceptance Speech' [Nobel Prize], 10 December 1989, https://www.nobelprize.org/prizes/peace/1989/lama/acceptance-speech/.
7   Elliot Sperling, 'The Mongols, Mao and the Dalai Lama', *International Herald Tribune*, 14 April 2008.
8   Huang Fensheng, quoted in Elliot Sperling, *The Tibet-China Conflict: History and Polemics* (Washington, DC: East-West Center, 2004), 9.
9   Bai Shouyi, *An Outline History of China*, 419.
10   Sperling, *The Tibet-China Conflict*, 10, citing *Concerning the Question of Tibet* (Beijing: Foreign Language Press, 1959).
11   *White Paper 1992*, 2.
12   Ibid., 4.
13   Wang and Nyima, *The Historical Status of China's Tibet*, 232, 260.

Epilogue: No Endgame in Sight

1   David Miliband, Written Ministerial Statement in the House of Lords on 29 October 2008. Available: hansard.parliament.uk/lords/2008-10-29/debates/08102936000006/Tibet.
2   Westad, *Restless Empire*, 323.
3   UN General Assembly Resolution A/RES/498(V) of 1 February 1951, Available: https://digitallibrary.un.org/record/211029?ln=en.
4   Stuart-Fox, *A Short History of China and Southeast Asia*, 165.
5   Xi Jinping, 'Speech at the Forum for Tibet-related Work, Beijing, 31 August 2020', *China Daily*, 31 August 2020.

Index